LIBRARY AUTOMATION
A State of the Art Review

LIBRARY AUTOMATION
A State of the Art Review

Papers presented at the
Preconference Institute on Library
Automation

Held at San Francisco, California, June 22–24, 1967

Under the Sponsorship of the
Information Science and Automation Division
of the American Library Association

Edited by Stephen R. Salmon

American Library Association

International Standard Book Number 0-8389-3091-3 (1969)

Library of Congress Catalog Card Number 73-77283

Printed in the United States of America

Third Printing, June 1970

Preface

From the very beginning of the American Library Association's Information Science and Automation Division, the primary function of the Division has been to provide leadership through education of its membership and dissemination of information about the new technology. Various means of performing this function have been considered: a journal to gather major articles in the field; a newsletter for current, topical information; a clearinghouse for information on projects and research in progress; regional and special institutes; and, of course, the Division's program at the annual conference. One of the most important ways of carrying out this function, however, was to be the holding of periodic Institutes on Library Automation, prior to the annual ALA Conference, which would review in depth the current state of the art, thus providing a synthesis of recent developments for those unable otherwise to keep abreast of rapid and widespread technical changes in this field. This book represents the proceedings of the first such Institute, held in the Civic Auditorium of San Francisco from June 22 through June 24, 1967.

Each session of the Institute was designed to concentrate on a particular area of automation activity, and in each case a moderator with broad experience in this particular area introduced a speaker with similar but complementary experience, who delivered a paper reviewing the currently operating systems in that area. Each speaker was asked to discuss only the general features or trends of automation in his assigned area, citing the details of particular systems only as examples of general trends or as significant deviations from them. The attempt, that is to say, has been to avoid compiling yet another collection of detailed project reports on individual systems and to attempt the synthesis mentioned earlier. One session, a full half day, was devoted to a brief course in library systems analysis, with a text, *Systems Study as Related to Library Operations,* by Paul L. St. Pierre and Edward A. Chapman (ISAD, in cooperation with John Wiley and Sons, 1967), provided through the courtesy of John Wiley and Sons. An evening session on the building implications of automation was held jointly with the Library Administration Division's Building Institute.

The arrangement of the book follows the program as it was presented, including the discussion periods, with two exceptions. First, several authors in checking the typescript made editorial changes in their presentations, and since in each case the changes made for a better or more accurate written presentation, I have included the edited version rather than the version actually delivered at the Institute. Secondly, the discussions have been edited rather drastically. Indeed, there was a temptation to leave out the discussions altogether, but to do so would have deprived the reader of the flavor of the Institute, and of some factual information and helpful insights as well. I have tried, therefore, in the Discussions to retain only matter which seemed substantive without adding unduly to the length of the text.

Matters which pertained solely to the organization and administration of the Institute have likewise been omitted. Thanks are due to the Resources and Technical Services Division, the Library Administration Division, and the Reference Services Division, who cosponsored the Institute and helped in its organization and administration. I am also indebted to Mrs. Sharon Schatz for assistance in checking references.

An extensive bibliography on library automation was distributed at the Institute and is referred to throughout the text. The Bibliography may be found on page 157.

Finally, it should be noted that one important aspect of the Institute could not be treated here because it was as intangible as it was real—the excitement and zest which permeated the sessions and spilled over into late-night discussions and which made the hectic schedule seem worthwhile. If these papers convey only a fraction of that excitement, their publication will have been worthwhile.

Washington, D.C.
February 14, 1968

STEPHEN R. SALMON
ISAD Provisional
President, 1966-67

Contents

Session 1:   *Keynote Address*

The Future of Library Automation and
Information Networks   1

    Joseph Becker, Director of Information
      Services, Interuniversity Communications
      Council

Session 2:   *Library Systems Analysis and Design*

Systems Study as Related to Library
Operations: Need and Planning   7

    Edward A. Chapman, Director of Libraries,
      Rensselaer Polytechnic Institute

Systems Study as Related to Library
Operations: Analysis, Evaluation,
and Design   13

    Paul L. St. Pierre, Assistant Director for
      Operations, Rensselaer Polytechnic
      Institute Libraries

Session 3:   *Buildings Implications of Library Automation*

How Library Automation May Influence
New Building Plans   30

    Joseph Becker

Building-Planning Implications of Automation   33

    Robert H. Rohlf, Coordinator of Building
      Planning, Library of Congress

Session 4:   *Acquisitions*

Moderator: Allen P. Veaner, Assistant
    Director for Automation, Stanford
    University Libraries

The Automation of Acquisitions Systems   37

    Connie Dunlap, Head, Acquisitions
      Department, University of Michigan
      Library

Session 5:   *Cataloging*

Moderator: Kenneth W. Soderland, Assistant
Director for Preparations, University of
Chicago Libraries

Automation of Cataloging Procedures   44
Wesley Simonton, Professor, Graduate
School of Library Science, University
of Minnesota

Session 6:   *Book Catalogs*

Moderator: Catherine O. MacQuarrie, Chief
Library Consultant, Professional Library
Services

Automated Production of Book Catalogs   55
Kelley L. Cartwright, Institute of Library
Research, University of California,
Berkeley

Session 7:   *Implications of the Library of Congress
Automation Projects*

Moderator: Stephen R. Salmon, Assistant
Librarian for Processing Services,
Library of Congress

Implications of Project MARC   79
Henriette D. Avram, Senior Systems
Analyst, Library of Congress

The Library of Congress Systems Study and
Its Implications for Automation of Library
Processes   90
Barbara Evans Markuson, Assistant
Coordinator, Library of Congress
Information Systems Office

Session 8:   *Serials*

Moderator: Howard W. Dillon, Associate
Librarian, Harvard University Graduate
School of Education

Automated Serials Systems in Perspective   131
Bruce W. Stewart, Data Processing
Supervisor, Texas Agricultural and
Mechanical University Library

Session 9: *Circulation*

Moderator: Foster M. Palmer, Associate
University Librarian, Harvard University

Automated Circulation Systems   138
C. D. Gull, Professor, Graduate Library
School, University of Indiana

Session 10: *Information Retrieval and Related Topics*

Moderator: Robert M. Hayes, Director,
Institute of Library Research, University of
California, Los Angeles

Trends Affecting Library Automation   149
Charles P. Bourne, Director, Advanced
Information Systems Division,
Programming Services, Inc.

Bibliography of Library Automation   157

LIBRARY AUTOMATION
A State of the Art Review

The Future of Library Automation and Information Networks

Joseph Becker

Director of Information Services
Interuniversity Communications Council

Inasmuch as this Preconference is in fact the first meeting of the newly formed Information Science and Automation Division of the American Library Association, it seems most appropriate to begin with an historical account of the progress of automation in libraries. In doing so, I hope to provide you with some perspective concerning future developments.

Several years ago, Brad Rogers reminded an audience of medical librarians that it was a librarian who first suggested the development of the punched card. The inventor was Herman Hollerith, a United States Census Bureau employee, who attributes his invention to a chance remark of John Shaw Billings, then Director of the Surgeon General's Library and later Director of the New York Public Library. At tea one Sunday afternoon in 1880, Billings said, "There ought to be a machine for doing the purely mechanical work of totalling population and other statistics." Within the year, Hollerith had designed the now familiar IBM [International Business Machines] punched card. He cut a card to the size of the dollar bill and assigned coordinate positions to represent the ten numbers. Paper does not conduct electricity, but air does; on this principle, Hollerith was able to effect mechanical responses by providing open electrical paths at selectively punched positions on the card. Since a punched hole represented the same number every time, it was possible to encode numerical information in the cards and to use them as input for mechanical calculations.

It is interesting to speculate what might have happened if Billings had presented his idea to Hollerith as a statistical device for solving the library problem rather than the census problem. Had he done so, my talk might have begun with a description of the 1890 version of MEDLARS (the Medical Literature Analysis and Retrieval System). Under such circumstances, the Information Science and Automation Division might well have been the first ALA division to be formed, and the librarians might be outstripping the mathematicians instead of the other way around.

Hollerith's invention led to the development of a billion-dollar industry. By the mid-1930's, several of the large universities in the country were installing punched-card equipment for student registration and accounting. Soon thereafter, imaginative librarians such as Ralph Parker started to experiment with these very machines to improve library circulation and serial record controls.

Although the literature records various early professional attempts to apply punched-card machines to library routines, such work during the 1940's and 1950's was rare, scattered, and outside the mainstream of library activity. However, several experimental efforts were made that are worth noting. Among them, for example, was Margery Quigley's punched-card circulation control system at Montclair Public Library in New Jersey. Ralph Shaw developed the Rapid Selector, using film as the processing medium instead of cards. Dorothy Alvord, at the King County Public Library of Seattle, Washington, rented a key punch, a sorter, and a tabulator, and with them evolved one of the first, if not actually the first, machine-produced book catalog.

Two events in the late 1950's and early 1960's gave further impetus to library automation developments. The first was general recognition and acceptance of the digital computer's ability to perform nonnumerical work. The second was the creation of the Council on Library Resources by the Ford Foundation to enhance understanding of the new technology and promote innovative research.

Information science and library automation are no longer topics of only occasional interest to librarians; they are fast becoming the central theme of professional work. Evidence of this trend is unmistakable. At the national level, the Library of Congress, the National Library of Medicine, and the National Agricultural Library are all engaged in technology programs designed to facilitate the exchange of machine-readable bibliographical information among libraries. Next week, on June 25, 1967, in San Francisco, the directors of the three national libraries are planning to announce the details of a recent automation agreement that is certain to have significant implications for every library in the country. At the state level, through the provisions of Title III, plans already exist to develop the arteries of communication that eventually will lead to the regional network of library activities. In addition, at the local level, the trend toward shared cataloging and centralized processing continues to grow among many library systems. Most of the impetus for these efforts comes from the new technology. It seems virtually certain that the role of the library as we know it today is destined to undergo further change.

I firmly believe that the future of library automation is inextricably tied to the computer and to new communications developments, and my purpose is to elaborate on some of the implications of this statement.

COMPUTERS IN LIBRARIES

Until recently, applications of the computer in the library were confined mainly to the support of technical processing and circulation functions. Several of these very important bread-and-butter applications will be presented to you in detail during the Preconference Institute. However, another, less publicized area of library application is beginning to emerge, wherein the computer is used not as an information processor but as a tool of library management. A computer program, for example, was written at Johns Hopkins that was capable of predicting the shelf growth of a classed collection. It used a random-number generator to simulate the pattern of book receipts in the library by class, and another subroutine kept track of the number of times various segments of the collection had to be moved to make room for new material. By assigning an average weight to each book, it was also possible to calculate the number of pounds or tons which had to be lifted by a page to fill the stacks to capacity. A mathematical model of this type enables a library director to interpret and judge the effects of various courses of action —such as new construction, large-scale weeding, or extensive reshelving— long before things reach the crisis stage.

Mathematical models are used most effectively to measure physical situations. When joined with the computer, it is possible to use a model for testing a hypothesis in compressed time. Thus, a library director can exercise his model on the computer, observe the consequences of his decisions, alter his strategy accordingly, and repeat the process until he is satisfied with the results. Combined with his intuitive judgment and his experience, these techniques can give the librarian increased confidence in deciding which course of action he should take in the real world.

Last semester, in my library science class at Catholic University, one of my students investigated the possible use of a computer program to predict the optimum distribution of a serials collection in order to minimize shifting in a fixed-area stack. Another used a computer to generate exception reports to library management whenever imbalances between budgeting, obligations, or expenditures exceeded planned thresholds.

Research work involving mathematical models and computer simulators has been reported in progress at Purdue, the University of California at Los Angeles, and the University of Chicago. I suspect that similar work is underway elsewhere and that in time this research will lead to remarkable innovations in library administration.

Aside from the housekeeping and management applications just described, research work is still underway to find ways of using the computer for reference work and information retrieval. Library reference work demands a high order of intellectual activity, and its subtleties have thus far proven too elusive for computer programming. I say "thus far" because I believe the time will come when some ingenious person will supply the missing algorithm that will make machines as vital to the support of the reference function as they already are to technical processing.

There are two principal obstacles to computer progress in the reference area, but I think they can be removed through continuing research and development. The first bottleneck is caused by a technical limitation that prevents the rapid conversion of printed matter into machine-readable form. In other words, the computer can be of little help to the reference librarian until the data it must work with have been put into digital form. The second concerns the lack of new intellectual concepts of information organization that are significantly better than the traditional methods of alphabetic subject headings and decimal classification. The real problem is to develop computer programs that not only organize information by subject but also are capable of logically reorganizing stored information in order to respond to the changing needs of library users. Once this has been done, however, it may become possible to extract underlying patterns of meaning from a complex mass of information. This is the ultimate objective.

The term "machine-readable" denotes the representation of nonnumerical information in the form of codes in punched cards, on punched paper tape, or on magnetic tape. In numerical data processing, the volume of data entering a computer is generally small, and very often the computer expresses its solution as a single number. However, when we process the full text of journal articles, books, or even catalog cards by computer, the volume of data that must first be transposed to machine-readable form is enormous.

The routine way to convert nonnumerical information into machine-readable code is to rekey the printed information one letter at a time, using a keypunch machine or a tape-operated typewriter. Both methods are slow, prohibitively expensive, and prone to error. To overcome these difficulties, character-recognition machines that scan the printed page and automatically convert each letter, word, and sentence to machine-readable code are being developed. This is not a farfetched idea. Character-recognition machines already exist that can scan a printed page and convert the ten numerals, special symbols, and the upper- and lower-case letters of a prescribed type font into equivalent machine code. For example, the squiggles we see in the lower left-hand corner of our personal bank checks are machine readable, as are the embossed numerals on our gasoline credit cards. Also, at a recent symposium on the computer and the humanities held by EDUCOM [Interuniversity Communications Council] and the National Endowment for the Humanities, Dr. Stefan Bauer-Mendelberg, President of the Mannes College of Music, described the musicologist's need for a machine capable of automatically scanning music scores and converting the printed notation into machine-readable code.

Published material is printed in a variety of type fonts, styles, and alphabets. As librarians, we are well aware of how impractical it would be to attempt to compel publishers to use a standard type font. Therefore, the technical challenge is to develop a machine capable of reading intermixed fonts—and this is an overwhelming assignment. Until this objective is achieved, however, it is unlikely that large quantities of printed information will be machine readable. It logically follows that machines are not apt to be of much help to the reference librarian until a much larger corpus of data can find its way into the computer.

Machine-readable information is beginning to be produced by some publishers and by scholars and researchers. Publishers generate machine-readable text as a by-product of manuscript preparation, and later use it to drive automatic printing devices. Certain humanistic scholars—for example, those interested in comparative literary style—are painstakingly keyboarding original material that is prerequisite to computer analysis. A fairly complete list of literary works in machine-readable form appeared recently in *Computers and the Humanities*,[1] and many of these digital sources may someday be part of every library's collection. In science and technology, organizations such as the Chemical Abstracts Service and the Institute of Scientific Information are beginning to offer new machine-readable data services. Future editions of source guides, such as Winchell,[2] should incorporate descriptions of these new resources so that reference librarians can make more active use of pertinent digital files.

A current trend within the library profession is to produce catalog data that are machine readable. Production of machine-readable catalog data is practical because it can be captured as a by-product of typing in the catalog department. Granted that we must first agree on standardized format and content —and this is a very formidable task—the gradual stockpiling of such data would eventually lead to the creation of a union catalog that can serve reference stations in many libraries through network communications. The embryo of this idea exists today in the MARC (Machine-Readable Catalog) system at the Library of Congress and in MEDLARS at the National Library of Medicine.

Once bibliographic data are available in machine-readable form, the next step is to communicate and display these data rapidly in a form suitable for use at the local library level. This is the responsibility of the communications network.

COMMUNICATIONS NETWORKS

Next, I wish to describe briefly selected elements of technology that may soon provide the means for remote access to digital and graphic information through interconnecting communications networks. The prospect of such an information network is attractive because it can potentially transform the library's traditional role as a passive receiver of information into a much expanded role as an active transmitter or distributor of information as well. The ability to broadcast information to those who need it when they need it is likely to turn libraries and information centers into communications centers. Some users who must commute to the library today may instead communicate with it tomorrow. How will this interaction take place? And what new technology will bring this change about?

The marriage of computers to electronic communications can provide important advantages for the dissemination of information. Since 1940, computer technology has progressed rapidly through several generations. The earliest computers were able to perform mathematical operations in a fraction of a second, a speed several orders of magnitude greater than manual processing. A second generation of transistorized computers became available in the late 1950's. Most of the machines we see around us today are products of this generation. They are faster, cooler, and more accurate than their antecedents, and possess greater versatility and capacity. Furthermore, these machines no longer merely compute; they are capable of manipulating with equal skill letters of the alphabet, words, and sentences.

The computer industry recently announced a third generation of computer hardware. Besides offering more computer power for the dollar, the new equipment has several important and unique capabilities. Its memory is large and can operate at

---

[1] "Literary Materials in Machine-Readable Form," *Computers and the Humanities*, 2:133-44 (Jan. 1968).

[2] Constance M. Winchell, *Guide to Reference Books* (8th ed.; Chicago: American Library Assn., 1967).

speeds measured in billionths of a second. However, its principal advantage consists in the fact that it can be connected with other computers and other electronic machines over standard communication lines. With the development of high-capacity, direct-access storage devices such as the 2321 data cell drive, recently announced by IBM, and Control Data's Multiple Disk File, we can now think in terms of storing large quantities of information at a central location, while at the same time having these data available to numerous users at distant locations. This is what is meant by being "on-line" with a central computer and "time-sharing its use. Project MAC [Multiple Access to Computers] at Massachusetts Institute of Technology is one example of a time-sharing network, and General Electric's DATANET-30 commercial, computer subscription service is another. While these two networks are at the present time used primarily for numerical computing, the same principles of operation can be applied to the sharing of files of information over similar networks.

Communications technology can extend the resources of a library and information center beyond its physical borders. During the past few years, a wide variety of new communications equipment and techniques have been introduced, and their impact on data-transfer methodology is growing rapidly. The *same* communication channel can be used to send printed and graphic materials directly to homes, offices, or libraries. The major communications common carriers, such as the Bell System and the Western Union Telegraph Company, are currently upgrading their facilities in order to provide these new services. Standard telephone line facilities, for example, though originally designed for voice communications, are already being used for transferring the digital language of computers from one point to another. As microwave links and satellites are added to common carrier facilities, they will gradually replace the coaxial cables now used for the transmission of video information. Last year, at Ashridge College in England, I heard Dr. W. J. Bray, who is in charge of the British end of the EarlyBird satellite system, describe how synchronous communications satellites can be used for global interlibrary communications. The American Telephone and Telegraph Company predicts that by 1970 more than half of the traffic transmitted over its lines will be in the form of digital data rather than of voice communications. The ability of libraries and information centers to engage in two-way multimedia communication with sister institutions and with individual users is extremely significant. This new factor can easily reshape the library's role and place in society.

The idea of remote direct access to central stores of digital information is not new. Computerized airline reservation systems, for example, have been in operation for many years. Eastern Airlines reservation network has telephone lines connecting more than five hundred points east of the Mississippi to a UNIVAC 490 real-time computer in Charlotte, North Carolina. Basic data concerning all Eastern flights are stored on a magnetic drum, called FASTRAND. A Uniset terminal, at each agent location, serves as an input device for entering the passenger's flight request. On command, the Uniset transmits the request to the computer by cable line. The computer looks up the flight, performs the required logical processing, and composes a suitable response by extracting selections of data from the FASTRAND drum and communicating them back to the reservation agent through the communications system. This feedback causes a green or red bulb to light on the Uniset, allowing the agent to give a corresponding yes or no answer to the prospective passenger.

The Massachusetts Institute of Technology has led an experimental effort to place at a user's fingertips the terminal equipment needed to interrogate a large store of information, under the control of a computer program, while numerous other users are simultaneously using it. Project MAC provides its users with much more than merely a binary response. For example, a user at a terminal in Ann Arbor can transmit his computer program and data to the central computer in Cambridge. The computer, in turn, interacts with the user, debugging his program when necessary, processing the data for him, and finally giving the answer to the problem. All this occurs while users at other terminals elsewhere in the country are similarly conversing with the computer for their respective purposes.

Although Project MAC was designed for processing numerical problems, Dr. M. M. Kessler of the MIT Library developed a working model of a nonnumerical, on-line retrieval system serving as many as one hundred remote consoles at distant points throughout the country over ordinary telephone wire. Bibliographic information from the field of physics constitutes the data base. Interaction between man and machine is free of intermediates and employs an inquiry language that closely resembles English.

Demonstrations of remote retrieval by computer were also featured at the Library/USA exhibit produced by the American Library Association for the United States Pavilion at the New York World's Fair, 1964-65. Any person anywhere with access to a teletype machine was able to interrogate ALA's electronic computer at the New York World's Fair for selected essays, bibliographies, translations, and current periodical references by subject. The service provided was identical with what the requester would have received had he been standing in the exhibit area in New York.

The teletype machine, incidentally, is far from new to libraries. The Free Library of Philadelphia used a teletype machine in 1927 for internal communication between the stacks and the circulation desk. Teletype has been said to couple the speed of the telephone with the authority of the printed word. One of the earliest library teletype networks was installed in 1951 at Michigan State Library. A disastrous fire had crippled the State Library, and teletype communications were used to link it with the Detroit Public Library, the University of Michigan Library, and the Grand Rapids Public Library in order to provide interim library service while the State Library rebuilt its own collection.

Shortly thereafter, other libraries began acquiring teletype machines; by 1965 the yellow pages of the teletype directory listed 130 library subscribers in the United States. Dr. L. J. van der Wolk, Director of the Bibliotheek Technische Hogeschool in Delft, Holland, reported in 1966 that 821 libraries throughout the world were in teletype communication. The number of installations in the United States seems to be growing steadily, and teletype networks are being used to negotiate interlibrary loans, to query union catalogs, to answer reference requests, and to carry on miscellaneous communication with other libraries.

Thus far I have reviewed examples of remote access to digital information. Let us now turn our attention to the methods which can be used for gaining access to stores of audio information from a distance.

A typical dial access system is in operation today at the University of Wisconsin Medical School for the retrieval of medical tape recordings. Physicians on the staff of the Medical School record 4- to 6-minute commentaries on current information having to do with various medical subjects. Tape content is changed and updated according to a preset schedule. Tapes include topics such as: "Surgery for Carotid Insufficiency" and "Intracranial Hypertension." A practicing physician in any state may telephone (Area Code 601-262-4515) at any time of the day or night and request that a particular tape be played. Although audio information represents a slow form of information exchange, technological advances have been made to compress speech without distorting its content. The Division for the Blind at the Library of Congress has experimental tapes that use this new technique. Two to three times as much information can be recorded per linear inch of tape in this way without loss of comprehension. Direct access to stores of audio information offers an inexpensive and practical method for updating information frequently and distributing it over an established, reliable telephone network.

An example of a hybrid digital-audio system can be found at Carson Pirie Scott and Company in Chicago. This department store issues dial cards to its customers for credit sales. The telephone number of the company's computer and the purchaser's account number are punched into the dial card. By depressing the dial card into a touch-tone telephone, any salesperson can automatically communicate with the central computer and cause it to examine the purchaser's credit history. The same touch-tone telephone can also be used by the salesperson to enter the dollar amount of the purchase into the computer by merely depressing the push buttons as if they were keys on a

cash register. Thus, the touch-tone telephone not only establishes contact with the computer, but also provides an on-line communications channel for further data input as needed. (The old rotary dial was unable to perform this function without extensive buffering electronics.) After the computer has compared the dollar amount with the purchaser's credit record, it determines whether any limits have been exceeded. Following this logical processing, the computer automatically composes a voice message for relay to the salesperson. An audio response unit connected to the computer contains a limited number of words and phrases which were prerecorded by a lovely voice. It thus becomes possible for the computer logically to sequence a set of phrases to constitute the intelligence of a full sentence. With a little imagination, combined digital and audio systems such as the one just described can be designed for use by libraries and information centers to satisfy a variety of information requirements.

To round out the story of direct access, a word should be said about the use of video techniques. Stores of printed and graphic information in libraries and information centers usually exist in one of two forms, either as hard copy or as film. In either case, remote video scanning can permit a user to inspect these materials selectively on a television monitor from a distance. For example, the Mosler Safe Company recently announced its SELECTRIEVER equipment, which provides automatic access to a single page among millions of frames on microfiche. The system finds the desired fiche, brings it to a holding station, scans it with a television camera, and transmits the intelligence to a remove television monitor. Printed material in books and journals can be similarly scanned and transmitted by either video or facsimile equipment.

Facsimile transmission is another method for sending graphic material from library to library. The original material can be either film or the printed page. Video type scanning at the sending station converts the intelligence on the original material into signals which can be sent over standard communication lines. At the receiving station, these signals are reconstituted to form a copy of the original message. Cost, time, and the requirement for a flatbed scanner are the current obstacles to wider use of facsimile transmission among libraries. However, with the introduction of wide-band telecommunication facilities, we can surely expect to see the trend change sharply. Within the past year, experimental facsimile networks have been installed in Hawaii, Nevada, New York State, and California.

As an extension of the use of video to provide remote access to information, several companies are developing video discs that will record many thousands of individual video frames of information; a single frame of video information could be the equivalent of a page of text. Since discs can be addressed digitally, it becomes possible rapidly to locate a particular frame without scanning the entire file sequentially. Ultimately, we can expect to see information systems capable of broadcasting video frames incrementally as well as continuously to television sets in homes and offices (which can be uniquely addressed by the transmitter). This form of television time-sharing could have a profound effect on the design of information distribution systems of the future, particularly if the utilization of standard television broadcasting facilities for this purpose proves feasible.

A library communications network utilizing many of the ideas described here may bring us a wholly new approach to library service—an approach in which librarians will increasingly share their resources with one another rather than concentrate on developing competitive collections. But technology alone is not enough. Technology in the service of imaginative and creative minds shows us a future bright with promise.

DISCUSSION

JOHN KOUNTZ, Orange County Library System: I was wondering if there has been any attempt made by ALA or ISAD to communicate with various industrial firms, such as Hughes Aircraft or Autonetics, or perhaps even IBM, who under government contract have developed information retrieval and information processing systems which may be adaptable to our uses.

MR. BECKER: As far as I know, no such formal relationship exists or has existed, but all military contractors are required by the Department of Defense to submit copies of their research findings to a central organization which then makes them widely available, provided they are unclassified.

MR. SALMON: ISAD does, of course, receive information, frequently not by solicitation, sometimes by solicitation; we do keep it on file at ALA headquarters, because we have been discussing for the last year or longer the establishment of a clearinghouse on library automation and related technology at headquarters.

As many of you know, this division has also cooperated with a similar type of clearinghouse function at the Library of Congress, called LOCATE [Library of Congress Automation Techniques Exchange], which also maintains information on actual library applications and on related technology.

Question: Are there differences in the various experiments for facsimile transmission in terms of systems or in terms of equipment?

MR. BECKER: I cannot answer the question about systems; I do know that the equipment is different. For example, the Xerox Corporation features long-distance xerography, which is called LDX, and there are some organizations that are using it in their experiments. There are other libraries that are using facsimile systems provided by the Alden Electronics Company and others provided by Western Union.

Systems Study as Related to Library Operations

Need and Planning

Edward A. Chapman

Director of Libraries
Rensselaer Polytechnic Institute

My paper deals with the topic of library systems study as related to the control and ordering of data and records which bulk so large in library operations. As I have told students in library orientation lectures, the library, among other things, is a big records factory with a great volume of internal data processing behind the books or information they receive from the library.

I know that the phrases "systems study" and "data processing" usually are related to the use of computer-based systems. It is true that a systems study is prerequisite to a well-designed, automated data processing system, but the end results of a systems study need not be a computer system. The organization of data-handling operations can and should be a matter of study, whether your operations are to be manual, semiautomated, or fully automated. There probably is not a single procedure or process in any library that cannot be performed more efficiently and effectively in the interests of improved processing of library materials, and in the interests of improved reader services. A particularly hard look should be given outmoded, time-consuming technical processing procedures. The pressures and demands being experienced by libraries are compelling arguments for work simplification, greater accuracy, speedier execution, and greater flexibility in adjustment to unpredictable requirements.

What we are talking about is the "make-ready" work that feeds the primary goal of the library, service to users. The systems of make-ready operations to be considered are the acquisitions system, the cataloging system, the serials control system, and the circulation control system, all of which are concerned with the production and handling of records and data without which the total library system would grind to a halt.

I shall give you an overview of the planning of a systems study from the viewpoint of library management and its responsibilities and functions in a systems study. Mr. St. Pierre describes in the following paper the role of the library analyst in executing a

systems study consisting of three phases: the analysis of the present operating data processing system; the evaluation of the efficiency, economy, accuracy, productivity, and timeliness of existing methods and procedures, measured against the established goals of the library; and the design of new methods and procedures to improve the flow of data through the system. Mr. St. Pierre treats in considerable detail the first major phase of a systems study (the analysis of the library's current procedures), giving guidelines on what this analysis is, how it is conducted, what results should be expected, and the techniques, methods, and tools used. The remaining two major steps (evaluation of current procedures and the design of a system) are discussed in general terms.

The Wiley manual you have received presents in some detail the concepts that will be treated in this meeting. It will serve as your guide, at home, in conducting a systems study. It contains sample survey worksheets for use in the analysis phase of a study.

You will not, of course, leave this session prepared to design a computer system, but with the manual as a guide you should be able to perform at least three functions:

1. To analyze and evaluate some of the basic manual methods and procedures in your library, and to design or redesign those methods for smoother and more efficient operation
2. To provide analysts and programmers the information each requires, and understand better what each will be looking for in analyzing your system and designing a new one
3. To evaluate the findings and recommendations of the analysts and to determine whether the implementation of such recommendations will satisfy the requirements you have specified for the system.

A systems study is little more than another way to say "let's get organized." Administrative and "housekeeping" functions and decision making require systematic study and development and should not be left, as is frequently the case, to the pragmatic approach, to on-the-job experience, or to intuition.[1] Most libraries are, or are becoming, complex organisms of interacting operations whose control and results cannot be left to intuition if the total operating system is to attain its primary goal of meaningful service to its community. Clerical functions merit special analysis and study. The application of integrated data processing procedures, based upon the recommendations of a systems study, should result in clerical workers or computers taking over the clerical work and jobs done by many librarians, thus freeing librarians for creative endeavor.

Walk into the acquisitions department of most any library today, and you will see a continuing growth in the backlog of requests for material. The open-order file will be bulging with outstanding orders; the accounting clerk will have a mounting backlog of uncleared invoices; and the section checking in books will contain shelves of uncleared books awaiting processing. Visit the cataloging department, and you will find an analogous situation: an increasing backlog of uncataloged materials. Increasing funds and staff shortages are forcing administrators to look toward solutions of such problems through modern data processing systems.

What are the principal symptoms of a library's inability to adapt to the pressures and increasing demands causing complexities in the library? These symptoms are: (1) increasing unit costs in processing library materials; (2) increasing backlogs of requests and of materials standing unprocessed; and (3) deterioration in the services needed and expected by the library's community. It is the responsibility of library management to evaluate continually each of the library's operating systems to determine whether one or more of the preceding symptoms exists. Except for minor adjustments in operations, if these symptoms exist, the library management will have to gain approval for conducting a systems study from his governing administration, including authorization of the extra funds required for such a study. In order to gain approval, library management must be capable of rudimentary analysis and evaluation of data processing systems. It is not sufficient for management merely to recognize that problems exist; in order to convince the library's governing administration that changes are needed, the library director will also have to present the reasons causing the breakdown of the library's systems and present preliminary recommendations for improving operations (see Bibliography No.323).

---

[1] The usual situation in this connection is well described in Mary Lee Bundy, "Decision Making in Libraries," *Illinois Libraries*, 43:780-93 (Dec. 1961).

ORGANIZING, PLANNING, AND CONDUCTING THE SYSTEMS STUDY

Let us turn now to the business of organizing, planning, and conducting a systems study. Since a systems study represents a major total library effort which often results in major operating changes, the entire library staff, under strong leadership by the administration of the library, must be fully involved in planning and conducting the study. The guidance, direction, and personal participation of the director of the library are also critical in planning and conducting the study.

Having received authorization to proceed, the director must first select and appoint the staff to make the study. There are two principles to be kept in mind here: a good systems study cannot be done on a part-time basis and the person selected to direct the study preferably should possess a combination of education in librarianship and training in the methods of systems analysis as taught in modern management courses. Since satisfaction of the latter prerequisite probably is not possible in most instances today, one of two courses is open: either to designate a library staff member to prepare himself for the conduct of a study or to bring in a skilled systems analyst unfamiliar with library organization. However long it may take, the outside analyst skilled in modern management techniques must become fully familiar with the library's problems and responsibilities and develop a rapport and identification with the supervisory staff.

The study staff, then, should consist of:

1. A library officer possessing responsibility and authority within the library's organization to take supervision of the study
2. At least one member, preferably a librarian, fully trained and experienced in the application of management-analysis techniques
3. At least one staff member, again preferably a librarian, skilled in electronic data processing methods if an automated system is contemplated
4. Clerical staff adequate to support the work of the study staff.

This staff develops with library management a detailed procedural plan and time schedule for the systems study itself. The first step of this planning is defining the problems to be studied; it is the responsibility of the library's management to supply a clear and concise statement of these problems, in the form of a written report, such as would have been prepared for gaining governing administrative support and financing for the systems study originally.

The next step, and the most critical in the planning and conduct of the study, is the definition of the library's goals. The statement of goals determines the major requirements which must be satisfied by the library, and which are basic in evaluating the current system and in designing a new system. If the goals are not precisely and correctly defined and understood in detail, the results can only be an inaccurate evaluation of current operations and the design of a faulty system.

Long-term planning is implicit in defining the library's goals. Since most libraries, as stated earlier, are in a period of dynamic growth which will persist, systems to satisfy long-term goals must be designed with the capability of handling increased demands. Thus, computer-based systems are suggested; such systems have the capability to grow less costly and more efficient as demands upon the library grow, while today's commonly applied manual systems become more costly and less efficient under increasing demands and do not possess the "standby" qualities of the computer system in adjusting to growing requirements.

The following are major goals of many libraries today:

1. To improve service to users through more efficient use of available professional talent, who are relieved of data processing functions
2. To provide prompter access to and greater use of the library's resources
3. To participate in library network programs of bibliographic data distribution and information transfer.

Once goals have been defined, the scope of the study must be established. At this stage, particular systems within the library that are to be studied are identified, in order to prevent the study from wandering into other systems with which management is not concerned at this juncture. Priorities are then established to determine the components needing early attention by the library's administration. It is important in specifying scope and priorities that the systems study staff not be too rigidly restricted but allowed enough flexibility to permit recognition of other areas which might be affected by the particular system directly assigned for study.

Management should also define any limits or restrictions to be placed upon the development of a system. It is important, obviously, for the study staff to know these limits prior to the systems analysis phase. Illustrative of limits and restrictions are:

1. The type of system wanted: manual, semiautomated, automated
2. The number and distribution of personnel to be in the system
3. Tolerable unit costs or total costs of operations of the system.

In further preparation, the study staff members must decide upon the methods and techniques to be used in the study in order to ensure a logical, systematic study, as well as a consistency of results and compatibility of findings.

After selection of the methods to be applied throughout the study, the criteria for each method selected should be adopted, thus assuring that the results reached by each study staff member are in agreement and allow uniform evaluation by the staff as a body. For example, if statistical work sampling is to be used, the confidence level to be accepted should be agreed upon in advance, with applicable sampling techniques being uniformly employed. Survey forms must also be designed for each of the surveys to be conducted in the study.

As terminal planning steps, the organization of the work of the study staff is set down, and a time schedule is prepared for completion of its assignment. The latter includes estimating the amount of work in each study assignment, measured by man days or man months; determining the type of skills needed for each assignment (managerial analysis, clerical, programming); defining clearly the responsibilities of each person in prosecuting and completing his study assignment; setting target dates for interim reporting to the library's management; and setting the target date for submission of the final study report. The time schedule is not only important to the orderly and expeditious prosecution of the study but to administrative knowledge and acceptance of how long current library operations will be affected by the study's demands upon operating time (see Bibliography No.321).[2]

As the plan for the systems study is being formulated, it is the responsibility of the director of the library to introduce the idea to the library staff, indicating the reasons for a study and its objectives. When planning is completed, the director should review the finished plan with the study staff and with other members of the library's administration. When he has approved the plan, the director of the library should make formal announcement to the library's community of the undertaking of the systems study, indicating the reasons for the study, its objectives and anticipated benefits, as well as explaining what problems the user may temporarily encounter during the period of the study.

The staff must be assured of the administration's awareness and sympathetic understanding of the disruption of each staff member's assigned duties and be assured of the administration's firm support of the study. It must be demonstrated to the staff that without the cooperation and participation of each member, the study cannot lead to results beneficial to the staff and the library as a whole.

Following the announcement of the starting date of the study, it is well to conduct a short staff training program detailing the techniques used in a systems

---

[2] The structure of this section on planning, which began on page 8, is based on James W. Greenwood, Jr., *EDP: The Feasibility Study—Analysis and Improvement of Data Processing* ("Systems Education Monograph," No.4 [n.p.: Systems and Procedures Assn., 1962]).

study. Discussion of these techniques will bring a better understanding of the study, generate the necessary staff interest in it, and furnish knowledge of what information the analyst will be seeking in his contacts with individual library staff members. The training program might also include a description of the potential use and contribution of computers in library data processing operations and library services.

It cannot be overstressed that staff understanding and support are prerequisites to a meaningful systems study. Support in this phase of organizational improvement efforts will be carried over into the successful implementation of the study's recommendations. This, of course, is true in any activity: engendering staff cooperation, willingness, interest, desire, and pride in work assures attainment of operating objectives.

The basic ingredients of a fruitful systems study, then, are: (1) precise knowledge of management's goals; (2) the full support and participation of management; (3) a rigorously objective attitude on the part of analysts and their acceptance as members of the library's professional staff; and (4) full staff involvement at all levels (see Bibliography No.321).

NEW PROFESSIONAL CAREER OPPORTUNITIES

The entire ISAD [Information Science and Automation Division] Preconference program, predominately concerned as it is with library automation, quite obviously suggests new professional career opportunities and a preparation supplemental to library education as we have known it. As mentioned in the beginning of this session, there are too few professional librarians equipped to analyze and evaluate their own problems and to design methods and procedures for more effective internal operations to meet the library's goals. Bob Hayes emphasizes this in his recent paper, writing in effect that librarians must acquire sufficient orientation to enable them to fit data processing into the context of library goals.[3]

Take this business of systems study we have been discussing: It is the beginning of a different administrative and organizational work pattern which must be constantly monitored in order to maintain and improve the library's ability to achieve the goals set for it. The analysis and evaluation of current methods and procedures must continue in order to ensure that they are in fact meeting the demands for information and action being placed upon the systems within a library; if not, methods and procedures must be modified or redesigned.

Thus a "new breed in librarianship" is arising, as Paul Wasserman puts it in his admirable essay "The Librarian and the Machine."[4] Members of this new breed are the library systems analyst, and the programming librarian in the case of computer-based library systems. The demand for such personnel, trained in managerial skills, creates enhanced career opportunities in librarianship itself. As you may recall, I conjectured that some alleviation of the professional manpower shortage problem can occur by releasing the professional librarian from data processing functions to the areas of professional services to library users and research in user requirements and improved methods of service. With housekeeping chores concentrated in the hands of specialists in data processing and automation, "librarianship may devote itself to one of its higher roles—education," as Louis Shores has written.[5]

Basic education in librarianship coupled with specialization in data processing and/or computer programming is suggested if not essential for the professionally oriented library systems analyst and programming librarian. The problems to be solved are not simply tied to managerial technology but also involve understanding of the professional objectives to be served.[6] Librarians must be able to analyze, evaluate, and design their own systems in terms of the requirements of librarianship. Otherwise the management and computer technologist, unaware or incompletely aware of the goals of librarianship, may unwittingly adversely influence organizational structures required for the attainment of the purposes of library service. As Wasserman writes in discussing the use of technological expertness by libraries, "the responsibility of the data processing person...must be subordinate to a management which is broader and more comprehensive in its approach to the program of the library. Even when those who are trained or experienced in data processing begin to assume general and broader library management responsibility, it must be for the ability which those so chosen manifest in these broader problems of organization than simply those tied to its technology." Thus it is advisable to look toward the library profession itself in the development of these new administrative positions in order to maintain balance in the composition of library administration leadership.

Every library should have on its staff at least one full-time officer whose fundamental responsibility is that of improving the library's systems and procedures and constantly modifying processes and procedures as demands or requirements placed upon the organization increase or change. As stated previously,

[3] Robert M. Hayes, "Data Processing in the Library School Curriculum," *ALA Bulletin,* 61:662-69 (June 1967).

[4] Paul Wasserman, *The Librarian and the Machine: Observations on the Applications of Machines in Administration of College and University Libraries* (Detroit: Gale Research Co., 1965). Dr. Wasserman's felicitous comments on the analyst's place and role in the library's organization are recognized subsequently by quotation marks unless otherwise noted.

[5] Louis Shores, "Epitome," *Journal of Library History,* 2:97 (Apr. 1967).

[6] Paul Wasserman, *op. cit.,* p.88; Thomas Minder, "Library Systems Analyst: A Job Description," *College and Research Libraries,* 27:271-76 (July 1966).

the size of a library is not a determining factor in deciding whether a systems study should be made. In the case of the one-man library, it is left for the librarian himself to acquire the requisite managerial skills. On the other hand, the medium-sized to large library organizations should think in terms of full-time staff specialists or a systems and procedure director with staff and divisional status.

Whether the systems analyst or director of auxiliary services is a line or staff officer, he must be one whose point of view and interests are coterminous with those of the library's director, and who is established and accepted as an agent of the director. The responsibilities of this position, in cooperation with library department heads, include:

1. Assisting management in continuous review and evaluation of operations and services to meet the established goals of the library
2. Designing and implementing new and improved procedures and operating systems for increased effectiveness, strengthened operating or management controls, and expedited performance of routine work
3. Developing operating manuals and reviewing, improving, and planning statistical and accounting reports for managerial control at all levels
4. Keeping abreast of new developments in data processing and of their application to library operations, together with associated equipment
5. Designing forms and evaluating the need for, and format of, proposed new forms
6. Conducting training programs for staff and management in the continuous application of systems study techniques to daily operating problems, and in the capabilities and use of the computer in operations and library services
7. Directing the design and programming of computer based systems and representing the library's interests in shared computer facilities.

Systems analysis, evaluation, and design, whether directed toward manual, semiautomated, or automated operations, will be for naught unless done by persons who are thoroughly trained or formally educated in librarianship. Although without experience, the library school graduate is prepared to learn the nuances of library service that can be gained only through experience; at least his schooling has made him aware of this contingency and he is prepared to develop professional attitudes. This cannot be safely said of one trained solely in managerial techniques.

Library schools in the main are beginning to recognize the need of at least an introduction to systems study and data processing in conjunction with the substantive aspects of librarianship, as a recent article revealed.[7] There is, however, a tendency to feel that the inexperienced library student, without sufficient prior knowledge of the components of a total library

[7] Robert M. Hayes, *op. cit.,* p.664.

system, would not properly profit from instruction in these phases of managerial science. Cannot this be said, too, of the student courses on library administration and library organization, where the application of principles can only be inferred and may be misinterpreted?

Paul Wasserman suggests that the library school, as doubtless some are planning, should offer programs in data processing to the practicing librarian at an intermediate level "not necessarily tied to any formal degree level," resulting in "some type of certificate midway between the master's and doctorate." I suggest conversely the offering, to management degree holders, of programs in the specific functions of systems in a library. The possibilities for development of modern methods at an administrative level should be attractive to these trained people. Such training is being offered by some libraries through in-service study programs; in institutions where both a library degree and a management degree are offered, some cross-discipline advertising and coercion could be profitable in making available to libraries management personnel with "know-how" in library operations.

In any event, a need exists which must be satisfied in the interests of meeting the services being increasingly demanded from the library. In the parlance of the market, library is indeed a "growth" stock, and its operations must be tailored to meet the expanding requirements of its users, the research worker, the student, and the public whose sights are being constantly raised by more and more people having modern educational preparation in increasing depth in more and more subjects.

In sum, the need for libraries to undertake systems studies is underlined by the fact that manipulation and control of data is a major element of the work within a library. Upon the systematics of data handling depends the effectiveness of internal operations in carrying out the library's functions and in meeting the library's goals. Modern library management must become aware of the need for a systems study through identification of existing data-handling problems and recognition of the pressures causing them. With the complexity of library operations multiplying, there is no recourse but for librarians to learn the techniques and tools of systems study and the skills to apply them. The library from its very beginning has perforce been extensively preoccupied with processing and control functions, but this is the computer age, not the typewriter age. We must abandon yesteryear methods and procedures to cope with the mounting pressure of reader demand.

DISCUSSION

Question: The examples of our three national libraries, as they have gone toward automation of their library operations, is an expression of a different philosophy than you have offered to the librarians here today. You have suggested that the people doing systems work should be from the library side, preferably, if not exclusively. Yet our three national libraries, while using as many librarians as they could, have gone in each case to a formal contract with an outside organization, to draw upon a wide variety of skills which those organizations offer and which the libraries have not been able to get from their own staffs.

I believe that if we restrain the development of automation in libraries to the views of the librarians, we will be much too restrictive. I believe we must obtain the views of the governing bodies and particularly of the needs of society for information. I am afraid that we as a library profession do not now see these in their fullest extent nor do we have the capabilities for all of the disciplines required to automate a library.

Now most libraries fall in the group between the one-man size (or one-girl size) and the national libraries, and they do not have the extensive funds available to them to go out on contract. They are going to have to compromise then and, in addition, train their own personnel as much as they can for automation. They are also going to have to seek, I believe, advice from outside corporations. A number of firms and individuals now have a considerable body of such information, and I believe it will be seen essential for these intermediate-size libraries to obtain this outside assistance as they attempt to automate their libraries.

If we do not go this route, I fear we will be limiting ourselves to what we can see in our own concepts, and our concepts won't be big enough for that.

MR. CHAPMAN: I don't think that our thesis is that

there shouldn't be help from outside, witness Rensselaer Polytechnic Institute, where Mr. St. Pierre, without a library degree, in a matter of some two years has acquired at least a semblance of understanding of library work.

Now, the converse can be true. What we are talking about is systems study not necessarily related to the development of computer-based systems.

MR. ST. PIERRE: I feel that the problem when you bring in the outside consultant to look at your problems is that he brings with him preconceived ideas of someone else's problems, and if he does not have sufficient time to spend within your own organization, he is going to solve your problems based upon someone else's solution. The reasons for the problems within the two organizations might be completely different. It is true that the national libraries have gone to outside consulting firms, but I think we will find (in Project MARC, for example) that they are now taking what was done during the original study and reprogramming it, reformatting it, in order to fit better the needs of the library profession.

I have also worked very closely with an outside consultant in the development of a large cataloging system which is not, in my impression, being done correctly and will have to be modified a great deal because, again, there was not sufficient time available for the consultant to spend within the library organization.

You cannot analyze a system by standing on the outside and looking in. You must become involved in it. The small or medium-sized library can usually take five or ten days of the consultant's time and that's all that he can afford, so they must depend, I think, upon their own people. I think we can train people to do this particular work.

Systems Study as Related to Library Operations

Analysis, Evaluation, and Design

Paul L. St. Pierre[1]

Assistant Director for Operations
Rensselaer Polytechnic Institute Libraries

DATA PROCESSING SYSTEM

A data processing system is defined as the organization and methods used to effect changes in the form and/or content of information in order to satisfy the demands placed upon the system. A data processing system's main functions are to manipulate, store, and retrieve information. It receives data upon which it performs certain predetermined operations and in so doing modifies the content and/or the form of the input in order to produce the desired results. Data processing systems are ongoing and dynamic processes consisting of groups of interrelated operations which tend to become increasingly complex as the volume of input and output requirements grows.

The complexity of any data processing system prohibits its study as a unit. The job of the study staff in the analysis phase is that of identifying the major activities of the system, i.e., the subsystems. A subsystem consists of a related group of operations which together satisfy one or more secondary requirements or demands placed upon the system and which contribute to the satisfaction of the system's primary requirements.

When the subsystems have been identified, the operations occurring within each subsystem must be isolated, and the functions and decisions associated with the manipulation of each input needed to prepare the desired output must be defined. Finally, the required actions resulting from the various decisions also must be defined.

These functions and decisions are the basic elements of a data processing system. The evaluation of a system consists of determining how well the functions are organized and performed and how appropriate the decisions are in satisfying the requirements of the system. In addition, the design of a new system must start with these basic elements.

Figure 1 illustrates the concept of a library data processing system, in particular an acquisitions system. Shown schematically is the combination of all the elements required to make up the acquisitions system operations. As previously stated, within this or any other system there is always a group of subsystems, each of which is designed for performance of particular tasks. The acquisitions system illustrated consists of the following subsystems: preorder search, ordering, receiving and checking, and accounting and reporting. As indicated, the subsystems depend one upon the other. For example, the ordering subsystem, taken as a unit, could not be meaningfully applied alone, for it would require the verified information supplied under the preorder search subsystem.

Let us consider the composition of any subsystem. Each subsystem consists of a group of logically interrelated operations, with each operation involving the performance of certain functions and/or requiring certain decisions upon which action is based.

Two operations in an accounting and reporting subsystem are analyzed in Table I. The level of detail in such an analysis as shown in this table depends upon the type of system being developed. If the design of a computer system is contemplated, the functions and decisions must be defined in sufficient detail to permit the programmer to program the system.

Figure 2 illustrates a total library system and its operating systems. The total system operates within an environment dictated by the goals of its parent organization or governing body. The objectives of a total system are "to organize administrative work flows from the viewpoint of the library as a whole, without regard for barriers of organizational segments," and "to develop data processing systems whereby source data are recorded once and thereafter perpetuated in various summary forms to meet ...operating...needs without repetitive processing."[2] Although these two aims can be accomplished to a limited extent by manual methods, it is the

---

[1] Mr. St. Pierre is now Chief, Systems Analysis and Data Processing Office, New York Public Library, New York City.

[2] Alan D. Meacham and Van B. Thompson, *Total Systems* (Detroit: American Data Processing, Inc., 1962), p.16.

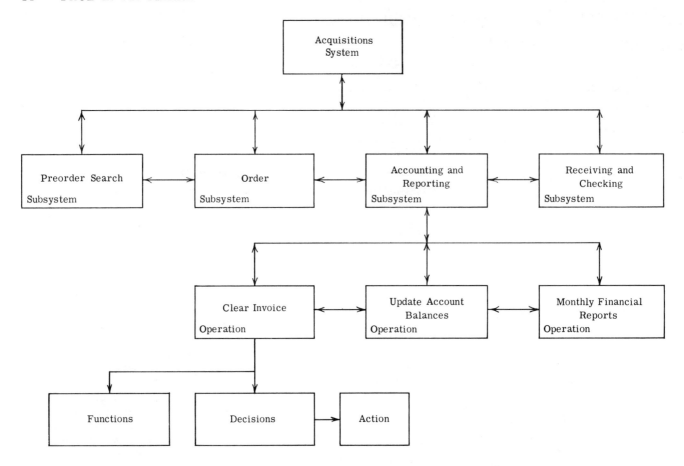

Figure 1. Acquisitions System

complexity of interaction among systems which is causing libraries to investigate the concept of a total system requiring computer methods.

The realization of the total system concept can only occur when the major operating systems have been so designed and integrated that the interaction and exchange of information are facilitated in a logical and systematic manner. Planning of individual systems is not an end in itself; such planning must always be within the context of developing a total system.

Within the library, the planning of a total system involves the developing of methods to prepare, control, and utilize three major record types: bibliographic, fiscal, and inventory. This requires the designing of integrated procedures for what are regarded as the six major library systems: administration and planning; acquisitions; cataloging; serials control; circulation; and reference. Integrated procedures are essential for relaying information from one system to another, so that a given system can adjust to satisfy the requirements of the total library system.

DETERMINATION OF THE REQUIREMENTS OF THE SYSTEM

The requirements of a system are the demands placed upon it for specified information and actions. Since the system's raison d'être is to provide information and take necessary actions, the system must be evaluated with respect to how efficiently, accurately, and economically it fulfills these requirements.

The study staff must translate the stated goals of the library into the requirements that the goals place upon each system and, in addition, must identify other requirements and their sources from:

1. Outside of the local organization: American Library Association rules for filing; rules for main entry; reports required by governmental agencies and professional groups
2. Outside of the library locally: accounting information required by central purchasing offices; user requests for information and services

TABLE I

THE LOGICAL INTERRELATIONSHIPS OF SUBSYSTEM OPERATIONS

Operation	Function	Decision	Action	Subsystem Tasks
X				Clear invoice for payment
		X		Is invoice correct and complete?
			X	Yes: clear invoice
			X	No: determine invalid data; correct or return invoice
	X			Assign proper account number to invoice
	X			Post the order, invoice and account numbers, and amount to invoice register
X				Maintain current balance on each book fund
	X			Post invoice amount to proper book fund
	X			Calculate new balance for each book fund
		X		Has book fund reached minimum balance (balance equal to or less than $100.00)?
			X	Yes: notify library director for authorization of additional funds or discontinue ordering

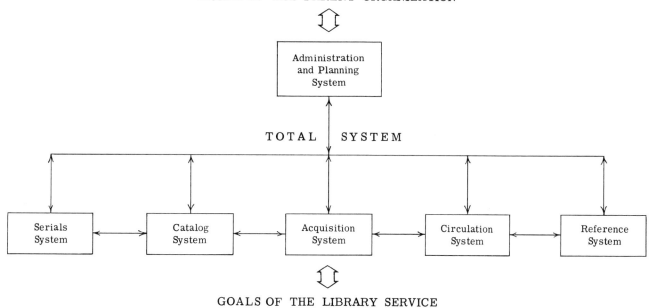

GOALS OF THE PARENT ORGANIZATION

Administration and Planning System

TOTAL SYSTEM

Serials System — Catalog System — Acquisition System — Circulation System — Reference System

GOALS OF THE LIBRARY SERVICE

Figure 2. Total Library System

WORKSHEET
For the Survey of Requirements

1. Prepare a copy of this worksheet for each of your requirements. 2. Attach a completed sample of each record or report.

System	Analyst	Date
Name of Person Interviewed	Position	
Name of Supervisor	Position	

Describe the Requirement:

Describe decisions you make in satisfying this requirement:

Describe what action you may take as a result of your decisions:

Describe the functions you perform in satisfying this requirement:

RENSSELAER LIBRARIES, TROY, NEW YORK

Describe how you use each bibliographical, fiscal, inventory and statistical record or report satisfying this requirement (use additional forms as necessary). PLEASE ATTACH A COMPLETED SAMPLE OF EACH RECORD OR REPORT; on samples circle in black information you use, in red information you add, and, in blue any information regarded unnecessary.

Figure 3. Worksheet for the Survey of Requirements

PRELIMINARY SURVEY WORKSHEET RENSSELAER LIBRARIES TROY, NEW YORK			
System	Analyst		Date
Brief Description of System			
Primary Requirement of the System:			
		Manual of Procedures Available	Yes ☐ No ☐

EQUIPMENT SURVEY			
Type of Equipment	Location	Special Features	% Utilization

PERSONNEL SURVEY					
Name Each Staff Position	Job Level	Special Skills Required	Name of Person in This Position	Job Level	Special Skills Available

In preparing the following analysis, every effort should be made to list the components in the order that they normally occur in the present system.						
	Type of Component					
Sub- system	Oper.	Func.	Dec.- Action	Name of Component	DESCRIPTION	Standard Rate

Figure 4. Preliminary Survey Worksheet

3. Within the library itself: other systems depending upon this system for information; the director of libraries requiring certain reports and statistics
4. Within the system itself: information required by a subsystem from another; information required within a subsystem.

The need for identifying sources arises in connection with the authority the study staff may or may not have in modifying, changing, or eliminating specified requirements.

The study staff should interview the following people to identify the requirements each one places upon the system:

1. The director of libraries
2. The users of the libraries
3. Within the parent organization, the heads of departments affecting library operations, such as purchasing and accounting departments
4. The head of each major operating system within the library
5. The head of the system being surveyed
6. The personnel within the system being surveyed.

Figure 3, "Worksheet for the Survey of Requirements," can be used as a guide and record in the interviews for determining the requirements placed upon the system by each interviewee. Whether a similar form is used or not, the following questions should be asked:

1. What bibliographic, statistical, and account records or reports are needed?
2. What system generates the requested records or reports?
3. What information must these reports and records contain?
4. Why and how is this information used?
5. Is the information received in usable or final form? If not, what functions must be performed to adapt it for use?
6. Is the proper information furnished for making necessary decisions? What are these decisions and their bases?
7. What actions are normally taken as the result of these decisions?

Each of the records and reports used must be thoroughly analyzed in the survey of outputs, a step in the analysis phase.

ANALYSIS AND UNDERSTANDING OF CURRENT PROCEDURES

With the requirements of the system definitely known, the study staff can proceed to the remaining steps in the analysis phase. Before the study staff members can ask intelligent and pertinent questions, they must have a working understanding of the capabilities and the deficiencies of the current system.

Figure 4, "Preliminary Survey Worksheet," is the worksheet used to record the basic data of the initial system study. The Equipment Survey portion should include information on:

1. Equipment used in the present system
2. Other equipment available in the library and outside of the library
3. Location of each item of equipment
4. Special features of any items of equipment, such as tape typewriter with punched card input and output
5. Percentage use of each item of equipment
6. Authorization and procedure required for use of equipment outside of the library and availability schedule of the equipment
7. Age and condition of each item of equipment.

The Personnel Survey section should provide from organizational charts, job descriptions and personnel classification schedules, and personal interviews, the following information:

1. Positions currently authorized in the system
2. Job levels (classification and grade of each authorized position)
3. Special skills required in each position
4. Name of incumbent for each authorized position, noting vacancies, or additional personnel not reflected in organizational chart
5. Actual job level of each incumbent
6. Special skills currently available
7. Whether job descriptions are accurate or outdated.

The bottom of the "Preliminary Survey Worksheet" (Figure 4) may be used by the analyst to organize his findings, as follows:

1. Indicate in the appropriate box, by a check mark, the type of component
2. Supply name of component if so identifiable
3. Supply description of each component
   a. Subsystem: Indicate major requirements. Identify the other subsystems and/or system with which it interacts
   b. Operations: Identify by name, the inputs and outputs of each operation together with the number of items received and the number processed, by day, or by week, or by month
   c. Functions: Describe procedures and methods for performing each function
   d. Decisions-Actions: Describe criteria for each decision and the resulting action taken
4. Standard rate: This is defined as the number of work units processed per unit of time. This should be determined for each function if practicable; if not, the standard rate for each operation must be calculated.

DETERMINATION OF OUTPUTS

The outputs of the system consist of the records and reports prepared or maintained by the system to

WORKSHEET
For the Survey of Outputs
1.   Prepare a worksheet for each output that is prepared or maintained.
2.   Attach a completed copy of each.

SYSTEM	ANALYST		DATE

NAME OF PERSON INTERVIEWED	POSITION

NAME OF SUPERVISOR	POSITION

NAME OF OUTPUT

TYPE OF OUTPUT	Bibliographic Fiscal	Inventory Statistical	Record	Report

Identify the requirement(s) which use the output:

Describe the functions you perform in preparing or maintaining this output:

Describe the decisions:

Describe the action taken:

RECORDS	Present size of file:		How many records added to the file:	_____ Daily _____ Weekly _____ Monthly
Type of file:			How file arranged:	
Are written rules available:	Yes No	How long is record kept in active file:		How long kept in inactive file:
How often is file referred to:			By whom:	
How much time required to prepare record:			How much time spent on filing:	
How much time spent in updating:				

REPORTS	How many copies:	What use is made of each copy and by whom:

How much time spent in preparing report:

What information, if any, is added to the output and where does the added information originate. Circle this information in red on sample:

Is any of the information in this output transcribed to other forms or records. Circle this information in blue on sample:

Does the information contained in the output appear on other records independently originated in the system. Circle this information in black on the sample:

Use this area for your comments; please do not forget to attach a completed form:

This area for the analyst's comments:

Figure 5. Worksheet for the Survey of Outputs

SUMMARY WORKSHEET FOR THE SURVEY OF REQUIREMENTS

SYSTEM	ANALYST		DATE
Name or description of requirement	Identify each output which is required to satisfy the requirement (report, records)	What operations prepare or maintain each of these outputs	What activities receive each of these outputs both within or outside the system

RENSSELAER LIBRARIES
TROY, NEW YORK

Figure 6. Summary Worksheet for the Survey of Requirements

satisfy the requirements placed upon it. During the survey of requirements, each output will have been identified. The purpose of the survey of outputs is to determine the methods and procedures involved in preparing and maintaining each output. The outputs of a library system may be categorized by type: bibliographic, fiscal, and inventory.

In using the "Worksheet for the Survey of Outputs" (Figure 5), the analyst must:

1. Identify the requirement(s) which the output satisfied in whole or in part
2. Identify the type of output: bibliographic, fiscal, or inventory
3. Determine the specific information contained in each output and the source of such information
4. Determine for each report prepared by the system:
   a. Who received the report
   b. Number of copies necessary
   c. Whether the report is intermediate or final
   d. Method of preparation
5. Determine for each record maintained by the system:
   a. How long the record is kept in active files or in inactive files
   b. The frequency of reference to a given record, and by whom reference is made
   c. What information is used from the record and how it is used
   d. Whether information is available in any other record of the system
   e. Whether information is added to this record continuously; if so, by whom and how often
   f. What the disposition of the record is if it is not permanent, e.g., that it is destroyed or transferred to another system
6. Determine how many outputs are prepared or maintained, and the time consumed in this activity
7. Identify the level of the system at which the output originates
8. Determine if information is needed from other systems to complete the output, and if so, from what systems and what information
9. Identify what functions of the system are concerned with generating the output
10. Determine what decisions are required in preparing the output
11. Identify what actions result from these decisions and the effect of such actions upon the outputs.

A sample copy of each actual output should be obtained from each person responsible for preparing it, together with answers to the following questions:

1. What information, if any, is added to the output and where does the added information originate?
2. Is any of the information in this putput transcribed to other forms or records?
3. Does the information contained in the output appear on other records independently originated in the system?

After completing the survey of outputs, the analyst should fill in the "Summary Worksheet for the Survey of Requirements" (Figure 6).

DETERMINATION OF INPUTS TO THE SYSTEM

The inputs to a system constitute the body of information upon which the system must act in order to fulfill its requirements. Each subsystem within any system is on a standby basis until it is triggered into action by the entry into the system of one or more inputs. Each input may require the performance of one or more functions and/or the exercise of required decisions which lead to predetermined actions.

Before the functions of the analyst are discussed, it is necessary to describe further some of the types, sources, and forms of input:

1. Types of input
   a. A *primary* input is one which activates a subsystem. This type of input usually involves major clerical, professional, or mechanical functions, decisions, and actions. In acquisitions, for example, a book purchase request triggers the preorder search subsystem. The receipt of a book activates the receiving and checking subsystem.
   b. A *functional* input is one which usually involves only minor clerical functions requiring no decisions. For example, notice of delayed publication requires only that the clerk post the new date of anticipated receipt to the open-order record.
   c. An *instructional* input is one which modifies or explains a primary input. For example, in cataloging, the cataloger will create a worksheet which gives directions to the clerk in processing nonroutine items.
   d. An *informational* input is one which potentially may become the basis for one of the preceding types of inputs. For example, a new filing code may be adapted to the local situation (instructional input).
2. Sources of input
   a. From outside the local organization
   b. From outside the library locally
   c. From within the library itself
   d. From within the system itself.
3. Forms of input
   a. Manual input, i.e., handwritten or typed forms
   b. Machine record, e.g., punched cards, paper tape, magnetic tape
   c. Verbal communications.

Figure 7, "Worksheet for the Survey of Inputs," is used to record pertinent input data. In this phase of the analyst's survey, he must follow the flow of each input through the system, obtaining answers to the following questions for each input:

WORKSHEET
For The Survey of Inputs

1.   Prepare a copy of this worksheet for each input received. An input is any item of information upon which, or, as the result of, you perform any or all of your assigned functions.

2.   Attach completed sample of the input.

NAME OF INPUT		
SYSTEM	ANALYST	DATE
NAME OF PERSON INTERVIEWED	POSITION	
NAME OF SUPERVISOR	POSITION	

Review the description of the types of inputs given below and check the one which best describes this input:

☐ PRIMARY INPUT: involves major clerical, professional or mechanical functions, decisions, and actions.

☐ FUNCTIONAL INPUT: involves only minor clerical functions requiring no decisions.

☐ INSTRUCTIONAL INPUT: modifies or explains a primary or functional input.

☐ INFORMATIONAL INPUT: potentially may become the basis for one of the other types of inputs. Please answer additional questions below on informational inputs.

If informational input, who makes the decision that it is to enter the system:

If you make the decision, on what is it based:

Which of the other types of input does it become:

Source of input:	Do you have authority over this source:	☐ YES ☐ NO
Form of input: ☐ Handwritten ☐ Punched cards ☐ Verbal input ☐ Typed ☐ Paper tape ☐ Other (describe)		
Is input used in its original form: ☐ YES ☐ NO	Does the input enter the system at your operation:	☐ YES ☐ NO

Describe decisions you make in processing this input:

Describe what action you may take as a result of your decisions:

Describe the functions you perform in processing this input:

RENSSELAER LIBRARIES, TROY, NEW YORK

How many do you receive: Daily ____ Weekly ____ Monthly	How many do you process: ____ Daily ____ Weekly ____ Monthly
How much time do you require to process this input:	What is the disposition of this input: Destroy ____ Forward ____ File
If used by other functions, to which do you send it:	If verbal input, do you record for later use by you or others: YES NO
If you do record verbal input, in what form:	What is the name of the form:
How long is this input kept in active files: How long kept in inactive files:	How often is this file referred to: Active ____ Inactive
How many of these forms are filed: Daily ____ Weekly ____ Monthly	Are written procedures available for the processing and control YES NO

What information do you add to this input -- where does it come from; if other form, name it.
Circle this information in red on sample:

Do you copy any information from this form on to other forms or records; if so why.
Circle this information in green on sample:

Is any of the information on this form unnecessary for your operation.
Circle this information in blue on sample:

Does any of the information on this form appear on other forms used in this system other than those mentioned above.
Circle this information in black:

Use this area for your comments: Please do not forget to attach a completed form:

This area for the analyst's comments:

Figure 7. Worksheet for the Survey of Inputs

1. What is the form of the input? Is it necessary that the form be changed for use within the system?
2. Where and how does the input originate?
3. At what level does the input enter the system? At what levels is it used?
4. What information from the input record is required at each such level?
5. Is information added to the input record for use at other levels or is a new input record created?
6. What functions, decisions, and actions are triggered by the input?
7. Is the input eventually an output of the system?
8. What is the final disposition of the input?
9. What files and records does the input affect?
10. Are there written procedures that describe the functions of the input? (Such procedures should have been obtained in survey step 2, the analysis and understanding of current procedures.)
11. What is the type of the input? The first two types, the primary and functional inputs, must simply be identified. On the other hand, the next two types of input, instructional and informational, must be analyzed. The use of the instructional input can and should be minimized by setting up procedures covering all possible nonroutine functions; in other words, every effort should be made to eliminate such inputs by developing standard procedures for these nonroutine functions. Regarding the informational input, it is essential for the analyst to identify the decisions and actions occurring both inside and outside the system which require the entry of the informational input into the system. Further, he must identify the highest level at which these decisions and actions occur. Finally, the analyst must decide which of the other types of input (primary, functional, and instructional) the informational input will become if accepted.

The analyst, upon completion of the survey of inputs, should systematically summarize the foregoing data obtained on each input, using a summary worksheet. (For model, see Figure 8, "Summary Worksheet for the Survey of Inputs.") What information in each input is necessary, and at what level of the system is it used? The analyst must be aware that one input document may affect multiple operations, and that it might serve as input to more than one level of the operation, or to more than one subsystem in the system. He must determine, at each level, what information in the input is required. Further, he must determine what the minimum amount of information is that will allow for the completion of the system at each level. For example, on a purchase form, it is necessary to have the complete author's name at the time we order the book; it is not a necessity at the time we search it because the purpose of searching is to verify the author's name.

The analyst must determine the disposition of an input document when it has served its purpose. Is it retained? Is it filed? By main entry, by call number, by title? If it is filed, what function does it serve? Too often it is found, particularly in libraries, that files are retained which serve little or no purpose. Hours and hours are spent in maintaining such files, which also take up valuable space.

The analyst must also determine whether the input is used at various levels in the system in its original form, or whether it is rewritten. If it is rewritten, why is it rewritten? Why cannot the input be used in its original form? If it cannot be used in its original form, can the form be changed? If changed, what is the effect at the originating source? The analyst must determine, in the case of verbal communications within the system, if this is the most effective form of input from one level to another or within the same level. Is the data that is transmitted through verbal communications something that is required later in the system, and therefore must be retransmitted by someone else? Is the information that is transmitted of importance to the system? Is the information that is transmitted an output of the system that is being passed up the line to be incorporated eventually in a report? If so, why is it not recorded on the report at the point where it originates, instead of up the line where the chances of error creep in? Are verbal inputs to the system allowed from outside the organization? A fundamental rule in any system is never to accept verbal input from outside the system. Having all the information available on the system, the analyst is prepared to proceed with the evaluation of the present system.

EVALUATION OF THE CURRENT OPERATING SYSTEM

The second phase of the systems study is evaluation of the current methods and procedures, upon which the analyst bases his report of findings and recommendations.

The analyst must determine that:

1. The present requirements are those which, in fact, are necessary for the successful operation and management of the system and the total system.
2. The current methods and procedures are adequate for processing the current as well as the anticipated work loads.
3. The outputs and controls of the system adequately fulfill requirements within the total system.
4. The inputs to the system provide sufficient data, in proper form, so that they do or can fulfill the current as well as essential requirements under current operating methods.
5. Staffing is sufficient and adequate in relation to present methods.
6. The equipment available allows application of efficient methods.

SUMMARY WORKSHEET FOR THE SURVEY OF INPUTS

SYSTEM ANALYST DATE

Name or Description of Input	Type of Input	Form of Input	Deposition of Input	Number Processed D, W, M	Originating Source	Input Point of Entry to System	What Operations Receive this Input					What Operations Require this Input				

RENSSELAER LIBRARIES
TROY, NEW YORK

Figure 8. Summary Worksheet for the Survey of Inputs

Having come to some conclusion about the adequacy of the present system in satisfaction of the foregoing factors, the analyst must:

1. Compute the cost of processing a unit of material through the system
2. Measure the productivity of the system
3. Determine whether the system provides data promptly for timely action
4. Evaluate the accuracy of information supplied.

Finally, the study staff must submit to management a written report precisely stating its findings, conclusions, and recommendations, i.e., design of a new system, modification of the present system, or continuation of the present system without change. The study staff must provide management with enough detail for it to make the correct decision in relation

to overall organizational goals. Depending upon these recommendations and the decisions of management, the study staff may or may not proceed to the culminating step of a system study, that of design.

For reaching his conclusions regarding current operating systems, the analyst has available the following "tools" obtained in the planning and analysis phases of the survey:

1. Managerial statement of goals
2. Current operating procedural manuals, if available
3. The worksheet prepared on each requirement (Figure 3)
4. Preliminary survey worksheet (Figure 4)
5. Worksheet prepared for each output (Figure 5)
6. Summary worksheet prepared for all requirements and associated outputs (Figure 6)
7. The worksheet prepared for each input (Figure 7)
8. The summary worksheet summarizing all inputs (Figure 8).

The worksheets, if completely executed, contain all the data the analyst needs for the evaluation of current procedures. It remains for the analyst, prior to evaluation, to summarize systematically this mass of data. To do this, he utilizes the method called "flow charting."

Flow charting is the shorthand of the systems analyst. It provides a set of standard symbols which can be used to represent the elements (functions, decisions, and actions), the inputs, and the outputs. The flow chart indicates graphically the flow of work through a system and the sequence in which action must be taken. As stated earlier, a system is a dynamic process which is continuously changing. Therefore, in actual operation it is difficult, many times, to understand the relationships that exist within a system. The flow chart may be compared to a snapshot, stopping the action within a system, thus allowing the analyst to evaluate systematically the old system or to design a new system. Examples of typical flow charts are shown in Figures 9 and 10.

The following symbols are those most often used in flow charting:

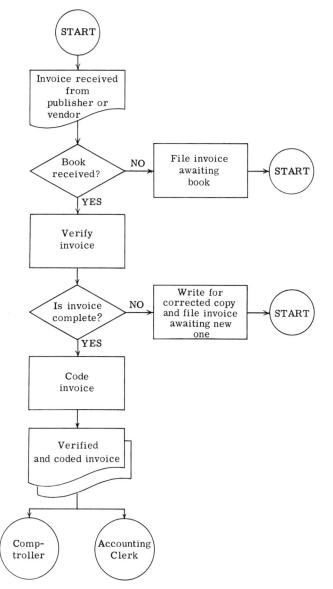

Figure 9. Flow Chart for Clearance of an Invoice

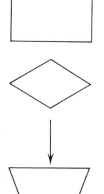

Process: represents a clerical or mechanical function such as: search catalog, type order, etc.

Decision: represents a point in a system where a decision must be made about what action is to be taken based upon variable conditions.

Flow of work: indicates the direction of flow.

Input-Output: represents any form or type of input or output media.

Connector: indicates the entry point or exit point from one component to another.

The following symbols may be used when more detail is desired:

Processing Functions

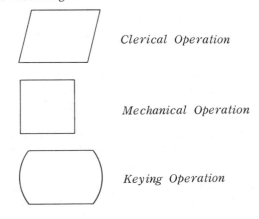

Clerical Operation

Mechanical Operation

Keying Operation

Form of Inputs and Outputs

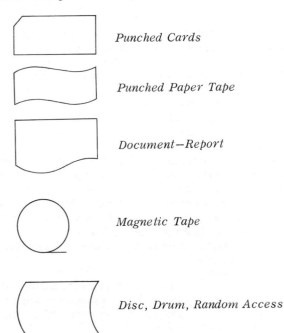

Punched Cards

Punched Paper Tape

Document—Report

Magnetic Tape

Disc, Drum, Random Access

The following general rules should be used in flow charting:

1. Conventional symbols should be used so that others may be able to follow it.
2. The system and/or its components should have a clearly defined beginning and ending in the chart.
3. The flow of work should always be in one direction, normally top to bottom or left to right.
4. No directional flow-line should be unconnected at any point.

5. The description in the symbols should be understandable to others, using terminology applicable to the system being charted.
6. Additional side notes should be used to provide a thorough understanding.

In his evaluation, the analyst must review the answers he has received in the first three parts of the survey and consider additional questions arising in his mind in the course of arriving at his conclusions. In testing his findings and conclusions, the analyst uses the flow chart as a simulator of the system and its components. By following the flow of work through its associated functions, decisions, and actions, he verifies or disproves what results are obtained under any and all possible operating conditions.

Each component, as well as the overall system, should be tested under various work loads to determine the maximum capacity of the system at which it can continue to fulfill its requirements. Does the work load and accompanying cost meet the standards of management's goals? In the acquisitions system, for example, three factors affect the work load: the number of requests received, the number of orders processed, and the number of books received. The magnitude of work loads throughout the system depends upon the volume of book purchase requests. By varying the number of requests entered into the system, the maximum capacities of the subsystems (preorder searching, ordering, receiving, accounting, and reporting) can be tested.

The analyst should also determine whether the current requirements of the system burden the manager of libraries or intermediate managers with too much statistical or other informational detail. Does management need all such reports, or can the modern principle of "management by exception" be applied for seeing that management gets only the information required at respective levels?

"Management by exception" is a principle whereby management receives only that information upon which action is indicated. For application of this principle, it is necessary that management be able to define the information required for taking action and to define the point at which such action may be taken. Application of management by exception is not confined to the top level of administration. For example, in the serials system, the serials librarian controlling the claiming of serial issues does not need to receive a report of all serial titles received in a given period in order to find out what issues have not been received; rather, he should have a report on those issues which should be claimed, i.e., those titles whose issues are more than thirty days overdue.

Each output must also be tested for sufficiency in meeting the internal and external requirements placed upon it. Do the outputs of the preorder search subsystem, for example, furnish sufficient bibliographic data to satisfy the requirements of the ordering subsystem? If a "total system" is one of management's goals, will the present outputs of the preorder search

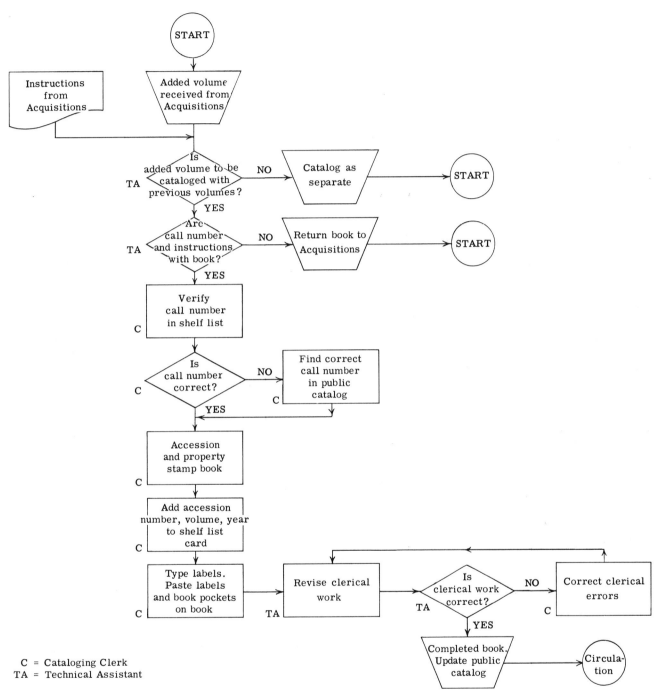

Figure 10. Flow Chart for Processing Added Volumes

subsystem furnish the necessary bibliographic data required by the cataloging system; and in both cases, are the data furnished in usable form? If not, what modifications can be made in the preorder search subsystem? What effect would such modifications have upon efficiency, capacity, and cost of the preorder search subsystem's operations? What effect would such modifications have upon the types of staff positions needed in the preorder search subsystem?

SYSTEMS DESIGN

A systems study does not necessarily result in an automated, computer-based system. Therefore, the study staff must not only be conversant with the techniques of computer-based systems but must also be thoroughly familiar with the techniques of sound manual procedures and the various types of supporting business machines (punched-card systems, accounting, copying, duplicating, etc., machines).

Further, even in the most self-sufficient and competent of computer-based systems, there is inevitably a substantial use of manual procedures in gathering information, in preparing the inputs to the computer system, and in processing the outputs of the system.

In designing a new system, the system requirements must first be identified. To do this, the analyst must analyze requirements in terms of a computer-oriented system, keeping in mind that, through programming, the computer system can be assigned many of management's routine decisions. He must also analyze for all possible applications of the principle of management by exception, in order to provide management only the data upon which action may be required and to determine and design reporting systems best serving management's needs.

Most libraries cannot justify the cost of maintaining a computer system for their exclusive use, and it can therefore be anticipated that libraries in general will be faced with designing their operating systems to fit the capabilities of the existing computer equipment of the parent organization. The characteristics of the available equipment must be determined, particularly with reference to the following:

1. Means of input available (punched cards, paper tape, telecommunication)
2. Means of storage available (magnetic tape, disc, bulk core, core memory)
3. Storage capacity available
4. Means of output available (printer, punched cards, paper tape, console)
5. Relative speed of machine components
6. Computer time available for library operations.

The total system should then be diagrammed, showing:

1. The primary inputs and outputs
2. The major activities of the system

3. The interface among the various subsystems comprising the total system, illustrating clearly the interface between manual-manual, computer-computer, and manual-computer activities.

Next, the system designer should determine the input information required to satisfy the system, taking advantage of the arithmetical, logical, and speed capabilities of the computer. To do this, he must evaluate the inputs of the present system and determine what additional inputs are required and what inputs are not required. Input media may also be developed at this point. New forms required to capture needed data should be designed, after determining within the characteristics of available computer equipment, the machine-readable media best adapted to the system's requirements (punched cards, paper tape, etc.), and evaluating and selecting the equipment to be used in the library to generate machine-readable input records (key punch, tape typewriter, optical scanner, etc.).

The reports necessary to satisfy the reporting system should then be defined, and the degree and frequency of these reports should be determined. The following must be identified at this point:

1. The information needed in each report
2. The source of this information
3. The bibliographic, fiscal, and inventory records to be maintained in this system
4. The information needed to update accurately each record, and the source.

After this, the analyst should determine the form best suited for each report within the limitations of available equipment and design each report for best satisfaction of the needs to be fulfilled. He must also determine for each record the type of storage media required for efficient processing (whether sequential or random processing), and evaluate and store the computer output. Each function required for successfully meeting the system's requirements must then be identified to enable the analyst to determine those functions to be performed under programmed control and those to be performed under manual control. The procedures to be followed in the performance of each function can then be described in full detail. Each decision required for successfully meeting the system's requirements must also be identified to enable identification of those decisions which may be delegated to the computer under programmed control. For these decisions, the criteria upon which each decision is based must be determined, and the source records and reports from which the information is obtained for making each decision must be identified. The actions to be taken as the result of each decision, and the functions and/or further decisions resulting from each action should also be identified.

At this point, the study staff must prepare the flow chart of the new system in sufficient detail to permit the programming of the computer-based parts of the system and to permit preparation of detailed instructions for the manual parts of the system. This flow chart can then be used as a simulator to test the new system under various operating conditions.

The system must be evaluated with respect to how well it satisfied the goals of the library and the requirements placed upon the system. Further, any system being designed should be evaluated with respect to how well it satisfied the following objectives:

1. Improving the service to the library user
2. Improving the public image of the library
3. Improving the quality, timeliness, and form of information to each management level
4. Eliminating duplication of effort within the system, as well as other systems within the library
5. Increasing the efficiency and effectiveness of each level of management
6. Improving the coordination between systems
7. Achieving economy of operation by providing one or more of the following:
   a. Increase in clerical and professional productivity
   b. Reduction in operating cost
   c. Elimination of unnecessary functions
   d. Utilization of personnel and equipment to the maximum level.

In this stage of the design phase, the study staff should continually modify the system until the objectives sought are realized. The final steps in systems design are to:

1. Establish the cost of installing the new system
2. Compare the cost of the old system with that of the new
3. Determine the staffing requirements of the new system
4. Prepare a summary report for the director of the library, outlining the salient features of the new system
5. Prepare a detailed procedural manual for each major activity in the system
6. Prepare a detailed procedural manual and time schedule for conversion to and installation of the new system
7. Program and debug the computer systems involved.

DISCUSSION

Question: You have been speaking about institutional-originated systems; is it feasible to use an adaptation of another system which is operational, and is it feasible to select empirically one or more items from other systems which are operational for your use?

MR. ST. PIERRE: I believe that we should be able to eventually develop standard systems that libraries can use. I hope this is the way the Library of Congress is going in MARC [Machine-Readable Cataloging].

One of the problems, I think, is that libraries are going to have to get together and decide that they will allow standardization. If we all want to have different

filing rules and if we all want to do this differently, we cannot have a standard. If we all want a different type of book catalog, with different information and different font, we cannot have standardization; but hopefully we should be able to design input programs for cataloging data that could be standard and could be adapted by various libraries.

On the point of taking specific parts of another system and incorporating it, I think until you have analyzed your own system to determine what the problems are, you're walking on dangerous ground.

Question: If I wanted to use a system that Bruce Stewart used at Texas A and M for circulation, which is quite effective in its operation, I see no reason to go back through all the analysis and design of such a system when it will fit very well to the needs of the kind of library which I am in. Can't you make open-end systems? What if I do not wish to print a catalog until I get through the acquisitions process? As long as I have substantially uniform data, I can add the rest of it on at some later time, can't I?

MR. ST. PIERRE: In designing a system, we said that we should look at what the other systems are doing, and Mr. Chapman stated that in the planning phase one of the purposes of planning is to designate what specific systems we want studied. The study staff should look at the cataloging system to see what demands it places upon acquisitions, so that the acquisition system that is designed will furnish data at the point in the future when we are ready to automate or design a new cataloging procedure. If the staff members do not look at cataloging and try to design an acquisition system within a vacuum by itself, they are not going to come up with a system which will be able to be integrated with other systems within the library. The system should be designed, in other words, as open ended, unless you are going to design the total system in one fell swoop.

Question: Do you have a method or a formula by which we could figure how much time it will take to do a system study like this?

MR. ST. PIERRE: I could only give you the time that it took at RPI [Rensselaer Polytechnic Institute] and the cost to us. We started our study in June of 1965, and turned in a final report in November of 1965. The original study took a period of six months.

Question: How many people were involved, and how large is your library?

MR. ST. PIERRE: Two people almost full time, and at some points other people became involved. As we said, we trained our librarians to be able to analyze their own problems. Our library is not big; we have a total budget this year of around $500,000, so it is not a large library.

How Library Automation May Influence New Building Plans

Joseph Becker

Director of Information Services
Interuniversity Communications Council

My purpose is to acquaint you with the new technology and to describe ways in which it may influence the design of library buildings. Three main technological developments have implications for libraries: the *computer, multimedia communications*, and *book transportation*. Accordingly, I will try to outline the requisite planning considerations.

Third-generation computers which are currently available are smaller than their predecessors, require less power to operate, and are designed to interface smoothly with communications. Each of these characteristics has implications for library building planning. Areas in libraries set aside for computer occupancy need not be large, requirements for special power can be minimal, and there is no functional reason which demands that the computer be located in proximity to main library service areas. When computers were introduced years ago, they were always placed on public display in prime space; however, third-generation machines can be located at points distant from the mainstream of library activity, with cables connecting the main computer to remote terminal equipment. Cables for the transmission of computer data from point to point within a building maintain signal fidelity as far as 2000 feet.

The physical area in which the computer is to be installed, however, will still require certain environmental protection. The computer area should be dust free, under temperature and humidity control, and constructed with a raised floor for out-of-sight interconnecting of various components. Because microminiaturized circuitry does not radiate much heat, normal building air conditioning will probably be adequate; nonetheless, danger from overheating exists with third-generation computers, and alarm systems should be included in planning. Although third-generation computers may be described as "soft spoken," noise from their surrounding impact printers and the hum of control electronics make soundproofing of the area mandatory.

The novelty and glamour associated with the computer are wearing off, and I suspect that the machines will gradually be moved out of public view. The possibility that they may even be located outside of the main library building should not be overlooked. Computer utilities, connected to service points by standard communications lines rather than cables, are becoming an integral part of the third-generation trend. The capability thus produced is known as being on-line with the computer and time-sharing its use.

Marriage of the computer to communications is a significant development. It means that the language of the computer can be exchanged over standard telephone lines, over teletype lines, through coaxial cables, via microwave radio broadcasting, and even by way of satellites. These same communication lines can be used to transmit line copy, pictures, or facsimile combinations of them both. As libraries engage more actively in teletype interlibrary loan and facsimile communications, building plans should give increased attention to providing a communication center within the library—an area that can serve as both a receiving and a transmission point for internal and external communicating. Equipment considerations here will vary, based on the complexity of the media used. Multimedia communication—i.e., audiovisual, digital, voice, and video—will certainly require more sophisticated communication terminals than, say, voice alone. Early development of a library communications plan will help to clarify the specifications for the web of cables and wires required to connect internal activities, as well as to predict the size and scope of the communications interface with external resources. Communications planning of this kind will help dictate the location and size of ductwork needed to distribute the wires and cables from a primary transmission source like the computer to points of use.

If communication is to become a key library function, then ways of organizing some of its operating elements will probably need to be reconsidered. For example, if "hot carrels" are to be spotted around the library to bring audio-visual resources to reader service points, then the proximate location of the audio-visual collection to the communications center becomes an important issue. Under such circumstances, a communications switching center will be needed to accept a request, locate the source of the material, and route or reroute the response to the appropriate reader service point. Also, if the library plans to transmit and receive large quantities of video information, it may even wish to consider having its own television transmitter and receiver. Broadcasting facilities of this kind need not be elaborate; many local police and fire departments own and operate limited networks, and it is just possible that libraries will someday consider this kind of transmitting too.

Operating a communications center and maintaining a large multimedia collection imply establishment of a processing laboratory for treating film and other media, and maintenance of a technical laboratory for repairing communications equipment and other hardware. These laboratory requirements should be taken into account along with initial planning of the library's photoduplication and microfilming services.

As a specific example of library planning, I want to describe one technological innovation in the field of book transportation which resulted in a tremendous systems gain even though it involved only very slight library building alterations. It is called Bibliophone and was introduced into the Bibliotheek Technische Hogeschool, Delft, Holland.

Moving a book from stack to reader is not substantially different from the process of supplying goods to customers from a warehouse inventory. Just as factories have introduced mechanized material-handling equipment to expedite the flow of goods from their inventories, so libraries have sought ways of delivering a book to the reader in the shortest possible time. For many years, large libraries have utilized horizontal and vertical conveyor systems to transport books from closed stacks to the issue desk in the reading room.

Several years ago, Dr. L. J. van der Wolk, Director of the Library, invited a young mathematician, Dr. J. Verhoeff, to take charge of the research department of the Library. Dr. Verhoeff suggested that new automation ideas be sought from architects who have had experience in mechanizing factories. He preferred to concentrate first on improving methods for the physical handling of books rather than on the application of computers to library operations. As a result of his efforts, the Bibliophone system was installed in the Library. It has been in operation now for three years and handles 270 requests daily from a collection of 120,000 books.

Bibliophone is an ingenious development combining the electronic principles of telephone switching and a new but simple type of book conveyor called the "spiral book chute."

Normally, in a closed stack system, a reader submitting a call slip must expect to wait twenty to forty minutes before the book is delivered. There are two reasons for the delay: first, the multiplicity of steps in the procedure of locating the book after a request is submitted; and second, "queuing time." Dr. Verhoeff's library innovations have drastically reduced the time between reader decision and book delivery. Today, the Library's service time averages *less than three minutes per request.*

Before describing how Bibliophone and the spiral book chute function, we must state two important facts about the library at Delft: it maintains closed stacks, and it shelves books by accession number rather than by subject classification. Thus each book has a fixed location in the stacks, and the collection grows by adding new books at one end.

In the system at Delft, the reader consults the catalog in the usual manner. When he decides on the book he wants, however, he reaches for a telephone instead of a call slip. Six telephones sit atop the catalog ready for his use. Instead of being connected to other telephones through a switching center, they form a part of a network of wires and light bulbs in the stacks. A number dialed at the catalog causes a small central switching mechanism to activate relays that send electric current over certain circuit paths of the lighting network in the stacks. Wires lead to each stack level, to each main corridor in the stack, and to each stack range.

The first four digits of a dialed call number cause a flashing light to go on at the designated stack level in the main corridor nearest the precise range where the book is located. A stack attendant, seeing the light flashing in the corridor, goes toward it. As he does so, he also sees, on a Nixi tube, a visible representation of the last three digits of the call number. (Nixi tubes are designed to display any number from 0 to 9; the tube is two inches in diameter and contains electric filaments preshaped to form any of the ten numerals.) The Nixi tube displays each of the last three digits of the call number one at a time and repeats them over and over again. By the time the stack attendant has reached the correct range, he has memorized the last three digits of the call number and can withdraw the desired book from the shelf if it is there.

Book in hand, the stack attendant proceeds to the spiral book chute. He deposits the book anywhere on the 3-foot-wide surface of the spiral. Gravity takes over and the book glides swiftly down to the issue desk. The angle and pitch of the spiral were computed mathematically so that regardless of its mass the book's acceleration is continually slowed as it descends. When it reaches the bottom, the book moves gracefully onto a horizontal conveyor belt that carries it a short distance to the issue desk for delivery to the reader. A book the size and weight of *Webster's New International Dictionary* can travel down several stack levels with the ease of a pamphlet.

Installing Bibliophone and the spiral book chute in an existing library is not difficult. A network of electrical wires running through ceiling conduits in the stacks to a telephone switching terminal is all that is needed. Thereafter, normal telephone wires connect the terminal to the phones at the card catalog. The installation of a spiral book chute requires that a hole 7 feet in diameter be cut in the floor of each stack; the chute itself is prefabricated.

Even if a library prefers to keep its books in classified order, the Bibliophone system may still be used. A small electronic drum memory attached to the switching terminal can automatically translate the class number of a book into the corresponding stack location. Data on the magnetic drum can be erased and replaced each time a major shift of books is made. Of course, when a new library is being built, it would be desirable to incorporate specifications for the Bibliophone and the spiral book chute into the architect's plans as early as possible; the John I. Thompson Company of Washington, D.C., is franchised to install either or both items in the United States.

Building-Planning Implications of Automation

Robert H. Rohlf

Coordinator of Building Planning
Library of Congress

Mr. Becker has described in his usual clear and complete manner some of the automation devices for libraries now and in the future, and it has been left to me to attempt to discuss how library buildings should be planned for those automation possibilities. I would like to begin by pointing out an amusing feature of our present-day concern about automation. Mr. Becker explained to you in some detail the Bibliophone as it is used at the university in Delft and how this kind of mechanical or semiautomated device holds promise for certain applications.

The following is from the minutes of a former library association meeting:

> The President then explained to the Conference a device for the automatic delivery of books which he had planned for use in the new [Harvard] building. At the delivery desk there would be a key board showing the digits to be combined into the various shelf numbers. As the number of the book wanted was struck by combination, it would appear by an automatic connection on the floor where the book was to be found. The attendant stationed there would take it from the shelf and place it in a box attached to an endless belt, whence it was tipped out at the other end into a cushioned receptacle close by the delivery desk, thus saving time, running, and expense.

This statement was made at the second annual conference of librarians in 1877. This evening, ninety years later, we are still discussing the same type of thing, but now we are calling it automation.

Discussing automated devices and their effects on planning in the future, I would like to divide my brief remarks into four areas, not all of which deal with building planning as such: the concept of some changes in library service, the problem of physical environment in library buildings, some specific physical requirements for fully automated systems as we can now see them, and some probable cost implications of automation insofar as buildings are concerned.

We must restrict our discussion to library planning now and in the next five to ten years. We are not talking about building planning thirty to forty years from now, although we must plan for thirty to forty years from now. First of all, I would like to discuss libraries in the sense of automated bibliographic files and limited facsimile reproduction. Because the directions were that our remarks were to be based on current library building planning, I am assuming that the book is still with us. It is proper to point out that the technology is here at the moment, of course, to reduce the Bible to the size of a pin and then to reproduce it page by page. However, considering that the cost would be $250 or more per page, and considering that the machines necessary to do this will take much more space than the Bible itself would, I am not going to discuss this technology because we must still concern ourselves with economics.

I mentioned that we would be concerned with limited facsimile reproduction. I qualify this by pointing out that we still have the problems of copyright and how they will be resolved. We also have the problem of cost. So, while it is tempting to discuss some of the very miraculous things which are taking place in the miniaturization of the actual material and in cross-country and even cross-continent facsimile transmission, my remarks are directed to the primary considerations which are here at this moment for libraries.

Now to the question of service. What type of library service must we plan buildings for in the next five to ten years that will still allow development for the future? First of all, libraries must be more "information outgoing"; by that I mean libraries will send information to people, whereas in the past, normally people came to the information. This change has obvious implications for building planning and for service. Another consideration is what will happen to the large main or central libraries, either university or public, in the future? I think that they will not only continue to be with us but that they will grow even larger and will increase in their services. We will have more storage buildings in the future, but the main libraries will still be with us and will be even more important then they are now.

However, I believe the branches—be they neighborhood, departmental, or divisional—may change. All library planners will have to consider whether or not their branch libraries might increase in number but decrease in physical size because of the possibilities of remote bibliographic access, print-outs, mail service, and perhaps a numerical reduction in the serial holdings necessary at multiple points.

Libraries should be able to send services out to businesses, to academic departments, and to area schools, but they will be sending out bibliographical information and requested follow-ups, for specific materials can then be fed back into the main library or into large area libraries or major divisional libraries to supply the material. In short, I think that libraries will be more outside oriented, not inside oriented. This conclusion assumes, of course, that library administrators and staffs will themselves become more outside oriented and think in terms of serving readers whom they may not see face to face but who may be only a voice over the telephone or a letterhead on the desk. This change is happening today in many libraries and it will accelerate in the future.

Given some of these service conditions, therefore, and given the ability to interrogate a library file by means of teletype-telephone or electronic data console, what are some of the environmental problems which library designers must not only consider but must successfully overcome in the future?

In the past ten to fifteen years, there has been a noticeable retreat from expansive, uninterrupted reading rooms to at least a visual breakup of the rooms into smaller areas by the use of smaller tables or groups of tables and more individual carrels or study tables. The rooms have been designed to maintain areas of expansiveness and yet to achieve some kind of personal, intimate feeling for the individual user.

One fact that is becoming more and more apparent to those people concerning themselves with the problem of planning space for automated service libraries of the future and of the present is that there is an increasing need for individual study space and individual bibliographic access. This will not necessarily mean more enclosed carrels as we see them or think of them today. It may mean simply more individual tables, although certainly an increase in enclosed electronic carrels is a necessity also. These individual reader spaces will come equipped with more wiring than existed in our grandfather's lifetime, simply because without this wiring the individual carrel and the individual table is useless for the special function which it will perform.

If you can envision rooms full of individual tables and rooms full of individual carrels, you can also envision a whole series of little boxes or blocks on the floor, a rather depressing scene, which the architect will have a real challenge to deal with aesthetically. The engineer will have a problem to allow for ventilation and the movement of air. The architect will have another problem to deal with in terms of light and the psychology of color. (Sometimes we are forced to wonder if all men are to be in boxes long before they are buried in them.)

Electronic carrels by their very nature are cocoons, but how many cocoons do we need or want in one room? This is a very real problem for the designer. I have seen some installations of individual carrels in larger rooms of which my first thought upon entering was of faceless men, and I wondered if some of the twentieth-century abstract impressionist painters were really prophets and if, while we may all have individual recesses, we will all become men without faces.

This is a future which I do not like to contemplate, and I give the challenge to the designers to overcome this problem and at the same time to the engineers to provide us with the electrical and mechanical facilities we need for library service—automation, video screens, facsimile reproductions, small computer consoles so that we can query the central bibliographic file from our study area—but to give us these things in such a way that we do not become faceless men. It has been pointed out that we need studies in depth on human engineering and behavioral studies to get persons and machines together in a way in which the machines are efficient and the people are happy. The challenge to architects will be to design these intimate electronic spaces and still provide us with space, color, visual beauty, and also a sense of the group or of humanity.

My third area of concern deals with some actual physical needs as I can foresee them at the moment. Formulas for reading space will of necessity have to allow for more space than those now used. It will take more square feet per reader on an individual basis—whether it be carrels or individual tables equipped with electronic devices—to achieve the same overall capacity as the 4-, 6-, and 8-place tables did in the past. Old reading space formulas will no longer be valid unless they take into account the need for increased individual study space. Another way to express the physical problems of the libraries of the future, insofar as their interior design is concerned, is that to a much greater degree than today, the libraries will become a series of spaces with connectors. This problem of the spaces and the design of the connectors is one of the prime interior design problems facing the library architects today.

The major share of my concern in the area of physical needs deals with flexibility and with electrical capacity. *Flexibility* is a word that has been used for some years now in library planning. It has often been pointed out that too much flexibility can be a bad thing, and that you cannot build full flexibility into a building because you simply cannot afford to or you do not really need to. On the other hand, libraries and librarians who have suffered for years with nineteenth-century totally inflexible buildings have emphasized flexibility in almost all postwar library buildings.

I am discussing flexibility in the sense that the prime need of today might be an inferior need in fifteen years and that a slight requirement today might be a very prime need in fifteen years. Our buildings must allow us to shrink or expand rooms and areas by moving or even removing walls. In this sense, we must have flexibility in our buildings, and I think that, by and large, libraries are achieving this.

Electrical capacity, a term used earlier, refers not simply to electrical power but more to electrical cables. One of the greatest considerations for library planning today is that of underfloor ducts, not conduits as we are used to thinking of them—3/4-inch pipe tubing or flexible tubing—but ductwork which is underneath the floor surface and which is nothing more than a tunnel framed in metal and laid in with the building floor when the building is constructed.

At one time, a single duct was used, then two underfloor ducts running side by side, and now some buildings are being planned and constructed with a 3-duct underfloor system. Let me describe these ducts briefly for those of you who are not certain what they are. They are a metal box, really. Each duct of a standard size will be approximately 3 inches across and approximately 2 inches deep. Today, there are super ducts on the market which measure approximately 2 inches deep and 7 inches across. One duct is used for telephone cabling, another duct is used for electrical cable, and a third duct is used for low-voltage requirements or for signaling controls. It is the third duct which is becoming so essential in modern library planning because this third duct, if properly sized and installed, is the duct which will carry the coaxial cables for the automation devices and, running side by side with the telephone ducts, will give the on-line accessibility that Mr. Becker talked about earlier.

These ducts have been spaced as close as 3 feet on centers. By that I mean that running in one direction every 3 feet on any floor you will have a series of these ducts. Sometime the spacing is on 5, 6, 10, 15, or even 20 feet centers, depending upon the use of the building and, most importantly, upon the amount of money which is available to work with. I know one engineer who insists that ducts should be spaced 3 feet on centers and I know another one who says that 10 feet on centers is adequate because, after all, the ducts themselves take up anywhere from 1 to 2 feet in width depending upon the type of ducts used. This is an individual question which must be resolved for each building.

Many buildings have a cellular steel floor which may also be used for wiring raceways. It is my experience, however, that most libraries do not have cellular steel floors, primarily because of library load-bearing requirements and of our desire for large spans which normally make this type of construction uneconomical for libraries. While these cellular floors may be used as raceways, there are certain precautions which must be taken with them and an underfloor duct is often used in connection with the cellular floor.

There was a time when telephones operated on 1/16-inch wires which were spliced together to form cables. Today the typical telephone instrument requires a 25-pair cable. For some telephones, such as those termed "call directors," the cabling has increased to 75-pair cable and the cable size has increased to 3/4-inch diameter. In the past, telephone outlets and electrical outlets needed to be spaced along the walls, and in most cities, codes require certain spacing for these elements; but in large library workrooms and large library study rooms, we do not have a great wall expanse in relation to floor area and therefore the power must come from either above us or below us. Those of us who have seen some installations where telephone and power lines are hanging down from the ceiling or snaking along floors have been singularly unimpressed with the appearance and also with the safety of such installations.

Some libraries have had to go in and rip up flooring shortly after the library was occupied because the desks or listening booths were never in the right places on the floor where telephone or power sources could come up to their particular location. I know of one new large university library that is really a superbly designed and functioning building. Yet a short time after occupancy, some functions were automated and exposed coaxial cables had to be pushed through spaces between the floor slab above and the suspended ceilings below. Such alterations are possible, but they are far from desirable.

Underfloor duct is replacing conduit in many cases, even though we may still use the perimeter wall outlets, but underfloor duct is a prime consideration every library planner must discuss today before the library is built; and it must be discussed not in terms of today's use but tomorrow's use, a tomorrow of perhaps only five years from now.

Another physical problem that is surprisingly overlooked in some modern libraries is the problem of a computer center and the raised floor which generally is required for such an installation. This problem arises, of course, only in very large systems which will have their own computers. Computer machinery requires air conditioning, and while the amounts required have decreased because of the change from the old vacuum tubes to transistors, air conditioning of a greater capacity than that needed for other rooms in the library is required for those where computers are installed. The computers also require very extensive cabling and electrical power. This power is normally supplied under a raised floor to a particular machine. Another important consideration is that computer tapes, and to a lesser degree some microforms, are extremely sensitive to temperature and humidity changes, becoming in extreme cases unusable or even able to damage machines using them.

Another physical consideration is that of the illumination level. As you know, the lighting engineers and particularly the lighting companies have been raising the recommended light level each year to the point where one company now says that we need 1000 footcandles in order to have good reading and working light. But what happens to the use of viewing screens or video screens when we have such intense illumination? Now there are certain areas where the need for light will decrease, but the power level will, of necessity, increase because of the machines which will be used. This question of light level must be studied seriously, and we must make certain that we do not end up with machines whose screens are virtually unreadable because of the extremely bright light levels in the room.

Another physical change which we must plan for in buildings is that of shelving. The increasing amount of microform materials will require increasing amounts of special storage and shelving space. Normally, this material does not shelve efficiently or economically on standard library shelving and certainly not in standard library stack spacing. Careful consideration must be given to the question of center stack spacing when storing microform materials, for while a fixed stack may be an efficient and economical way to store books the fixed stack range based on the standard spacings of the past is not efficient for most microform storage. In effect, it would be very unfortunate to build any large library today where all storage shelving must be permanently fixed on a structural space. We must devote at least some portion, say one third as a minimum, to completely freestanding storage.

The problem of weight has been raised. Weight may be a problem with a computer facility which is going into an average office building, since offices are built on only a 50- to 60-pound live-load factor; however, the acceptable pound per square foot live-load weight for a library would be sufficient to handle computer machines now on the market, and the probabilities are that the machines will become lighter in the future, rather than heavier.

The last item to be discussed briefly is the unfortunate problem of cost. It should be fairly obvious to everyone that a fully electronic library will be a more costly one, physically, than the traditional library. We cannot build in sophisticated air conditioning and power requirements for machines and people, electrical flexibility, and telephone and audio flexibility, requiring extensive ductwork and conduit without increasing costs. These costs can be as much as $1 to $5 per square foot more than for a conventional

library. It is possible, of course, that we will develop some cost savings in other ways in the future, but, for the present, we are forced to be virtually all things to all men and our costs reflect this.

It is safe to assume that storage costs will be less for microform materials than they are for standard materials. We are able to store more in the storage unit, but I must point out that the unit will cost more. In addition, microform storage areas should have very effective and sophisticated humidity and temperature control, and this is costly.

The cost of an electronic carrel and its equipment is obviously going to be much greater than the cost of an individual study table. The exact increase in its cost will depend upon how complete these carrels are in terms of equipment and access devices, but it will certainly exceed the cost of a 3 feet by 2 feet individual study table. One thing that disturbs me is that so far no designer has effectively tackled the challenge of designing an attractive electronic carrel from the ground up. All we see are electronic modifications of present study table designs.

I would like to add another disturbing problem here. In theory, an electronic carrel is quiet. But what happens in a large space with perhaps several hundred of these going at one time? How quiet will they be or how attractive? We may have an increase in acoustic cost because of this potential problem.

There are certain cost trade-offs, of course. How much does it cost us, for example, to store catalogs in card form in large catalog card rooms or areas, compared to what it would cost us to store them on magnetic tape or to have access to another's magnetic tape or drum?

There may also be totally different cost items tomorrow. For example, I understand that Bell Laboratories is now studying the possibility of developing a computer service similar to a public utility. There would be one computer center, or perhaps several regional centers, owned by the Bell Telephone Company. The consumer could rent a keyboard from Bell Telephone Company and then have access to the Bell Laboratories computers. Perhaps this will make our libraries empty in the future, but I rather doubt it.

In summary, we should not be planning buildings now that in only ten years will be obsolete or will be as encumbering to our successors ten years from now as the Carnegie plans were to most of us. The Carnegie plan buildings, however, served well for at least their first twenty to thirty years, and some of them were efficient much longer than that. Our challenge today is to see if we can do at least as well in view of onrushing technological change. We can do so only if we have the full cooperation, support, and imagination of everyone involved in the planning process. If we can intelligently and imaginatively present the service problems to our architects and engineers, they can solve the physical problems better than we.

The Automation of Acquisitions Systems

Connie Dunlap

Head, Acquisitions Department
University of Michigan Library

Although the use of mechanical or semiautomated equipment in libraries can be traced to the 1930's when Ralph Parker introduced punched-card procedures at the University of Texas and to the 1940's when the Order Division of the Library of Congress began using punched cards, widespread interest in the use of machinery did not take place until the 1960's when computers became available in many institutions. Only a small percentage of the libraries in the United States have automated systems in operation at the present time, but because of the rapid growth of libraries and a shortage of personnel, many institutions are developing automated systems in an attempt to keep pace with an ever increasing work load.

It is generally agreed that automation studies should be conducted within the framework of a single system, for the implementation of many separate functions can create serious problems when these functions are integrated into the whole system. However, it is also possible to become so involved in systems studies that the actual programs are never implemented. Further, since all systems require a great deal of study, and hence a great deal of time, it is both possible and reasonable to implement some subsystems independently without seriously affecting the whole project even though the entire system has not yet been developed. This is especially true of large research libraries where the organization and systems are highly complex and where a complete automation project requires study over a long period of time. Many research libraries are state institutions where money is not available to hire a staff sufficiently large to develop a total system within a reasonable length of time. Yet, by implementing programs in areas of greatest need, it is possible to derive years of benefit from the individual parts while awaiting completion of the entire project. Moreover, it is quite possible that the entire system does not require automation or that complete automation would not be economically feasible. Necessary changes to integrate an existing function with the new can be made at the time additional programs are implemented or as an institution acquires more sophisticated equipment which necessitates reprogramming or which permits expansion or refinement of established procedures.

Some functions of acquisitions lend themselves readily to mechanization or automation, for they most nearly approximate the functions of the business world for which much of this type of equipment was originally designed. Data processing people are quick to decide that this type of processing is completely routine. If the system is small, this may be true; but in a large system, processing becomes very complex because of the tremendous amount of detail, and because the possibilities for error are virtually infinite. To guard against oversimplification of the problem, it behooves the librarian about to embark upon automation to learn something of programming in order to be able to determine if the system will really provide the desired results. Systems studies directed toward automation are beneficial even if the decision is made to retain manual procedures, for such studies require critical analysis of all routines with greater precision than is generally needed in purely manual operations. Computers can provide access to records from various approaches, and information can be made available in minutes to hours instead of days to weeks. Unfortunately, the reverse is sometimes true as well. The computer can also provide information in such profusion that the system can break down because the part of the output requiring human action is so overwhelming that it would take a whole army to handle it.

MECHANIZED AND AUTOMATED SYSTEMS

Libraries considering the use of machines can choose between simple mechanized procedures or more sophisticated automated systems, depending upon the needs of the organization. In general, *mechanization* refers to the use of tabulating equipment such as collators, sorters, and accounting machines. Systems employing this type of equipment are relatively simple but often very effective. The term *automation* suggests a concept of integrated systems in which various configurations of electronic data processing equipment are used to perform a series of operations from a single input.

Basically, there are three types of mechanized or automated acquisitions systems: (1) unit record systems employing tabulating equipment, (2) off-line systems using computers and allied equipment, and (3) on-line systems with input-output stations connected to a remote central computer.

The simplest systems make use of unit record equipment, generally consisting of a key punch, a collator, a sorter, and an accounting machine such as the IBM 403 or 407. In this kind of system, there is no memory storage of information. A deck of punched cards containing bibliographical, financial, and sometimes specialized information is used to provide various types of output. For example, the cards may first be sorted by vendor to print purchase orders, then sorted by fund or account to handle bookkeeping, and finally sorted alphabetically and merged with all other unfilled orders to print an outstanding order record. Sometimes the card decks themselves are used as an orders-receivable file. When the ordered item is received, the card deck for the item is manually pulled; and by punching the actual price paid for the volume, the financial card from this deck is used to update the accounts. By adding catalog information, the cards can be manipulated to produce stickers for book pockets, spine labels, and circulation cards as well as book lists and book stock statistics. Situations in which the volume is not great can be well served by the use of tabulating equipment; and although not as glamorous as computers, this type of machinery can perform a real service for the small or medium-sized library.

The University of Missouri uses unit record equipment, but this system has several unique features. Instead of using the usual accounting machines, Missouri uses an IBM 858 Cardatype which reads tab cards "and also receives input information from a keyboard; it is capable of adding, subtracting, and multiplying. Information read into or developed in the machine may be read out to a typewriter or a keypunch or both. It is possible to attach as many as four typewriters, each preparing distinctive documents" (see Bibliography, No.107). The purchase orders are prepared on the Cardatype and extra slips are used to order Library of Congress cards, to provide an entry in the public catalog, etc.

The collator is used to search, for claiming purposes, orders which have not been received. A claim slip is printed automatically which can also be used to claim an invoice. Another feature is the ability to maintain an active desiderata file. "With only a few exceptions, undelivered items are merely transferred from the order procedure to the desiderata procedure. All necessary information is already stored in the punched cards which had been used to prepare the original purchase order. They are now used to prepare requests for quotation and are subject to the same systematic control as is applied to outstanding purchase orders" (see Bibliography, No.108).

The Suffolk County (New York) Cooperative Library (see Bibliography, No.115) began its mechanized operations by using the standard series of tabulating equipment with the added feature of an IBM 514 Reproducing Punch with mark sense. After operating under this system for about a year, the IBM 403 Accounting Machine was replaced with a UNIVAC 1004, which is a step about halfway between tabulating equipment and a computer with capabilities similar to an IBM 1401. The system was further refined by the addition of tape drives which would permit the production of catalog cards directly from storage in the 1004 and which would make it possible to improve existing operations by taking advantage of increased information store. The Suffolk cooperative system is a good example of a library which began with simple procedures and which expanded and developed them as the needs of the system changed.

Another library that has made a successful adjustment from mechanized procedures to a more sophisticated system using an electronic computer is Joint University Libraries in Nashville, Tennessee.[1] The first system was put into operation in February 1965, using standard tabulating equipment plus an IBM 526 Printing Summary Punch. All procedures were easily converted for use with the IBM 1401 with a 4K memory. The purchase order packet provides slips for the catalog department to be used as a shelf list record, a slip for the binding routines, and a stiff sheet which is filed in the public catalog. This slip and one in the volume are stamped with an identification number to provide control while the volume is in process. Before the purchase orders are printed, the data are run through an edit program to detect errors and to call attention to duplication. Three by-products of the new procedures are the production of a new book list, claims, and the facility for desiderata searching. Catalog information is added to the on-order tapes which are then sorted by call number. A new tape is produced which prints the list on multilith masters. Desiderata have been added to the master tapes. Such items are printed by subject area to be used as want lists.

At the present time, probably the type of system most commonly used is that employing computers off-line. There appear to be as many variations of this type of system as there are libraries using it. The computers themselves come in many sizes and can be used with a variety of auxiliary equipment. The obvious advantages of computerized operations are speed, accuracy, and the ability to store and manipulate data. There are, however, disadvantages of

---

[1] Eleanor F. Morrissey, "A Mechanized Book Order and Accounting Routine," *Southeastern Librarian,* 15: 143-48; (Fall 1965) Eleanor F. Morrissey, letter dated May 3, 1967.

computerized systems other than cost. After listening to representatives of equipment manufacturers and data processing personnel extoll the seemingly limitless capabilities of these wondrous machines, it is easy to be lulled into a false sense of security. While it is true that a system is only as good as its design, programming, and input, the computer can—and does—make its own mistakes! Rigid controls should be placed on all parts of the program, for it is often much more difficult to get at information after the fact in an automated system than it is in a manual system.

The punched card is the most common type of computer input, although some systems use paper tape (which is generally a by-product of typing the purchase order or some other document) or magnetic tape produced by a keyed data recorder, thereby eliminating the punched card entirely. In an off-line system, the input is batch processed and many activities are handled simultaneously. As the input enters the central processing unit, it may be used to update or manipulate previously stored data or to provide a new output document. In most systems of this type, while purchase orders are being printed, funds are being encumbered, bibliographic information stored, statistics gathered, etc. Information may be stored on magnetic tape or a combination of tape and a random-access device such as a disc or drum. These latter units are most commonly used for book fund accounting, statistics, and vendor address files as they obviate searching long tapes for selected short pieces of information.

Because great quantities of data can be stored and manipulated in a computer-based system without human intervention, these systems are necessarily much more complex than those using unit record equipment. At Yale, for example, there are 32 computer products representing approximately 25,000 decisions weekly. The most important of these are an "in-process list arranged by author, an order number listing, registers of weekly fund commitment, notices to requesters of the status of their requests, notices to dealers and staff members of action which should be taken, and periodic and special graphs and reports of activities within the system." Yale has also developed a machine monitor "which is performed by the same computer that does the processing; but from a systems point of view, it is an entirely different activity. The computer monitors flow of material on the basis of information about material in the system and on the basis of minimum rate of flow. If a user's request lags in pre-order searching longer than the maximum period, the machine monitor will inform the supervisor that the particular request must be processed and the monitor will continue to notify the supervisor until a purchase order is issued. Similarly, the monitor will print out claim notices to dealers when material has not arrived on time, and following a predetermined number of claim notices, the monitor will direct the supervisor to issue a cancellation of the order" (see Bibliography, No.83).

In addition to handling great quantities of material for acquisitions, computer-based systems can provide information for catalog or circulation departments. Many systems add call numbers or other catalog information to the original data to provide book cards for circulation procedures or to produce catalogs in book or card form.

On-line systems are not yet in use for acquisitions procedures, and it appears likely that most institutions will find an application for this particular purpose too expensive to consider. Washington State University Library[2] is currently developing an on-line system using an IBM System/360 Model 67 for technical services which is to include all functions of ordering, receiving, searching, cataloging, book catalog or catalog card production, and book marking. At the present time, it is proposed to use on-line input for acquisitions procedures and to batch process the printing of purchase orders and the on-order record. IBM 1050 Data Communications System terminal devices will be used to type bibliographic and order information directly into the computer. When the system becomes operational, the on-order file will be searched by machine. It is anticipated that ultimately the entire catalog will be stored in the memory bank and that bibliographic searching will be handled entirely through the computer.

The University of Chicago is developing an on-line data-handling system encompassing all functions in the library.[3] Studies are just beginning on the acquisitions procedures, but a completely on-line program is envisioned to make all order information immediately available. It is anticipated that there will be two classes of orders: rush orders which will be processed immediately and less urgent orders which will be printed overnight or the next morning. If a title is being ordered from a proof slip, complete catalog information is added at the same time processing information is entered. At the present time, an interim operation is being used, but when the programming is completed, input data will be formatted by the computer.

SUMMARY

Although the "push button" library is still far in the future, there is no question that libraries will have to find ways to do things faster, cheaper, and more efficiently if they are to keep pace with the ever increasing demands placed on them. Automation probably offers more promise for the future in the area of acquisitions than in any other area, with the exception of circulation control, because of the relatively simple programs required. Immediate relief will not be felt by those developing systems, for a great deal of hard and exacting work is required to

---

[2] Thomas Burgess, telephone conversation, May 11, 1967.
[3] Thomas Burgess, telephone conversation, May 9, 1967.

design automated procedures. This is only the beginning; close scrutiny must be given a new system to ascertain that it is actually providing the information and performing the functions intended. In the long run, however, as systems are refined and as more technically trained people become available, automation holds a bright promise for the future.

It will not be an easy road to follow. The work is hard, but with a little luck, the rewards are many. To those who are about to embark upon systems studies and automation, be of stout heart, and good luck!

DISCUSSION

MR. WEISBROD: You referred to the uneasy feeling that system developers might be experiencing now as similar to that of catalogers wondering about duplication of effort.

I was wondering if, in the course of developing the survey which you so clearly presented, you noticed any obvious duplications among the systems you happen to look at. Generally, my experience is that everybody feels that his problems are totally unique and that nobody else's solution comes anywhere near solving his problems.

MRS. DUNLAP: It's perfectly true. Certainly no one system that was developed for another or perhaps in conjunction with several institutions working together could be adapted intact by any other institution, either because of local house rules or because of peculiar situations. However, with acquisitions there are enough common things so that even though the system could not be adapted and perhaps could only be used in very minute parts, it could still save a tremendous amount of work if someone wishing to develop the system had the benefit of all of the mistakes and all of the trials and tribulations that everybody else had already gone through. While he may throw nine tenths of the system out, as not being suitable for his situation, at the same time he would have learned a great deal of what not to do. I think that, perhaps, is a benefit of having a canned program. Another is in saving probably a great deal of time not just in the design of the programming, but in the actual programming by the data processing people themselves. It could save a tremendous amount of time if they had the benefit of other programs to work with and work from.

GUENTER JANSEN, Director of the Suffolk Cooperative Library System: I wonder if in your investigations, you found any efforts to standardize the fields of input into the computer or into automatic data processing equipment by the various people who used the acquisitions automated procedures.

I am thinking of some specifics. For example, we started, as you mentioned, about five years ago, using punched-card equipment where we keypunch

into certain columns of tab cards: author, title, publisher, and so on. Our 250 member libraries would like to use the Bowker punched cards rather than do their own orders, but the Bowker fields do not meet our fields and this presents problems.

We are also using a Flexowriter and producing a paper-tape input into the UNIVAC 1005 to produce catalog cards, but the Project MARC [Machine-Readable Cataloging] fields of the Library of Congress are not the same fields that we use as input for our computer. It seems to me with every acquisition center in the country devising its own fields, we need to have some effort toward standardization, as we already have in cataloging codes, in selection of main entry, and so on. I wonder if there have been any efforts made to standardize this particular aspect of electronic data processing as regards acquisitions.

MRS. DUNLAP: First of all, let me say amen to your statement. So far there doesn't really appear to have been much attempt at standardization; again, I think, because everybody has been more or less going off on his own, not realizing that by getting together with a number of people standardization would be possible. COLA [Committee on Library Automation] is, in one sense, trying to exchange some of this information so that it will be available, and, of course, now ISAD [Information Science and Automation Division] will be doing a great deal of this as well as some of these other things I mentioned.

In the past, there has been almost none of this. In the future, I think there very definitely can be and very definitely will be. The Institute of Library Research is trying specifically to develop programs in cooperation with other libraries so that this information can be relayed; so that perhaps there can be some sort of standardization of things such as fields, as machine language, and what not; and so that the information is readily transferrable and readily communicable.

Moderator VEANER: COLA is an informal group of people who have hands-on experience in various library computer applications.

MARY ELLEN JACOB, Sandia Corporation, Livermore: I want to make a comment about this business of common data fields. A number of the AEC [Atomic Energy Commission] libraries got together about two years ago and discussed this problem, because a number of them did have the funding and they did have automated equipment. The conclusion we reached was that because their equipment was not identical, it causes problems for the libraries to use the same fields. But we did find that we could decide on certain basic elements that belong in the catalog: author, title, and so on. I don't think there's any disagreement among librarians as a whole; they more or less decided this in setting up a catalog card.

So what we did was set up a medium of exchange.

We used a unit record card, because this is a standard medium that can be used even with tab equipment, and we set out certain basic identifying information and used it as a medium of exchange rather than trying to have each installation use the same fields. If libraries, as a whole, could do this, I think they'd be a lot further ahead than worrying about having the same identical data fields.

Moderator VEANER: I think we are probably at the stage of the electric light industry, maybe of about 1880 or 1885, when there were dozens of different kinds of sockets and bulb ends so that if you wanted to buy a bulb, you had to buy a special socket to go along with it. In other words, we simply lack standardization because we are in a pioneering period.

MISS MARTIN: This is another point that I'd like to make about sharing systems. I know that we at Harvard have looked at other systems that are in operation and liked what we have seen in many of them. But one problem is configuration of equipment, not only in the identification of data fields but just bringing in programs and systems as a whole. Many people have the use of discs. We do not. Therefore, we can't use any of the programming that has been done for them. If we use anything, we just have to use routines and generalized system flow instead of the actual programming.

I would also like to know if you have any data or any information on how many people who actually have operational acquisition systems have been able to use the information that has been acquired during the ordering process for the catalog department. I have my doubts about this; it somehow seems that all this information has to go through a tremendous amount of revision before it can get through the catalog department, and the decision to use the information gathered during the ordering process for the basis of cataloging data is, in my point of view, questionable.

MRS. DUNLAP: I think this depends entirely upon the kind of system you are talking about. For very small libraries—small public and perhaps small college and university libraries—where probably the bulk of the material is American-imprint trade publications with relatively little that is highly complex as far as the cataloging aspect is concerned, not a tremendous amount of foreign material and not many of the very complex serials and corporate entries and so on, I think that probably it is highly useful to utilize the information that is acquired at the time they are doing the acquisition searching. Now, in a system such as yours, or in any other large research library, this would be almost impossible. First, because of the nature of the material used; second, because probably a great deal of it will be ordered prepublication, before any kind of bibliographic information is available; and third, because as an expedient for ordering,

it will deliberately be ordered under something other than what the catalogers will ultimately use.

HENRY BENDER, IBM Systems Development Division Library, San Jose: We have had considerable success in standardizing the cataloging format among the various IBM libraries in different parts of the country. We are also working with this idea of carrying the data from the ordering phase into the cataloging phase, and we find, of course, that revisions are necessary when the book comes in. But if the data has already been keypunched or already been stored (ideally in a random-access, real-time, on-line system), it can be gotten to quite easily, thereby avoiding re-inputting items like the author and the title which generally are spelled correctly the first time.

MARGARET AYRAULT, Library School, University of Hawaii: Something Mrs. Dunlap said gave me a little pause. She was talking about our need to use computers—with which I agree—but also the need to do our operations more cheaply. It seems to me that it should be clear that it may become cheaper per unit only when you are able to handle enough to get the unit cost down. Is this not true, that for a long time it's going to be more expensive?

MRS. DUNLAP: It may always be more expensive, as a matter of fact. What I really meant to imply was that it would also be more efficient, if not necessarily in terms of money, certainly in terms of human resources. Automation—particularly if the system is at all complex—is fantastically expensive.

In our own system, for instance, when I see the data processing bills each month, I am absolutely horrified. I went into fits of hysteria at first and I wasn't sure in my own mind whether automation was really all that expensive or whether it just seemed to be because I was being reminded of the cost every single month instead of just once a year as I had been before, when we figured personnel costs annually and then tended to forget them for the rest of the year. So, in order to try to find out, we did some cost studies in which we found that, although we really expected the computerized system to cost us more for several more years to come, at the present time, it is actually a little bit cheaper. We are saving 7 cents an order over and above what it would have cost, or at least what we think it would have cost, had it been under a manual system.

This is pretty difficult to determine, of course, because the projections from our old manual system are no longer completely valid, and obviously it is not 100 percent accurate. Some of the old statistics we had from the manual system were not quite as good as some of the ones we have now, so that the comparison still is not too valid. But for us, money was not the only consideration; being a state institution, we are obliged to try to do things as economically and effectively as we possibly can, but because we are terribly, terribly overcrowded, space was also of prime importance to us. And because we are still a pretty small town, we don't have a big labor market and people are extremely hard to get; so we have to rely very heavily on students and student wives. As a result, our turnover rate is really quite fantastic. We get tremendously competent people, almost always overqualified for what they are doing, but because they are here only for a year or two while their husbands are in school, they go very quickly. So we felt that a great deal of the savings that we would realize from such a system really would be almost impossible to calculate, because it would come from the people that we would never have to hire and rehire and train and retrain.

MISS AYRAULT: I had one more question. I was very interested in your statement about the computer making its own mistakes, and I wondered if you could comment on the sort of thing that has turned up so that we can have some idea to keep in mind of what can happen with the machine.

MRS. DUNLAP: It sometimes is a little difficult to get an explanation from, say, data processing itself about just what went wrong and why it went wrong; but, like many other people, we have been going through the throes of trying to install a new computer, and any of you who are going through this know what it's like and know that it is quite a trial.

When I speak of the computer making mistakes, it may not be the computer per se; it may be, instead, the software. As far as I am concerned, that's the computer. I don't care why or what particular part of it doesn't work; if the whole job gets sort of garbled or botched up, to me, the computer has done it. There have been a number of instances in which the software in the new computer has just failed miserably. We are absolutely certain that it is the computer and not the program because before we got the new computer, the program had been running really extremely well for over a year. Almost all of the flaws had been worked out, but as soon as the new computer was installed, we began having more and more difficulty. Certain parts of the system that had worked beautifully without a flaw for over a year, all of a sudden, blew up. In that case, it was not the system at fault; it was either the computer or the software combined with it.

Each month it got to be something a little bit different. We would get the problem solved and then something that had been running along smoothly for a year and a half would blow up again. That's why I say the computer can and does make its own mistakes. Very often the data processing people would comment that they sometimes knew why, but very often they didn't know why, probably because the new computer is such a complex machine and still pretty new.

SCOTT WHICHER, University of Oregon: Could you

explain why you believe an on-line system for acquisitions would be too costly?

MRS. DUNLAP: Because computers cost too much. Their system, generally speaking, is on-line, but they are still batch processing as far as writing purchase orders, printing an orders-by-fund list, and that sort of thing. They are using the on-line capabilities for bibliographic searching. Generally speaking, I think an on-line system for acquisitions would be much too expensive for the simple reason that it would be really an inefficient use of the computer. Most of the steps involved can be handled just as well and more efficiently by batch processing.

Moderator VEANER: I might add that the number of man-years required to design an effective, efficient on-line system is quite substantial.

CAROL BROWN, Conservation of Human Resources, Columbia University: I'm not a librarian; I'm here to do manpower research on contract with the National Advisory Commission on Libraries. I'd like to ask a question about the computer as a labor-saving device. Whose labor does it save? Whose labor does it increase? And what are the different skills that are required of the people in a library once it has an automated or even semiautomated system?

MRS. DUNLAP: Basically, it will save the time of clerical assistants, because it does the sort of dull routine tasks like filing and what not. It saves a lot of supervisory time, quite obviously, by eliminating the need to supervise and train individuals and so on. The big problem is getting the system in, getting it settled, getting it debugged, and so on; this takes key supervisory time, and this is where it hurts.

MISS BROWN: Once you get it going—now that you don't need these clerks—do you need other people, such as programmers, key punchers, systems analysts?

MRS. DUNLAP: One way or another, yes, depending upon the institution. Many libraries have librarians who have gone into systems and programming to such an extent that they themselves are doing the actual programming. Most of them are not, however, and, for the most part, I think it is really important only that the librarian know enough to be able to communicate, to understand, and to be able to read the program to make absolutely certain he is really getting what he wants.

MISS BROWN: What about smaller libraries that want to hook into a big system, or want to have automated equipment themselves? Do they have difficulty finding people with the computer skills?

MRS. DUNLAP: I gather they are very difficult to find.

KEN DOWLIN, Arvada, Colorado, Public Library:
Can you give me a sketch of any efforts to coordinate data transmission systems with jobbers or publishers for direct access to their inventories? I am thinking of perhaps using a DataPhone to get a quick read-out from a publisher's inventory records on when the books will be ready.

BRETT BUTLER, Stacey's: Los Angeles Public Library has just announced that it has set up a Data-Phone direct to Baker and Taylor's Reno offices for their main branch ordering. I don't know much more about it than that, but it was in the papers in Los Angeles.

What we are doing is a little different. We are trying to integrate some cataloging information in machine-readable form with the approval plans that we work so that the people who get new books from us can also get input to their machine records at the same time in an analogous manner.

Moderator VEANER: My intelligence agent reports that there are people from the Los Angeles Public Library here. Perhaps one of them can tell us what Los Angeles Public is doing with Baker and Taylor via Teletype or 1050 link [IBM 1050 Data Communications System].

STANFORD OPTNER, Los Angeles Public Library:
Every week a transaction tape is prepared from the book lists which have been scanned by the branch system of 61 libraries and by the 13 central departments. This transaction tape is placed in a sequence which we have worked out with Baker and Taylor, and when our files are updated so that we add these new books to our open-order file, we punch out a deck of cards. This deck of cards contains all the necessary conventions to make it possible to transmit over a telephone line. We take the deck of punch cards and introduce it to the 1050 reader—which doesn't operate at 14.8 characters per second as it's advertised, but at an effective rate of 7 characters per second. I say that because it takes somewhere in the neighborhood of four hours of transmitting to pass the information

from the data service bureau of the city of Los Angeles to the Baker and Taylor point of receipt, which is currently Reno, Nevada.

The information transmitted to Baker and Taylor comes to them in their format. When they have a computer set up in Reno, they will be able to take the cards, which are automatically punched at their end of the circuit, and introduce them to their computer reader. Then they can automatically pass these requests for books against their inventory and develop an output tape which says, "These we have; these we don't. These are on order. These we never heard of," and so forth.

They will generate a deck of cards, as a result of passing our input against their inventory. Those cards will be introduced to their 1050 reader, and they will punch back to us a day later or two days later the result of this massive file maintenance. This system has been operating for about four months, and we think it has great promise.

BOB MacDONALD, University of British Columbia:
There have been several reasons mentioned for considering automation, and I direct a question specifically to acquisitions. Besides conserving manpower and having a more effective acquisitions operation, have you not found that you have also obtained better information concerning the management of the library, in the form of statistics and more timely information, as another reason for considering automation?

MRS. DUNLAP: Certainly such a system gives this possibility; and there are a number of things that we plan to program into our present system, things that we can't now do because we are already at capacity in core. We do plan to make various and sundry surveys, not only for management purposes but also to see that we are providing the kind of service to the library community that we should be; to see what kind of service dealers are really giving us, for example; and also to do a number of cost studies both in terms of book materials and in terms of personnel and other operating expenditures.

Automation of Cataloging Procedures

Wesley Simonton

Professor, Graduate School of Library Science
University of Minnesota

This paper represents an attempt to identify and organize the major activities and processes involved in the automation of cataloging as they have emerged in the various experimental or operational projects carried out thus far, followed by an attempt to identify some of the major questions which must be answered before automation of cataloging can be extended beyond its present limits.

The paper is limited to the theoretical and practical problems encountered in the automation of the cataloging record, with undue emphasis, perhaps, on the former. It is, by assignment, only incidentally concerned with the relation of cataloging to other individual library processes, such as acquisition and circulation, or with the place of cataloging in general automated library systems. It concerns itself with hardware primarily in relation to theoretical questions and does not attempt to assess considerations of cost. It is based primarily on the published literature, supplemented in part by information supplied by a number of individuals whose gracious and thoughtful assistance can be acknowledged only in general terms.

First, a brief definition of "automation of cataloging": Automation of cataloging involves (1) the preparation of a record which can be read by a machine (and possibly also by human beings), which renders explicit some or all of the information which has traditionally been a part of the record prepared by the cataloger; (2) the input of that machine-readable record into one or more of a number of machines of widely varying capabilities; (3) the manipulation of that record by the machine. The processes involved in this manipulation may range from a simple reproduction of the record to a complex set of operations involving the rearrangement, the sorting, and the printing of the data. The storage of the records in the machine may be *momentary,* as in the case of systems employing unit record equipment; *temporary,* as in the case of batch processing systems in which the records are subjected to certain prescribed actions with specified results; or it may be *relatively*

permanent, as in the case of on-line or on-demand systems in which all or parts of the record are available, over protracted periods of time, on demand by an individual user.

GOALS AND TECHNIQUES OF CATALOGING

Any consideration of the methods, problems, and challenges involved in the automation of cataloging must also begin with as clear a definition as possible of present and ideal goals and techniques of cataloging. The following summation is suggested.

The cataloging process involves:

1. Determination of those individuals and/or corporate agencies responsible for or identified with a document. This identification is for two purposes:
   To provide access to single documents
   To identify all documents "authored" by or identified with a given individual or corporate agency.
2. Selection of one individual, one corporate agency, or the title, as the main entry for the work. (Throughout this paper, the term "main entry" is used only with this meaning, that is, the *heading* chosen as the main entry. It is never used with the meaning of the basic catalog card giving all the information necessary to the complete identification of the work.)

Official guidance in performing these two operations has been provided by the *A.L.A. Cataloging Rules for Author and Title Entries*[1] and, more recently, by the *Anglo-American Cataloging Rules.*[2] Hopefully, the rules provide the necessary amount of guidance to effect the consistent application of consistent principles in the selection of main and

[1] American Library Association, Division of Cataloging and Classification, *A.L.A. Cataloging Rules for Author and Title Entries;* ed. by Clara Beetle (2d ed.; Chicago: ALA, 1949).

[2] American Library Association, Library of Congress, Library Association, and Canadian Library Association, *Anglo-American Cataloging Rules,* North American Text (Chicago: ALA, 1967).

other entries, resulting in uniform interpretations and uniform bibliographical records. The degree to which this hope has been realized has been discussed by many authors and the results are not necessarily of interest here.[3]

3. Provision of a description of the physical object

Official standards are presently provided in Part II, Description, of the *Anglo-American Cataloging Rules,* based on the earlier *Rules for Descriptive Cataloging* of the Library of Congress, for fulfilling the two objectives:

> 1) to state the significant features of an item with the purpose of distinguishing it from other items and describing its scope, contents, and bibliographic relation to other items: 2) to present these data in an entry which can be integrated with the entries for other items in the catalog and which will respond best to the interests of most users of the catalog.[4]

Lack of uniformity of practice in this area may be said to result more frequently from conscious variation from official positions than is the case with questions relating to entry, as descriptive cataloging principles are more likely to be subjected to official variations in individual libraries, either generally or for specific types of materials.

4. Provision of entries under the title and/or series of which the document is a member, as appropriate

5. Provision of subject access through—
Natural language (i.e., "subject headings")
Classification

6. Meaningful arrangement of the several records of a document in the various files maintained.

THE STATE OF THE ART

The following discussion of the state of the art of the automation of cataloging is organized in terms of the six goals and techniques enumerated above. An attempt will be made to summarize the present state of the art, citing appropriate examples as illustrative only and with no attempt to identify all examples for a given question or issue.

First, with regard to the third goal, the description of the document as a physical object in those catalogs prepared by public and special libraries: The reduction in the extent of the description should probably not be viewed merely as a result of automation, but in part, at least, as a reflection of the traditional policy of many of these libraries of shortening the bibliographical record for more economical processing and the supposed convenience of the patron. However, there is no doubt that the reduction of the entry

has also been influenced by a conscious or unconscious attempt to reduce machine-processing time because of the considerable costs involved. This concept applies both to catalogs produced on unit record equipment and those produced on computers. Examples of this sort of shortened entry may be seen in the catalogs of the Baltimore County Public Library[5] (see Bibliography, No.163), the Los Angeles County Public Library (see Bibliography, No.194), the Boeing Scientific Research Laboratories Library (see Bibliography, No.200), and the Lawrence Radiation Laboratory Library (see Bibliography, No.193). On the other hand, catalogs produced by university and research libraries have tended to repeat the traditional description as prescribed in the official rules. Examples here include the catalogs of Florida Atlantic University (see Bibliography, No.177, 197), of the Ontario New University Libraries Project (see Bibliography, No.160, 171), and of the Stanford University Undergraduate Library (see Bibliography, No.170).

Questions relating to the first objective of cataloging—that is, the provision of catalog entries for a given document—may be considered under three headings: (1) the number of entries to be provided, (2) methods for identifying the relationship of the individual or corporate body named in the heading to the document, and (3) the necessity of identifying one of the entries as the "main" entry.

With regard to the number of entries provided for a document, again we can identify variation on either side of the "official" position—that is, either fewer or more entries than prescribed. This variation may, in large measure, represent a traditional type of library practice rather than a new practice dictated by consideration of machines. Thus, the Baltimore County catalog, reflecting traditional public library practice, provides fewer added entries for an item than called for by official rules, and the catalog of the Technical Information Center of Lockheed Missiles and Space Company provides more added entries—under items such as source, contract number, and report number —reflecting the needs of the special library.[6] Again, catalogs produced by university libraries have tended to provide the same number of entries for an item as prescribed officially.

With regard to the identification of the relationship of a given individual or corporate agency to a document, current automated catalogs have not added any new designations to the traditional ones of editor, translator, joint author, etc. As entries for "sponsors" have been added on occasion to these catalogs, they have usually been treated as "general secondary" added entries, with no indication in the heading of the specific relationship of the agency to the document.

---

[3] Johannes L. Dewton, "Grand Illusion," *Library Journal,* 86: 1719-29. (May 1, 1961).

[4] *Anglo-American Cataloging Rules,* p.189.

[5] Baltimore County Public Library, "Book Catalog and Card Catalog: A Cost and Service Study" (1967).

[6] W. A. Kozumplik and R. T. Lange, "Computer Produced Microfilm Library Catalog," *American Documentation,* 18: 67 (April 1967).

EXAMPLES OF "NO MAIN ENTRY"

STANFORD UNIVERSITY - J. HENRY MEYER MEMORIAL LIBRARY

Angell, Robert Cooley
    The use of personal documents in
    history, anthropology, and sociology.
    By Louis Gottschalk, Clyde Kluckhohn
    and Robert Angell. Prepared for the
    Committee on Appraisal of Research.
    Social Science Research Council, 1945.
    243 p.   H61.G6

Gottschalk, Louis
    The use of personal documents in
    history, anthropology, and sociology.
    By Louis Gottschalk, Clyde Kluckhohn
    and Robert Angell. Prepared for the
    Committee on Appraisal of Research.
    Social Science Research Council, 1945.
    243 p.   H61.G6

Social Science Research Council.
    Committee on Appraisal of Research.
    The use of personal documents in
    history, anthropology, and sociology.
    By Louis Gottschalk, Clyde Kluckhohn
    and Robert Angell. Prepared for the
    Committee on Appraisal of Research.
    Social Science Research Council, 1945.
    243 p.   H61.G6

The use of personal documents in history,
    anthropology, and sociology. By Louis
    Gottschalk, Clyde Kluckhohn and Robert
    Angell. Prepared for the Committee
    on Appraisal of Research. Social
    Science Research Council, 1945.
    243 p.   H61.G6

Figure 1. Examples of "No Main Entry," Stanford Undergraduate Library Book Catalog

The main variation relating to identification of relationship is seen in those catalogs predicted on the "no main entry" concept (see Bibliography, No.113, 136, 181, 216). As examples, we may identify the Boeing catalog, the Lawrence Radiation Laboratory catalog, and the Stanford catalog, in which the unit description of the document is repeated under each entry with nothing more than the individual entry preceding the description, as opposed to the traditional practice of imposing the main entry between the added entry and the description. Figure 1 illustrates the application of the "no main entry" concept in the Stanford catalog, with four entries for a work, identical except for the heading, and with no clue as to whether the cataloger has selected Angell, Gottschalk, Kluckhohn, or the Committee on Appraisal of Research of the Social Science Research Council as the main entry.

Automation of cataloging has introduced no major change with regard to title and series added entries other than the more liberal provision of partial title entries of the sort characterized by Lubetzky over a quarter of a century ago as constituting the "fifth column" of the catalog.[7] Again, this development is seen most frequently in catalogs of special libraries and perhaps reflects nothing more than dissatisfaction in this type of library with the traditional limitations on partial title entries. The ease with which partial title entries can be produced by machine and the development of KWIC [Key-Word-in-Context] indexes have intensified this trend.

Unless this provision of additional partial title entries is viewed as reflecting a criticism of or change in traditional subject cataloging procedures, automation has as yet had virtually no impact on subject cataloging procedures except for those systems in the field of medical literature, such as MEDLARS [Medical Literature Analysis and Retrieval System][8] and the State University of New York Biomedical Communication Network,[9] which provide or contemplate greater "depth" in indexing in the form of more numerous subject headings for a document, with subject analysis attempted at the "chapter" rather than the "book" level.

Three questions relating to the "meaningful arrangement" of records are: (1) the number of files maintained, (2) whether "unit" or "variable" records are provided in these files, and (3) methods of arranging entries in the single or multiple files.

[7] Seymour Lubetzky, "Titles: Fifth Column of the Catalog," *Library Quarterly*, 11: 412-30 (Oct. 1941).

[8] Scott Adams, "MEDLARS: Performance, Problems, Possibilities," *Medical Library Association Bulletin*, 53: 144 (April 1965); General Electric Company, *The MEDLARS Story at the National Library of Medicine* (Washington: U.S. Department of Health, Education, and Welfare, Public Health Service, 1963), p.3.

[9] Irwin H. Pizer, "The Application of Computers in the State University of New York Biomedical Communication Network" (paper presented at IBM Customer Executive Program, Endicott, N.Y., April 10-14, 1967).

With regard to the number of files maintained, most automated cataloging installations have rejected the dictionary catalog—in which all entries for an item are interfiled in a single file—in favor of the divided catalog, with two or more files. Three major patterns of division may be identified. First, a three-part catalog consisting of authors (including added entries), subjects, and titles. The automated catalogs of public libraries generally reflect this practice (with the addition of separate juvenile catalogs). The catalogs of Florida Atlantic University, of the Lawrence Radiation Laboratory, of Lockheed, and of the St. Louis Junior College District (see Bibliography, No.175) reflect this pattern. Second, a two-part division into authors, and subjects and titles, as seen in the Boeing catalog. Third, a division into two files, one of the authors and titles, the other of subjects, as seen in the Stanford catalog.

With regard to the question of how much information concerning a document is presented at each access point, it may be noted first that most book catalogs reproduce the tracing—that is, the record of added entries—only in the main entry record. A number of the book catalogs produced to date have introduced a further variation in the amount of physical description provided at the different access points. First, a number of catalogs provide a full description of the document only in the main entry (or register) record, with a briefer description in the other records. This briefer description is a unit description, that is, it is identical under each of the entries. This form of catalog may be seen in virtually all of the public library catalogs, the catalogs of Boeing and the Lawrence Radiation Laboratory, in the catalog of the St. Louis Junior College District (in the form of a full description in the register), and in *The Elementary School Library Collection, Phases 1-2-3.*[10] A second pattern combines a full description in the main entries with a variable description in the other files. Thus, in the catalog of the Ontario Project, the added entries, title entries, and the subject entries, and in the Los Angeles County catalog, the subject entries are more complete (by virtue of inclusion of an annotation) than the author entries, which are in turn more complete than the title entries.

Questions relating to methods for arranging entries in the single or multiple files of the catalog are most appropriately discussed in connection with book catalogs and will be treated only briefly here. Because of the complexity of the official rules for entry and for filing, maintenance of the files in the prescribed order demands the application of a high degree of sophisticated knowledge. It is clear that dividing the catalog reduces the dimensions of the problem somewhat; this fact no doubt accounts in part for the predominance of divided catalogs in automated systems. Beyond this, these systems have accepted certain of the constraints of computer filing, with recognition of the limitations involved. It is also clear, however, that a fundamental choice must be made between revision of the form of certain of our entries and acceptance of new filing patterns, on the one hand, and the expenditure of considerable editing and/or programming time in an attempt to retain the traditional entries and patterns, on the other hand. The first approach is reflected in the computer filing code of Hines and Harris (see Bibliography, No.211). The second is seen in the Inforonics report by Nugent on the Library of Congress filing rules[11] and in the general discussion of the question in the report by Cartwright and Shoffner on the catalogs of the California State Library (see Bibliography, No.159).

HARDWARE AND METHODS

Following this review of the effect of automation on traditional cataloging goals and techniques, a few words are in order concerning hardware and basic methods of initiating automated or semiautomated procedures. With regard to hardware, four types of equipment which have been utilized in the cataloging process may be identified. The first of these is the automatic typewriter, utilizing paper tape. Notable success has been achieved at the University of Missouri (see Bibliography, No.148) and Washington University of St. Louis (see Bibliography, No.145) in the use of these typewriters for the production of catalog cards. In these installations, original copy is typed with two by-products, hard copy for proofing and paper tape, which, after any necessary corrections, is used to actuate the typewriter to produce catalog cards with headings added. Paper tape may also be an input medium for more sophisticated systems.

The second method involves card-actuated cameras and photocomposition. In this process, a camera is used to photograph automatically one, two, or three lines of information at the top of a card. The cards enter the camera through an automatic feeding device, and the camera automatically adjusts to mixtures of cards with one or more lines of print. A sheet of film is exposed, the negative is developed, and column lengths are stripped up into page formats. Photo-offset plates are prepared from the film negatives, and listings are duplicated and assembled in finished form. The major advantages of this method include the possibility of employing varied type faces, with more easily read entries, and a more efficient utilization of space (see Bibliography, No.183). The best-known example of the use of this method is probably the second stage of the Los Angeles County catalog (see Bibliography, No.194). The main disadvantage

[10] *The Elementary School Library Collection, Phases 1-2-3* (2d ed.; Newark, N.J.: Bro-Dart Foundation, 1966).

[11] William R. Nugent, "The Mechanization of the Filing Rules for the Dictionary Catalogs of the Library of Congress," *Library Resources and Technical Services* 11: 145-66 (Spring 1967).

from the point of view of automation is the fact that no machine-readable record is created.

The third method, involving the use of unit record equipment, requires the preparation of a number of punched cards for each title cataloged, including separate cards for each heading or entry, and the manual manipulation of these cards in sorters, collators, and line printers. A number of the early book catalogs were produced in this way, notably that of King County, Washington (see Bibliography, No.204), and the first Los Angeles County catalog (see Bibliography, No.210). This method does produce a machine-readable record but suffers from the disadvantage of requiring the storing and repeated handling of a large number of punched cards.

The fourth and most sophisticated method involves the use of a computer and the creation of a magnetic-tape record, usually generated from punched-card or paper-tape input. The tape record is then subjected to sorting, rearranging, and printing by the computer.

As indicated, the key punch and the automatic typewriter, generating respectively punched cards and paper tape, have served as the major input machines for most automated cataloging systems to date. The hope of utilizing some form of optical scanning device remains unfulfilled to this point, with the exception of work at Johns Hopkins University, in which it was found economically feasible to retype bibliographical records in a single font and then use an optical scanning device to create a machine-readable record (see Bibliography, No.250).

In those systems utilizing unit record equipment or computers for the automation of cataloging, a machine-readable record is created by recording the bibliographical information in a rigidly controlled format, with machine codes to identify the meaning and/or location of the item on the catalog record. Typically, one punched card is prepared for each line of the catalog record, with 40 characters per line yielding a record 4 inches in length at the rate of 10 characters per inch.

Figure 2 illustrates a typical machine record as prepared at Florida Atlantic University. The worksheet or "input record," as it is called, is divided into several sections, representing among other items the various sections of the catalog record: main entry, conventional title, title and edition, imprint and collation, subject tracing, other added entry tracing, and call number. Each of the sections is uniquely identified by coding in the control field of the punched card. These codes identify the information and govern subsequent manipulation of the information by the computer. Thus, the main entry is identified by "10" and the conventional title by "22," respectively, in columns 67 and 68. If any section of the record requires more than one line, the sequence of the lines must be indicated, as illustrated here by a code in column 70. The result, then, is the creation of a machine-readable record with the various segments of the record clearly identified for machine manipulation. Acting upon these instructions, the computer is able to reproduce sections of the record as appropriate, rearrange the record as appropriate, and produce author, subject, and title catalogs.

As already indicated, the major output devices include automatic typewriters and line printers, either unit record or computer driven. More sophisticated devices, as yet little used in library operations, provide photo-optical or electronic character generation. Photo-optical character generation is illustrated by GRACE, the unique Graphic Arts Composing Equipment employed in the MEDLARS system for the production of *Index Medicus*. This equipment has the capability of handling multiple type fonts, styles, and sizes and of mixing them in the same line. Electronic character generation is provided by the S-C 4020 high-speed microfilm recorder of General Dynamics Corporation. The S-C 4020 displays alphanumeric data on the face of a special cathode-ray tube, which is then photographed with a high-speed camera on standard 35-millimeter film. This system is employed in the Lockheed catalog.[12]

With regard to the physical housing of catalog records, we have already identified a trend toward substitution of a book catalog, machine produced and manually consulted, for the card catalog. In order to provide up-to-date records, it may prove desirable to supplant the catalog either by a card record, in shelf list or main entry form, as in the case of the Baltimore County catalog, or by one of two sorts of lists. The first of these is a list of titles "in process," that is, titles mainly in the acquisition stage, in which as soon as an item is cataloged it is so identified in the "in process" list, as seen in the PIL [Processing Information List] of the International Business Machines Research Library at Yorktown Heights, N.Y. (see Bibliography, No.109). The second kind of list is a "recent accessions" list, available in the interim period between editions or between edition and supplement of the book catalog, as seen in the Lockheed system. A more radical change in the physical housing of the bibliographical record is seen in the Lockheed catalog, in which records are maintained on microfilm in cartridges rather than on 3-by-5 catalog cards. Increasing concern with the feasibility of producing a book catalog for a file of any considerable size is seen in the expressed goal of most current research projects to produce an "on demand" file, machine produced, machine maintained, and available for consultation at any time.

As a footnote to the state of the art, it is interesting to note that there are now in existence a number of fairly substantial files of machine-readable records, namely, 11,000 titles in the Columbia-Harvard-Yale Medical Library Project; 14,000 titles anticipated in the MARC [Machine-Readable Cataloging] project by June 1967; 35,000 titles at Washington

---

[12] Kozumplik and Lange, *loc. cit.*

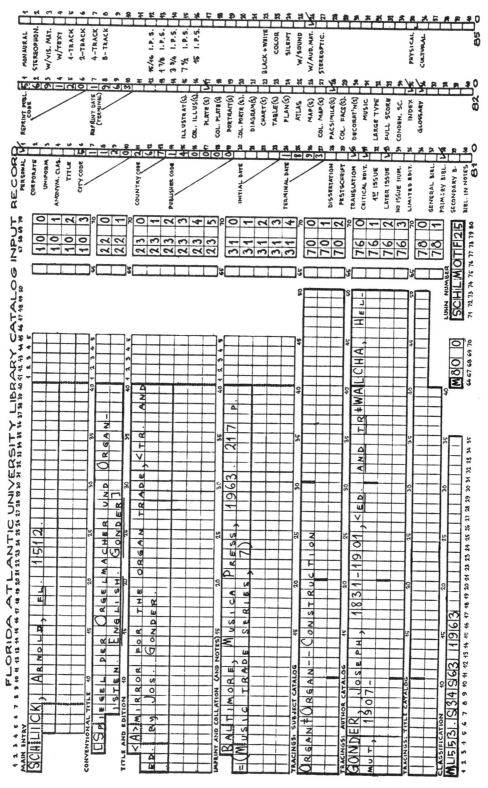

Figure 2. "Input Record," Florida Atlantic University Library Catalog

State University in Pullman; 40,000 titles in the Stanford catalog; more than 100,000 titles at Los Angeles County; and more than 150,000 titles at Lockheed. Although the content and the format of these files differ in some major respects, it is obvious that we are approaching a point at which there exists a considerable number of collections of data for experimentation and research.

THE FUTURE

To predict future developments at a time when the MARC program of the Library of Congress (see Bibliography, No.221), which is manifestly central to the automation of cataloging in the United States, is hardly more than a year old, is clearly presumptuous, but a few thoughts concerning the questions and problems involved in future developments may be in order nonetheless.

Markuson has suggested that we shall probably reach agreement on a standard format for the machine-readable bibliographical record by 1968.[13] To attain this goal, we must have firm answers to a number of questions relating to the bibliographical record. For the most part, these questions are not new, but the impact of the machine forces us either to reconsider our earlier answers or to provide an answer in those cases in which we have begged the question. The best recent identification of these questions is that provided by Avram and Markuson at the Anglo-American Conference on the Mechanization of Library Services in 1966 (see Bibliography, No.217) in which the following list of bibliographical questions was presented:

1. Does the formatting of entries for efficient machine processing affect the bibliographic function of the entry?
2. Should certain data, now implicitly stated in the bibliographic entry, be made specific? For example, should the language of the title and the text, the kind of author (corporate, personal, etc), and other attributes of a particular work be described explicitly?
3. To what extent do certain filing practices need to be retained in machine systems?
4. How many access points to the bibliographic data should be provided in a machine system? Should these include increased depth of subject indexing, more name entries, chapter headings, place of publication, etc? Which items could be reduced to codes for efficient searching, and how shall these codes be structured and maintained?
5. What diversity of cataloging practice actually

exists throughout the world? What impact does this diversity have on the development of a standard for international data interchange? What classes of practices present the most difficult areas for analysis and agreement and how might fruitful attempts to study and solve these problems be undertaken?
6. To what extent could a standardized format be developed which would be hospitable to description of materials in different media— monographs, serials, slides, motion pictures, phonograph records, maps, etc?
7. To what extent could a standardized format be developed which would be useful for a variety of library operations such as acquisitions, cataloging, circulation, bibliographical work, etc. To what extent would the development of such a format permit the creation of a complete bibliographic record of an item as a result of collecting data input from many separate library operations?

The following consideration of these questions is organized under four topics: Content of the Machine-Readable Bibliographical Record; Structure of the Machine-Readable Bibliographical Record; Effect of Machine Operations; and Access and Display of the Bibliographical Record.

Content of the Machine-Readable Bibliographical Record

It is clear that the machine-readable bibliographical record must contain at least the following items: (1) a description of the document; (2) a record of the entries under which the description of the document is to be filed, with perhaps an identification of one of these as the main entry; and, as appropriate, (3) an "authority" record, containing certainly a record of the cross references necessary in connection with the name entries provided, and perhaps including the references necessary in connection with the subject entries (see Bibliography, No.221).

The description of the document will probably be based on the traditional rules, supplemented perhaps by the results of the work of the USASI [United States of America Standards Institute] Z - 39 [Committee on Library Work and Documentation] SC - 2 Sectional Committee on Machine Input Records.[14] A probable major change here will be the provision of certain types of information in explicit rather than implicit form, as in the past. The most obvious example of this sort of change is the identification of the language or languages of the document.

However, there remain other basic questions

[13] Barbara Evans Markuson, "The Library of Congress Automation Program: A Progress Report to the Stockholders," *ALA Bulletin*, 61:654 (June 1967).

[14] Information from certain preliminary memoranda from this committee, currently engaged in a research study involving the analysis of bibliographic data from the viewpoint of developing standards for machine input of bibliographic records, has been made available by Mrs. Henriette Avram.

relating to the content of the bibliographical record which must be answered. Specifically, should and can we provide for automatic production of records of varying length for a single document, as appropriate for varying needs? That is, can the "checklist" and the "bibliographical" function of the record be accommodated in a single record; can we provide from a single record both a title-a-line description and the detailed description traditionally associated with rare books?[15] Another manifestation of this problem may be seen in the variation between local needs and national needs. Undoubtedly we need a national bibliographical record for each item, in at least traditional length, but it is a question whether each library in the country needs for its own records a duplication of that national record.

At the same time, we must be mindful of the possibility of introducing new elements into the bibliographical record, as seen most notably in the suggestions of Bry and Afflerbach, who propose the inclusion of such items as identification of the nature of the document (research report, conference proceedings, scope, etc.), indication of the sponsorship of the document, a record of reviews and controversies engendered by the document, and some evaluation of the document.[16] To date, these questions have not been seriously considered by the library community.

Atherton's outline of the general problem of compatibility of present codes and sets of rules provides a good beginning for consideration of the problem of compatibility.[17] For a dramatic illustration of the variations between bibliographical records prepared by "librarians" and "documentalists" (assuming the existence of such a dichotomy), compare the *Anglo-American Cataloging Rules* with the **COSATI** *Standard for Descriptive Cataloging of Government Scientific and Technical Reports*.[18] Clearly, much work needs to be done relating to entry and description to say nothing of subject headings.

Structure of the Machine-Readable Bibliographical Record

At present, the bibliographical record consists of four main parts: (1) the main entry, (2) the body of

the entry (title, edition, and imprint), (3) the collation (i.e., the physical description), and (4) any notes necessary to expand the description or provide further information concerning the document. The body of the entry consists of certain prescribed items, arranged in a prescribed order; it is based primarily, but not completely, on information appearing on the title page and usually, but not always, presents this information in the same order as it appears on the title page.

There are a number of considerations, some obvious and some subtle, which follow from the fact that the body of the entry is preceded by the main entry. The most obvious of these is that a statement of authorship appearing on the title page, in either explicit or implicit form, is frequently omitted from the body of the entry, and thus from the bibliographical record, because it has already been presented implicitly in the main entry.

It is possible to conceive of two major changes in the structuring of the bibliographical record as a result of automation. The first of these, proposed by a number of authors in recent years, is that the description of the document need not be tied to a single main entry (see Bibliography, No.113, 136, 181, 216). Evaluation of this proposal must include discussion of the likely effect on the obvious and subtle considerations mentioned above.

The other possible major change would be limiting the information in the body of the entry to information on the title page, and observing more closely than at present the order of that information as it appears on the title page in the hope of securing a more uniform content and organization of the information, with a resulting greater likelihood of effective machine searching or consultation of that portion of the bibliographical record[19] (see Bibliography, No.224).

A third, less significant change in the structuring of the bibliographical record is suggested in the preliminary work of the **SC-2** committee, in which it is proposed that the functions of notes be more clearly identified, in order to permit more efficient machine manipulation and interpretation of the information presented in note form. Three reasons for identifying different kinds of notes are presented: (1) to permit generation of entries from notes; for example, a phrase such as "prepared in cooperation with" would identify either joint corporate authorship or affiliation; (2) to provide for inclusion or exclusion of the note from the record, depending on varying needs at different access points; thus, availability notes might be pertinent in a finding list, and annotations might be desirable when the approach is by subject; (3) to provide special formatting, for example, positioning "title romanized" notes after tracings.

[15] J. W. Jolliffe, in *Brasenose Conference on the Automation of Libraries:* Proceedings of the Anglo-American Conference on the Mechanization of Library Services; ed. by John Harrison and Peter Laslett (London and Chicago: Mansell, 1967), p.95.

[16] Ilse Bry and Lois Afflerbach, "Bibliographical Challenges in the Age of the Computer," *Library Journal,* 90: 813-18 (Feb. 15, 1965).

[17] Pauline Atherton, "Is Compatibility of Authority Files Practicable?" in Simon N. Newman, *Information Systems Compatibility* (Washington: Spartan Books, 1965), p.69-81.

[18] U.S. Federal Council for Science and Technology, Committee on Scientific and Technical Information, *Standard for Descriptive Cataloging of Government Scientific and Technical Reports,* Revision No. 1 (Washington: 1966).

[19] H. H. Fussler, in *Brasenose Conference on the Automation of Libraries,* p.82; C. Dake Gull, "The Impact of Electronics upon Cataloging Rules," in *International Conference on Cataloguing Principles, Paris, 1961: Report* (London: 1963), p. 285-87.

Effect of Machine Operations

Avram and Markuson (see Bibliography, No.217) have posed the following list of questions relating to machine operations:

1   How can a multiplicity of languages be efficiently encoded for machine processing and how can they be transferred back to the original language for output printing?

2   How should bibliographical data be structured for efficient storage and retrieval? To date most work has been done on the problem of formatting for machine production of traditional library products such as book catalogs, printed catalog cards, and lists. The problems of file design for actual machine search and retrieval on special elements of bibliographic data will need intensive study if large-scale automated library systems are to be achieved.

3   What coding schemes most efficiently permit the machine identification of data elements in the record? That is, can data be so structured that the computer can recognize, by the configuration of codes, a particular item of data and process it in a variety of ways?

4   What are the trade-offs between frequency of use of data, the organization of the machine files, the configuration of the particular equipment available, and the use of minimal coding techniques for storage of the data? By minimal coding one attempts to store the most data in the least space, but in some cases one has the concomitant problem of processing the data upon request back to their original form. There is some point at which a balance has to be reached for the sake of system efficiency.

5   What relationships exist between the manner in which bibliographical data are formatted and encoded and the terminal devices (display consoles, typewriters, teletypewriters, etc) which one might wish to use?

For present purposes, a useful definition of a computer is the one which identifies it as "a device capable of accepting information, applying prescribed processes to the information and supplying the results of these processes."[20] In terms of the automation of cataloging, we may equate "accepting information" with receiving the machine-readable bibliographical record and storing it, either temporarily, while "prescribed processes" are being applied, or permanently, to be supplied later. In the process of receiving the information, the computer may also perform certain editing operations. Cox, Dews, and Dolby (see Bibliography, No.2) have listed as possible editing operations the following:

1)   the detection of missing information (for example, are author, title, date of publication all present?)

2)   the detection of invalid codes (for example, the presence of numbers in names or letters in dates)

3)   the detection of over-long or over-short fields

4)   the detection of out-of-order information

5)   the detection of unreasonable literal sequences, for example, the sequence BTR at the beginning of an English word or the sequence RTB at the end of an English word.

The basic prescribed processes performed by the computer include formatting data, reproducing all or prescribed portions of the data at various points, and sequencing, that is, sorting or alphabetizing the data. In addition, a number of other processes which might be "prescribed" have been suggested in the literature. These include: (1) reporting the number of items under a given access point when it reaches a certain point; for example, the number of titles under an author (see Bibliography, No.159) or the number of entries under a subject heading; (2) automatic generation of subject entries for place subdivided by subject from headings in the form subject divided by place (see Bibliography, No.111); (3) automatic updating of terminology (see Bibliography, No.111); (4) exploration of relationships between subject headings and classification (see Bibliography, No.111); (5) construction of a chain index to the Dewey classification (see Bibliography, No.113); and (6) preparation of name and subject heading authority lists with appropriate indication of the structuring; that is, "see" and "see also" entries for the items in the list.[21] In supplying the results, the machine can either print or display all or a portion of the information relating to the record at any number of predetermined access points.

The basic work on formatting the bibliographical record for machine handling is being performed in the MARC project. Here 38 possible portions of the record have been identified, 18 of which are placed in "fixed" fields, with information of predetermined length, readily accessible for machine processing. The other 20 are placed in variable fields, that is, fields whose length cannot be determined in advance (see Bibliography, No.221). Experimental work at the University of Chicago is notable for: (1) the rejection of the fixed field concept; (2) the concept of three input modes: "condensed," "BCD" (Binary Coded Decimal), and "format"; and (3) experimentation with a search code (based on portions of the author's name, title, place, and date of publication) which hopefully will permit machine searching of the title for determination of the inclusion of a given item.[22]

---

[20]U.S. Bureau of the Budget, *Automatic Data Processing Glossary* (Washington: Govt. Print. Off., 1962), p.12.

[21]U.S. National Agricultural Library, *Report of Task Force ABLE* (Washington: Govt. Print. Off., 1965), p.22-23.

[22]University of Chicago Library, "Memorandum on Automation Project" (March 1967).

Access and Display of the Bibliographical Record

Questions relating to the content of the bibliographical record, its structure, and its machine handling culminate in considerations of access and display. Preautomated cataloging theory regarding the number of access points (that is, the number of "entries" for a document) and the amount of information concerning the document to be displayed at each of these access points has inevitably been influenced in large measure by the unit card concept. As in other affairs, it is sometimes difficult to assess the relative importance of theory and hardware. If cataloging is to be automated, we must reconsider or reaffirm our answers to two basic questions: first, what constitutes the ideal description of a document; and second, how much of this ideal description should be presented under how many access points? A subquestion of the second question is: should the same amount of information be presented at each access point?

On the basis of evidence and informed reflection to date, there would seem to be serious questions relating to the feasibility of producing book catalogs containing more than 100,000 titles, particularly if the full entry for an item is displayed at each access point. If, then, we seek to produce book catalogs because of their many well-known advantages, it may be necessary or desirable to consider some division of or reduction in the recording of our resources. Possible criteria for division include date of publication (see Bibliography, No.159, 167), subject (as in the case of the Harvard shelf lists (see Bibliography, No. 111, 125)), and selectivity (i.e., "best books") (see Bibliography, No.167). As a means of reducing the amount of information at some or all of the access points, Weinstein and George have suggested the creation of a complete bibliographical record for an item, programmed to produce computer-generated indexes to the record, with the indexes displaying only a portion of the complete record.[23] Markuson has suggested that our bibliographical record may be arranged in accession number order with complete information at that point and indexes to the record (see Bibliography, No.219). Parker has suggested that the catalog of the future may be held on-line in the computer, with printed indexes available off-line.[24]

Among those who have written most persuasively for a completely on-line system, with the catalog machine produced, machine stored, and consulted through a console, we may include Bregzis, who has written of the "reactive catalog" (see Bibliography, No.110), and Swanson, who proposes "dialogues with a catalog" (see Bibliography, No.137). The feasibility of their

plans, both in terms of theoretical problems relating to the bibliographical record and the practical problems relating to hardware, will doubtless serve as the focus of much work during the next decade.

SUMMARY

At the risk of oversimplification, it may be suggested that a fair degree of success has been achieved in the automation of cataloging procedures: (1) in newly established or newly cataloged libraries, most of them relatively small, in which automation could be initiated at the same time that cataloging was initiated; (2) in libraries with relatively few existing cataloging records which it was necessary to convert to machine-readable form; or (3) in situations in which the likely increase in library services made possible by automated procedures was judged valuable enough to justify the cost of local planning and programming time. For such situations, a fair consensus exists with regard to procedures for recording and manipulating bibliographical records in machine-readable form.

In the automation of cataloging, traditional rules, policies, and procedures of cataloging generally have been observed; however, a number of variations may be noted, some based on different theories of cataloging and some based on the hope of more efficient machine procedures. At the present moment, when national if not international standards for machine-readable bibliographical records are being established, it is particularly important that the basic tenents of cataloging be reexamined and either reaffirmed or revised in the light of the opportunities presented by automation.

DISCUSSION

MR. VEANER: May I just make a brief comment concerning the use of forbidden combinations? Our British colleagues suggest having the computer inform us when this may occur, and I think we may be running the risk of trying to get the computer to do our intellectual work for us, unless we are going to send this computer to graduate school and have it become competent in every possible subject. As an instance, we cannot validly say that the combination of the figure "7," followed by the letter "X" is an invalid combination. I believe this is a surname among some of our Black Muslim colleagues. Likewise the combination cited, "BTR," would be a perfectly valid transliteration of a Hebrew place-name, and it's quite likely to appear as an article title or even a book title in, say, the publications of the American Oriental Society. I think the real answer is that there would be no really forbidden combinations in our intellectual activities.

PAUL LeBANNON: I have been for several years a cataloger for commercial library processing firms.

[23]Edward Allen Weinstein and Virginia S. George, "Computer-Produced Book Catalogs: Entry Form and Content," *Library Resources and Technical Services,* 11:185-91 (Spring 1967).

[24]R. H. Parker, in *Brasenose Conference on the Automation of Libraries,* p.42.

I am currently with the firm of Masterlist in San Diego, which produces and has been producing for four years automated book catalogs for libraries and school districts.

One of the problems we catalogers have with our customers is the business of updating standards for author entries, descriptive cataloging, and subject heading. Many of our customers still abide by what you call the traditional rules of cataloging. My point is that many of our traditional rules have been enforced because of the requirements of the 3-by-5 card catalog format. My feeling is that the time is going to come when all the entries, descriptive rules, and subject headings are going to have to be geared to the need of a modern society, of modern users, of modern terminology. What is your feeling on that matter?

MR. SIMONTON: I would agree with what you are suggesting, although I would hope that perhaps catalogers and users of catalogs have not been quite so reactionary as you have suggested.

Basically, this is what I was talking about when I said that preautomated cataloging theory has been based on the unit card concept, and it is very hard to distinguish those of our practices which follow from the 3-by-5 concept. Theory and hardware get intermixed.

STEVE FURTH, IBM: Several people referred to optical character recognition devices which could be used in library operations, and the question of using such devices for the conversion of catalog cards has been briefly mentioned.

In view of what you have said, I wonder if you could comment on the practicability of reading a card catalog that has been produced within the last 25 or 40 years into any kind of optical character recognition device which could recognize the characters. What would we do with the information? There's no explicit coding; there are none of the things of formatting that you have so clearly pointed out are necessary. I am raising this question because I think it should be discussed, and I think it should be put to bed once and for all; there is no magic in converting card catalogs by any mechanical means.

MR. SIMONTON: I would have to agree again. You are certainly quite right that there is nothing to be gained by reproducing our present records when they are not formatted for machine handling.

LOIS NEWMAN, Rand Corporation Library, Santa Monica: I am interested in what Mr. Simonton had to say about the Anglo-American cataloging code and the COSATI cataloging code. I think there is going to be a great problem because COSATI just came out with a revised edition which is very different from the Anglo-American cataloging code. I don't think we are ever going to be able to solve the dichotomy between the report literature and cataloging.

MR. SIMONTON: I think it is true that we have a basically different approach to these two types of records. If we include in our machine-readable record some identification of the nature of the document, then we may be able to achieve more compatibility. If the machine knows, for example, that it is dealing with a technical report, it may accept different entries or it may handle it in a different way than it does when it is told it is dealing with a book.

Automated Production of Book Catalogs

Kelley L. Cartwright

Institute of Library Research
University of California, Berkeley

This will be a discussion of methods—mechanics, if you will—including some pitfalls, some headaches, and what I think are some good and bad ways of doing things. An adjustment in the title is necessary, however, since we cannot properly speak of "Automated Production of Book Catalogs," but only of partially automated production. There is no machine into which we can stuff books and journals at one end and produce finished book catalogs at the other, and none appears to be on the horizon. It might be well, therefore, to define what we mean by an automated system. In the present context, a partially automated book catalog production system is one in which either the catalog information itself, or the physical medium upon which it is stored, or both are manipulated by machines, thus relieving human beings of some important part of the effort required to produce a book catalog.

In order to discuss more fruitfully the aspects of book catalog production in which techniques of automation can be of assistance, it might be well to divide the process into a number of steps. I would like to identify nine of these.

The first is the *provision of the citation*. This is the intellectual process we call "cataloging" and includes descriptive cataloging, subject cataloging, and classification. This aspect of the process has not been and cannot now be automated, although some of the work that has been done in the fields of automatic indexing and classification offers some faint hope of assistance.[1] Automation can help, of course, in some of the housekeeping jobs that support the cataloging effort, such as maintenance of authority files, classification schedules, and shelf lists.

The second major step in book catalog production is the *keyboarding of the citations*. This may be done by the cataloger himself, a clerk, or a typesetter; and the machine may be a standard typewriter, a paper-tape punch, a key punch, or a typesetting machine; but

at some point in the process, human fingers actuate the keys of some kind of machine.

The third step is the *editing* of what has been keyboarded. The object of this step is to detect errors and correct them, so that what finally is printed in the catalog corresponds to what the cataloger specified.

The fourth step is the *creation of multiple entries* from the single citation with which we have dealt up to this point. In standard cataloging terms, this means that we create the main and added entries in the form in which they are to appear in the catalog.

The fifth step is necessary if we are to have a divided catalog. That is the *sorting of the entries by type*—into author, subject, and title groups if we are going to divide the catalog in that manner.

The sixth step is the *sequencing of the file*, which involves putting the cards in order—chiefly alphabetical order—so that they can be integrated into the existing file, which has previously been put into the same order.

The seventh step is to *merge the new entries* into the existing file. This is simple if we have solved the problem of getting our entries into the proper sequence in the first place.

The eighth step is the *creation of the page masters*. Every page of a book catalog begins life as an original master page, of which the pages that finally appear in print are copies.

The ninth and final step is the actual *production of the book*. This usually involves reducing the master page to the desired final size, producing an offset master, printing, collating, and binding.

I would like to concentrate on all the steps after the first one and before the last. The first is not now a good prospect for mechanization, and the last is a very standard printing operation. Consequently, what should interest us here are those activities that take place between the time the cataloger finishes cataloging and the page masters are sent off to the printer.

I am aware of three major categories of book catalog production systems in which machines are used

[1] An excellent summary of the work to date is: Mary Elizabeth Stevens, *Automatic Indexing—A State-of-the-Art Report* (Washington: National Bureau of Standards, 1965).

ABBOT, CHARLES GREELEY
  Adventures in the world of science. 1958
  (Autobiographical)
    64010031   B A
ABBOT, WALDO
  Handbook of broadcasting; the fundamentals of
  radio and television 4th ed. 1957
    64010032   621.384 A 1957
ABBOTT, ANDREW
  Key to better memory. 1959
    64010033   154 A
ABBOTT, ARTHUR LAURIE
  National electrical code handbook. 10th ed.
  1960
    64010035   621.3 A 1960
  National electrical code handbook. 11th ed.
  1963
    64010034   Ref 621.3 A 1963
ABBOTT, ASHLEY
  Creative figure photography. 1960
    64010036   778 A
ABBOTT, BERENICE
  World of Atget, by Berenice Abbott. 1964
    66021090   779 A
ABBOTT, EDITH
  Some American pioneers in social welfare. 1937
    64010037   920 A
ABBOTT, EDWIN ABBOTT
  Flatland. 5th rev. ed. 1963.
    66014138   513 A 1963
  Flatland. 6th ed. rev. 1952
    64010038   513 A 1952
ABBOTT, FRANK FROST
  Common people of ancient Rome. 1911.
    66017179   913.37 A
  History and description of Roman political
  institutions. 3d ed. 1911.
    66014174   354.37 A
  Roman politics. 1963
    64010039   354.37 A
ABBOTT, GEORGE
  Damn Yankees. 1956
    64010040   812 A
  Mister Abbott. 1963
    64010041   B A
  New girl in town. 1958
    64010042   812 A
  Pajama game. 1954
    64010043   812 A
ABBOTT, JACOB
  Harper establishment. 1855
    65017942   Ref 655.1 A
ABBOTT, JOHN STEVENS CABOT
  History of Maine. 1875
    66021004   974.1 A
ABBOTT, PERCIVAL WILLIAM HENRY
  Teach yourself algebra. 1942
    64010044   512 A

Sample 1. Author catalog.

AACHEN--HISTORY
  Sullivan, Richard Eugene Aix-la-Chapelle in
  the age of Charlemagne 1963
    64058491   943.423 S
AALTO, HUGO ALVAR HENRIK
  Aalto, Hugo Alvar Henrik Alvar Aalto 1963
    64010015   720.9471 A
  Gutheim, Frederick Albert Alvar Aalto 1960
    64032080   720.9471
AARON WARD (DESTROYER, 3RD)
  Lott, Arnold S. Brave ship, brave men 1964
    65017119   940.545 L
ABACUS
  Kojima, Takashi Advanced abacus 1963
    64039091   511.2 K
  Kojima, Takashi Japanese abacus 1954
    65017051   511.2 K
  Yoshino, Yozo Japanese abacus explained 1963
    64065475   511.2 Y
ABAILARD, PIERRE
  Gilson, Etienne Henry Heloise and Abelard 1960
    64030281   B H
  Meadows, Denis Saint and a half 1963
    64044822   920 M
  Sikes, Jeffrey Garrett Peter Abailard 1965.
    66019233   189.4 S
ABAILARD, PIERRE--POETRY
  Whitman, Cedric Hubbell Abelard 1965.
    66012102   811 W
ABBEYS--ENGLAND
  Cook, Olive English abbeys and priories 1960
    64021734   726.7 C
  Gasquet, Francis Aidan, cardinal Greater
  abbeys of England 1908
    64029700   726 G
ABBOT, CHARLES GREELEY
  Abbot, Charles Greeley Adventures in the world
  of science 1958
    64010031   B A
ABBOTT, EDWIN ABBOTT. FLATLAND
  Burger, Dionys Sphereland 1965.
    66011458   513.82 B
ABBOTT, GEORGE
  Abbott, George Mister Abbott 1963
    64010041   B A
ABBOTT LABORATORIES
  Kogan, Herman Long white line c1963
    65012779   338.4 K
ABBOTT, ROBERT S
  Ottley, Roi Lonely warrior: the life and times
  of R S Abbott 1955
    64048739   B A
ABBREVIATIONS
  Buttress, Frederick Arthur World list of
  abbreviations of scientific, technological and
  commercial organizations 1960
    64018494   421 B

Sample 2. Subject catalog.

Samples 1-2. Baltimore County Public Library. *Catalog.* 1966. Methodology: Upper- and lower-case computer print-out. Full page size: 8 1/2 x 11 inches. 2 columns per page.

to assist in one or more of these steps. These are what we may call EAM systems, sequential-camera systems, and computer systems. "EAM" stands for Electronic Accounting Machines, and these include such equipment as keypunch machines, sorters, collators, interpreters, and accounting machines. A number of catalogs have been produced with this technology, in such places as Los Angeles County, Baltimore County (see Samples 1 and 2), King County (Washington), the University of Rochester, and the New York State Library. I am not sure whether any of these libraries are still using this technology; I do know that several of them have abandoned it in favor of either a computer method or a sequential camera method.

Very briefly, an EAM system operates as follows. The catalog information is punched into cards. These cards are then put into an accounting machine, and the information punched into them is printed out and proofread. When an error is detected, the proper card is pulled from the file and a new one is punched with the correct information. The corrected card is put into file in place of the incorrect one. The entries are then sorted, either by machine or by hand, and these newly sorted entries are merged into the existing file, if there is one. When we are ready to print the catalog, the entire file is again printed out on the accounting machine, a page at a time. The end product may be a printed page, ready to be photographed and then reproduced by offset printing, or it may be a direct-image offset master. In any case, we are done with it; it is ready to go to the printer.

If we go through the sequence of steps in book catalog production that we enumerated earlier, we will find that systems such as these offer us very little help in the editing step and extremely little in the process of creating multiple entries from the original single entry; and the latter only if we are willing to accept some rather severe limitations.

We can sort entries by type for the purposes of a divided catalog in these systems. We can also file entries, but the procedure is slow, unwieldy, and subject to human error. Furthermore, the filing must be very simple and straightforward unless we use cumbersome manual methods to make it more sophisticated. Once the entries are in order, the merging of new entries into existing files is quite simple and straightforward. Creation of page masters, too, is fairly simple, although it too can become a cumbersome process if anything but the simplest page format is desired.

You may gather from all this that punched-card or EAM systems do not appear very attractive as methods of producing book catalogs. The reason, quite simply, is that these machines are very limited; they involve much human intervention and much physical handling of cards. Furthermore, anything that can be done on these machines can be done on a computer, with much greater speed, with far less susceptibility to human error, and, most importantly, with vastly more flexibility. An EAM system is still a possible way to produce book catalogs, but the circumstances in which it would be a reasonable alternative to a computer system would be very special indeed.

An example of a book catalog produced by a system such as the one I have just described is shown as Sample 3.[2]

Another method of producing book catalogs which is in fairly extensive use at the present time is the sequential-camera method. Several commercial firms are now prepared to produce such catalogs for libraries. There is no reason, of course, why an individual library cannot produce these for itself; the major reason that the services of commercial firms are generally used is that the initial investment in equipment is quite high, and most libraries cannot use this equipment on anything like a full-time basis.

The system works approximately as follows. The catalog entries are typed onto cards, using a machine such as the Varityper, which has a number of fonts and type sizes available. These cards are then man-

ually proofread, or they may first be reproduced by a photographic method. In the latter case, proofreading is from a printed sheet; in either case, however, when an error is found, the card in question is pulled. It may be corrected by erasing and retyping, or a new card may be made.

At this point, certain information is punched into these cards. This information will generally include a unique identifying number for each title, as well as, for each entry, a number assigning it a sequence in the catalog. Please note that this is the only machine-readable information on these cards; the catalog information itself cannot be read by machine.

Sorters and collators are now used to sort this material into file sequence, on the basis of the sequential numbers that have been provided, and to merge new entries with the existing file. These cards, now in the proper sequence, are put into the sequential camera, a device which photographs, in sequence, the typed portions of the cards. The product is a photographic negative, which is cut and formatted into pages, and then sent to be printed by a photolithographic process.

The sequential-camera system has one great advantage over punched-card systems: the final product is considerably more attractive than the final product of a punched-card system. In addition, the photographing of the cards proceeds at a much faster rate than does printing them on an accounting machine. Furthermore, companies with experience in this method of production have developed efficient procedures for stripping the negatives and formatting the page master.

Another advantage of sequential-camera systems over computer systems is that the cost of getting started is less with the sequential-camera system. Designing a computer system presents some complex problems. In the end, I believe that these initial costs will be repaid in most systems of any size, but there is no doubt that the initial cost is high. Already, however, there are commercial organizations prepared to provide computer-produced book catalogs on a basis similar to that on which other firms provide sequential-camera catalogs. I believe that in the next few years more of these companies will appear and that some noncommercial institutions such as processing centers will also attain the capacity to offer such services. When this occurs, the costs to an individual library of setting up a system to produce a book catalog on a computer will be comparable to the cost of initiating a sequential-camera system.

The final product of a sequential-camera operation can be seen in Sample 4 from the Fairfax County (Virginia) Public Library and Sample 5 from the Los Angeles County Library. These are without question more attractive than the products of simpler punched-card systems and of most computer systems. They are also more legible and certainly easier to scan. This method of production has some very serious drawbacks, however. Let us again discuss these in

---

[2] In order to preserve the type size of the originals of the samples presented in this paper, all samples (except Sample 20) are partial pages.

```
GRAYDON ALEXANDER    MEMOIRS                                          1822  973.309  G78A
GRAYDON ALEXANDER    MEMOIRS                                          1846  973.309  G78A2
GRAYDON NELL S    TALES OF EDISTO                                     1955  975.791  G783
GRAYJACKETS                                                           1867  973.782  G78
GRAYSON FRANK Y    HISTORIC OHIO RIVER                                1930  977.    G784
GRAYSON WILLIAM J    REPLY TO PROFESSOR HODGE ON STATE OF            1861  973.71  G78
    COUNTRY
GREAT BARRINGTON MASSACHUSETTS    VITAL RECORDS                       1904  H974.41  G78
GREAT BRITAIN    DIPLOMATIC CORRESPONDENCE CONCERNING TEXAS           1918  976.4  G78
GREAT BRITAIN ARMY    ORDERLY BOOK FOR KING#S AM. REGIMENT                  A973.333  QG786
GREAT BRITAIN BOUNDARIES IN AM. COMRS. FOR    MEMOIRES 4V.            1757  W971.10  QG78
GREAT BRITAIN COUNCIL FOR VA.    DECLARATION OF STATE IN VA.          1620  A975.5  D29
GREAT BRITAIN HOUSE OF COMMONS    PAPERS RELATING TO AM.              1810  S973.48  G786
GREAT BRITAIN LAWS    ANNO REGNI GEORGII 111                          1765  V973.3111G786
GREAT BRITAIN PARK    PROCEEDINGS OF PARL. RESPECTING N. AM.          1941  973.2  G78
    5V.
GREAT BRITAIN PARLIAMENT    EXAM. OF BENJAMIN FRANKLIN                1767  N933.3111G78F
GREAT BRITAIN PARLIAMENT    EXAM. OF JOSEPH GALLOWAY                  1779  973.314  G78A
GREAT BRITAIN PARLIAMENT    EXAM. OF JOSEPH GALLOWAY                  1855  973.314  G78
GREAT BRITAIN PARLIAMENT    NORTH AMERICAN BOUNDARY                   1840  973.57  QG78
GREAT BRITAIN PARLIAMENT    PROTEST AGAINST BILL TO REPEAL           1796  V973.3111G78P
    STAMP ACT
GREAT BRITAIN PARLIAMENT    PROTESTS OF PEERS ON WAR                  1782  973.31  G78?
GREAT BRITAIN PARLIAMENT    TWO PROTESTS AGAINST BILL TO             1796  973.3111G78?
    REPEAL STAMP ACT
GREAT BRITAIN PARLIAMENT    WHO VOTED AGAINST BILL TO REPEAL         1766  973.3111G78
    STAMP ACT
GREAT BRITAIN TREATIES    TREATY OF AMITY                             1796  973.43  G78
GREATER AMERICA                                                       1898  973.8997G78
GREATER AMERICA ESSAYS IN HONOR OF HERBERT E BOLTON                   1945  970.  B69A
GREATER KANSAS CITY FED. BUS. ASSN.    FED. GOVT.                     1939  977.8411G78
GREATOREX ELIZA P    OLD NEW YORK                                     1875  974.71  QG78
GREBANIER FRANCES    PURITAN CITY                                     1938  974.45  516G
GREELEY HORACE    AMERICAN CONFLICT 2V.                               1866  R973.7  G79
GREELEY HORACE    AMERICAN CONFLICT 2V.                               1866  G973.7  G79A
GREELEY HORACE    GREELEY ON LINCOLN                                  1893  973.709  L7G2
GREELY ADOLPHUS W    REMINISCENCES OF ADVENTURE AND SERVICE          1927  973.9109G79
GREEN ARNOLD    NEW ENGLAND#S GIFT TO THE NATION TOWNSHIP            1875  N973.361  G79S
GREEN BENJAMIN F    IRREPRESSIBLE CONFLICT BETWEEN LABOR AND         1872  973.711  G79
    CAPITAL
GREEN CHARLES R    EARLY DAYS IN KANSAS                               1913  970.3  G79
GREEN CHARLES R    EARLY DAYS IN KANSAS 5V.                           1914  978.1  G79E
GREEN CHARLES R    US AND OUR NEIGHBORS                               1901  978.1  G79
GREEN CONSTANCE    HOLYOKE MASSACHUSETTS                              1939  974.42  H76
GREEN CONSTANCE W    HISTORY OF NAUGATUCK                             1949  974.67  N297G
GREEN COUNTY WISCONSIN                                                1884  977.586  H67
GREEN DUFF    FACTS AND SUGGESTIONS                                   1866  973.5  G79
GREEN EDWIN L    RICHLAND COUNTY                                      1932  975.7  G79
GREEN FITZHUGH    OUR NAVAL HERITAGE                                  1925  973.  G79
GREEN FLETCHER M    LIDES GO SOUTH                                    1952  975.7  S72E4
GREEN FRANK B    HISTORY OF ROCKLAND COUNTY                           1886  H974.728  G79
GREEN HORACE    GENERAL GRANT#S LAST STAND                           1936  973.82  ZG7G7
GREEN HORACE    LIFE OF CALVIN COOLIDGE                               1924  973.915  ZC7G
GREEN JAMES A    WILLIAM HENRY HARRISON                               1941  973.58  QZH7*
GREEN JOHN W    JOHNNY GREEN OF ORPHAN BRIGADE                        1956  973.782  G79*
GREEN LUCY G    DE FORESTS AND WALLOON FOUNDING OF                   1924  974.71  G79
    NEW AMSTERDAM
GREEN MASON A    SPRINGFIELD MEMORIES                                 1876  974.42  S764
GREEN PHILIP L    PAN AMERICAN PROGRESS                               1942  980.  G79
GREEN RALEIGH T    HISTORICAL NOTES ON CULPEPER COUNT  VA.           1900  975.5  G79
GREEN SAMUEL A    BOUNDARY LINES OF OLD GROTON                       1885  974.44  G8A7
GREEN SAMUEL A    DIARIES KEPT BY GROTON SOLDIERS IN WARS            1901  973.26  G79
GREEN SAMUEL A    EPITAPHS FROM OLD BURYING GROUND IN GROTON         1878  H974.44  G88A
    MASS.
GREEN SAMUEL A    GROTON DURING INDIAN WARS                          1883  974.44  G884
GREEN SAMUEL A    GROTON DURING REVOLUTION                           1900  973.3444G88C
GREEN SAMUEL A    GROTON HISTORICAL SERIES 4V.                       1899  974.44  G881
GREEN SAMUEL A    HISTORICAL ADDRESS                                 1876  N973.361  G798H
GREEN SAMUEL A    HISTORICAL ADDRESS 2.ED.                           1876  N973.361  G798*
GREEN SAMUEL A    NATURAL HIST. AND TOPOGRAPHY OF GROTON MASS.       1912  974.44  G88Z2
GREEN SAMUEL A    NORTHERN BOUNDARY OF MASSACHUSETTS                 1891  H974.4  G79
GREEN SAMUEL A    REPRODUCTIONS RELATING TO BOSTON                   1901  974.46  FB76*
GREEN SAMUEL A    TEN REPRODUCTIONS RELATING TO NEW ENG.            1902  974.  FG79
GREEN SAMUEL A    TEN REPRODUCTIONS RELATING TO VARIOUS             1903  974.  FG79T
    SUBJECTS
GREEN SAMUEL A    THREE HIST. ADDRESSES AT GROTON MASS.             1908  974.44  G8825
GREEN SAMUEL A    TWO CHAPTERS IN EARLY HIST. OF GROTON MASS.       1882  974.44  QG88
GREEN THOMAS J    TEXIAN EXPEDITION AGAINST MIER                     1845  976.4  G79
```

Sample 3. New York State Library. *Checklist on American History.* 1960. Methodology: Punched cards, printed on an IBM 407 accounting machine. Full page size: 10 1/2 x 16 inches. 2 columns per page.

terms of the production steps we enumerated before. While this system can provide a very legible print-out for proofreading purposes, correction of errors is still entirely manual. Making a correction involves finding the proper card, pulling it, correcting it or re-typing it, and reinserting it into the file. In addition, it may involve typing more than one card. The creation of multiple entries from the original citation is also entirely manual—that is, each separate entry in the catalog is required to be typed in its entirety.

Division of the catalog entries by type, for the purpose of producing a divided catalog, may be either manual or mechanical; if it is mechanical, however, certain information indicating type of entry must be punched into the card. Filing, too, is an entirely manual process. Some person must determine where each new entry is to go in relation to other entries in the file, and must assign a sequence number on the basis of this determination. Extensive records must be maintained indicating which sequence numbers have already been assigned. Once the numbers have been assigned, the process of actually arranging the entries is, of course, mechanical. So, also, is the process of merging new entries into the existing file.

A very serious drawback to this system is its rigidity. The catalog information is not in machine-readable form; therefore, it cannot be manipulated by machine at all. Furthermore, the format of the page

428.64   The **silver** elephant. Collier-Macmillan 1964 (Collier-Macmillan English readers) Material created for the Collier-Macmillan English Program by the Materials Development Staff of English Language Services, Inc.
H

Silverberg, Robert
951   The Great Wall of China. Chilton 1965
H   T M G   R W

Silverman, Jerry
787.61   The folksinger's guitar guide. v.1– Oak Publications 1962– Contents: v.1 An instruction manual. Based on the Folkways record by Pete Seeger.—v.2 An advanced instruction manual.
v.1   H
v.2   H X T M G D R W P J C.

Simak, Clifford D. 1904–
SF   They walked like men. Doubleday 1962
H X T   G   W P J
SF   Why call them back from heaven! Doubleday 1967
H X T M G D R W P

Simkins, Francis Butler 1898–
975   A history of the South. Knopf 1953
M G   R W   J

Simmons, Charles
Powdered eggs, a novel. Dutton 1964
X T   D R   P J

Simon, Edith
270.6   The Reformation, by Edith Simon and the editors of Time-Life books. Time 1966 (Great ages of man)
H X T M G D R W P J C
R270.6 ——H

Simon, Neil
812   The odd couple. Random House 1966 A play.
H X T M G D R W P J C
782.8   Coleman, Cy. Sweet Charity. Random House 1966
H X T M G D R W P J C

Simons, Eric N.
942.04   The reign of Edward IV. Barnes & Noble 1966
M G   R   P J

Singer, Louis C. 1912– ed
784.49   Glass, Paul and Singer, L. C. eds.
♦   Songs of the West. Grosset 1966
H

Singleton, Esther d 1930 ed and tr
910   Wonders of nature, as seen and described by famous writers. Collier 1911
G

Siniavskiĭ, Andreĭ Donat'evich see **Tertz, Abram** pseud

Sinkankas, John
549   Mineralogy for amateurs. Van Nostrand 1964
M   D R W P J

Sinnott, Edmund Ware 1888–
577   The bridge of life; from matter to spirit. Simon & Schuster 1966
H X T   D   P

Sinton, William M.
522   Miczaika, G. R. and Sinton, W. M. Tools of the astronomer. Harvard Univ Pr 1961
T   J

Sitts, Paula Elizabeth
The glad season; boyhood in the Cariboo of British Columbia. Dutton 1967
X   M G D R

Six great modern plays. Dell 1956
808.82   Contents: Three sisters, by Anton Chekhov.—The master builder, by Henrik Ibsen.—Mrs. Warren's profession, by George Bernard Shaw. —Red roses for me, by Sean O'Casey. —All my sons, by Arthur Miller. —The glass menagerie, by Tennessee Williams.
H   R

Skelton, Raleigh Ashlin ed
R526.8   Bagrow, Leo. History of cartography. Harvard Univ Pr 1964
H

Skinner, Burrhus Frederic
150   Science and human behavior. Macmillan 1953
T   J

Sample 4. Fairfax County (Va.) Public Library. *Author Supplement*. March 1967. Methodology: Sequential camera. Full page size: 9 x 12 inches. 3 columns per page.

cannot easily be changed, except within certain narrow limits. You will notice, for example, certain important differences between the format of the entries in the Los Angeles County Library catalog and the Fairfax County Library catalog. The differences are important, since they affect the usefulness and the cost of the catalog. Yet neither of these catalogs can be changed in important ways without extensive retyping of the original entries and reinserting new cards into the existing card file.

The sequential-camera method also shares an important disadvantage with simpler punched-card systems. In both, large and ever increasing quantities of cards must be physically handled in order to produce the catalog. This handling becomes more and more cumbersome, more and more expensive, and more and more prone to error as the size of the file increases.

Far and away the most serious drawback of such systems, however, is their very limited ability to make effective use of catalog copy produced elsewhere. No doubt, most users of a sequential-camera system base their cataloging upon the cataloging provided by the Library of Congress. LC is now distributing machine-readable catalog copy on an experimental basis. I am ready to assert that this experiment will turn into a routine service of the Library of Congress—not because I have inside information, but because the provision of this service at this time is so eminently and obviously desirable as to be inevitable. Yet I fail to

RENOIR, JEAN
F759.4   Renoir. Hachette, 1962. 428 p.
R418   English translation has title "Renoir, my father".

RENWICK, WILLIAM LINDSAY
820.9   English literature, 1789-1815. Clarendon Pr., 1963. 293 p. Bibliography.

RESNICK, SEYMOUR
860.8   Highlights of Spanish literature; a bilingual anthology with Spanish and English
            on facing pages. Ungar, 1963. 463 p. Bibliography.

RESOURCES FOR THE FUTURE
            SEE ALSO
711   Wingo, Lowdon. Cities and space.

REWALD, JOHN
            SEE ALSO
759.4 P678 Pissarro, Camille. Camille Pissarro.

REXROTH, KENNETH
811   Homestead called Damascus. New Directions, 1963. 48 p.
            Previously appeared in the "Quarterly review of literature", volume 9,
            number 2, 1957.

REYNOLDS, BERTHA CAPEN
361.3   Uncharted journey; fifty years of growth in social work. Citadel Pr., 1963.
            352 p. Illus. Bibliography.

REYNOLDS, ERNEST EDWIN
92 B746   Bossuet. Doubleday, 1963. 285 p. Port.

REYNOLDS, MAYNARD CLINTON
371.21   Early school admission for mentally advanced children, a review of research and
            practice. 1962. 56 p.

REYNOLDS, PAUL REVERE
029.6   Writing and selling of non-fiction. Doubleday, 1963. 198 p.

REYNOLDS, QUENTIN
909   With fire and sword; great war adventures. Ed. and with an introd. by
            Q. Reynolds and R. Leckie. Dial Pr., 1963. 383 p. Illus.

RIAN, EDWIN HAROLD
208   Christianity and world revolution. Harper, 1963. 237 p.

RIASANOVSKY, NICHOLAS VALENTINE
947   History of Russia. Oxford Univ. Pr., 1963. 771 p. Illus., maps.
            Bibliography.

RICCIO, ANTHONY C.
371.1   Teaching in America. Merrill Bks., 1962. 517 p. Illus.

RICE, DAVID TALBOT
709.02   Art of the Byzantine era. Praeger, 1963. 286 p. Illus. (part col.) plans.
            Bibliography.

Sample 5. Los Angeles County Library. *Author Supplement*. March 1964. Methodology: Sequential camera.
Full page size: 8 1/2 x 11 inches. 2 columns per page.

see how libraries producing catalogs with a sequential-camera method will be in a position to make effective use of this service when it becomes a reality. It appears probable that both commercial and noncommercial processing centers will in the near future be able to provide computer-produced book catalogs on a basis as routine as the one on which sequential-camera catalogs are now provided. These catalogs will probably be less expensive and will appear increasingly attractive to libraries now producing book catalogs by some other method. Libraries, therefore, which have been producing catalogs by the sequential-camera method will be faced with the difficult decision of whether to change—and I

think that for most of them change will eventually be inevitable. When they change, they will be faced with the necessity either to begin a brand-new catalog or to convert the holdings that they have already listed in their book catalogs. Of course, conversion may be simpler to the degree that the holdings in their backlog are included in available machine-readable catalog files. Nevertheless, there will be agonizing and expensive periods of change involved.

These remarks are not made in criticism of librarians who have decided to produce book catalogs by the sequential-camera method. Each such person made the decision to embark on a book catalog project in terms of his own circumstances, of the resources available to him—resources both of money and of trained manpower—and of the state of the library art. I do not therefore say that a library that decided on the sequential-camera method made a bad decision, nor do I say that libraries which fail to apply the rules correctly can be detected by the computer. The application of the rules for encoding languages can also be checked to some extent by the computer. There are many other examples which could be mentioned. In any case, it seems to me that the computer can give us important assistance in the proofreading of catalog data. This help appears to be most readily available in proofreading just those portions which are most difficult to proofread manually, the fixed-field coding.

When the information has been proofread and the cataloger or editor is satisfied that the data are correct, the further processing steps are almost entirely performed by the computer. The computer reads the unit record information, determines what added entries need to be made, and makes them. It then segregates the entries by type, in order to produce separate files for the various parts of the divided catalog, if a divided catalog is being produced. It then places the entries into the order specified by the filing rules, merges these newly sorted entries into the existing file, and prints page masters.

The process can be described quite easily. In fact, it works smoothly once it has been established and its initial shakedown period is completed. Computers are very fast, very accurate, and increasingly less expensive to use. Nevertheless, the ideal system for producing book catalogs by computer has not been established, nor has there been a system yet with which experienced analysts cannot find some fault. This is not because either librarians or systems analysts or programmers are stupid; rather, it is because the new technology has raised some serious intellectual questions in the realm of cataloging itself and practical questions in the realm of production methods. My purpose is to discuss principally the latter.

Let us go through the steps of producing a book catalog by computer and discuss some of the various methods that have been adopted and some of the pitfalls that lie in the way. I would like to begin at the very beginning, with the cataloging process itself. The reason is that machine manipulation of catalog data can be accomplished only if these data are encoded in a fairly complex manner. I believe that this necessity must eventually affect the cataloging process itself, since encoding this information may in many cases require special knowledge or capacity which only the cataloger has, especially in foreign languages. The cataloger may be the only person on the staff capable of making the distinction; therefore, he will probably be called upon to make it if it needs to be made. Another very important way in which automation will almost certainly affect the cataloger's work routine is that eventually he must be responsible for keyboarding the information in machine-readable form. At the present time, he must record his decisions in some way, and this is usually done by typing. If he is going to have to type anyway, and since he has some of the special knowledge required to encode the information in machine-readable form, it seems only reasonable that his recording of his decisions should be in machine-readable form.

Of course, there are some important problems involved with getting this machine-encoding step back into the hands of the professional cataloger. In all book catalog-production installations with which I am familiar, it is not the cataloger but a clerk who keyboards the material on a device which produces a machine-readable record. The devices themselves are generally keypunch machines or paper-tape typewriters. One of the objections to keypunch machines has been that they provide only for upper-case letters, so that using them to keyboard information which eventually is to be printed in upper and lower case has involved some fairly cumbersome encoding methods. However, keypunch machines are now available on which input of upper- and lower-case information is quite simple. The key punch retains the disadvantage that the cards it produces are discrete physical entities, which must somehow be so identified that they can be restored to their place within the group of cards to which they belong if they are separated or out of order. On the other hand, keypunch machines are sturdy and not expensive. Furthermore, keypunch operators are fairly easy to come by these days and do not command high salaries. Yet another attraction is that virtually no computer installation lacks the ability to read punched cards, which is not the case with paper tape.

Paper-tape typewriters, on the other hand, do not produce discrete physical entities like cards; rather, they produce a continuous roll of punched tape. Therefore, the problem of keeping the material in order does not exist. The keyboards of these machines are very nearly standard typewriter keyboards, which means that they routinely provide for both upper and lower case, and are quite familiar to any typist, although special training in the unique aspects of these machines is required. Another advantage of paper-tape typewriters is that one of the products of typing is a hard copy; that is, a sheet of paper which people can read. The typist has a continuous visual indication of what she has typed. Therefore, she is able to make corrections as soon as she is aware of having made an error, and this procedure, while it is not painless, at least exists, which is not the case with keypunch machines. The existence of a hard copy may also mean that the step of printing a copy for proofreading may be unnecessary. Finally, while there are several companies that have had considerable experience in building paper-tape typewriters, it is my impression that some of these machines are not as reliable as the steady and dependable key punch.

There are other methods of creating machine-readable input. One of these is optical scanning.

Unfortunately, there is not now available a machine which can read a Library of Congress printed card, but there are machines that can read a far more limited character set. This, however, means that someone must keyboard the information before the optical scanner can read it. Another family of input devices includes those which input directly to magnetic tapes. Some of these are particularly attractive because they produce a product—that is, magnetic tape—which most computer installations have the capacity to read, and also because they have provisions for making corrections at the keyboard quite easily.

I have had experience with an input device that goes directly to magnetic tape. From the user's point of view, the best thing about it was that it was not very different from a normal typewriter. Errors were easy to correct. These characteristics may make these machines very attractive when we come to the point of actually moving the input stage back to the catalog department. At that point, it will be desirable to allow the cataloger to operate as much as possible as he does at present, without learning new techniques that are not a part of his more important professional skills.

In practical terms, however, the choice of an input medium nowadays generally boils down to a choice between a key punch and a paper-tape typewriter. Frankly, I believe the choice of one over the other is by no means obvious. One of the main reasons is that the keypunch machine has usually been used with techniques inappropriate to the keyboarding of catalog data. Every installation that I have seen which uses keypunch machines has been hampered by what we might call the 80-column-card mentality. A whole array of techniques and ways of using the 80-column card developed quite early and was based upon the fact that most of the data consisted of fixed-field numeric information. Catalog data, on the other hand, are generally composed of variable-field information. Sometimes a subject heading is 10 characters long; sometimes it is 50. Yet again and again one encounters keypunch installations in which a 10-character subject heading must have a card all to itself, even though it may be followed by another card which has nothing but a 20-character author added entry. This is one example of inefficiencies which result because computer people have the same tendency that most human beings have, to think in the ways they have always thought, even though the situation in which they are operating may have some very different characteristics.

I believe that the entire area of keyboarding techniques and systems should be investigated carefully in the context of the special kinds of information which are involved in a library book catalog-production system. The emphasis should be upon the operator in such an investigation. Things should be made as easy as possible for her, in order to increase her efficiency. The emphasis should be upon allowing her to develop a natural text-typing rhythm. Thus, if code

symbols must be inserted into the text, they should be the symbols that lie most readily to hand on the keyboard of the input device. If the programmer finds other symbols more desirable from his point of view, he can convert them internally; but at the point of input, the emphasis should be upon the operator's efficiency.

The 80-column-card mentality is not the only reason why catalog input systems are not as efficient as they could be. Another is the curious and anomalous fact that computer people—and particularly programmers—often do not like to use computers. Again and again, when one looks at book catalog-production systems, one discovers that when a choice exists between having a computer perform a certain portion of the work and having human operators perform it, the decision has been made to give the job to human beings. Computers, of course, cannot do everything; but when the choice is between placing an additional burden upon the computer and placing an additional burden upon the human operator, my predilection is to give the job to the computer. Naturally there are circumstances in which this does not make sense, and each circumstance should be investigated on its merits. Let me give you an example.

In every computerized book catalog installation that I have seen in which keypunch machines are used as the input device, when an error is detected the offending card is pulled and a new card is punched. My opinion is that once keypunch cards have been created, they should be read onto magnetic tape, or perhaps into a random-access device, and then discarded. After that, if it is necessary to find a part of the information and change it, the computer should do the searching and should make the change. If this is done, it is no longer necessary to correct an error by punching an entire card. Only the correction needs to be keypunched and inserted in place of the incorrect portion of the entry. Thus, several corrections could be input on a single card, saving a considerable amount of the effort expended on rekeypunching. The possibility of introducing new errors is also reduced. Most importantly, the handling of cards—cumbersome, time consuming, and prone to error—is eliminated.

After proofreading, we presumably have a clean product. Therefore, the computer can now perform the next step in the sequence, which is creating the various entries from the protean body of data which it has been fed. I have no specific comments to make upon this procedure. It is quite straightforward. The only problem I see is that we librarians need to give considerable thought to what the content of catalog entries ought to be, since the amount of information printed in a catalog entry directly affects not only the usefulness of the entry but also the cost of the catalog. In this connection, I strongly recommend that you give careful consideration to the implications of a catalog of the type represented by Samples 6 and 7, from the East Bay Cooperative Library System (Hayward, California) catalog.

In this catalog, all entries are in a brief index form. They include the call number of the item and its location within the system. These indexes are backed up by photographic copies of the original LC catalog cards, which are bound in volumes. However, these photographic copies are not arranged in any order. They are added to the bound volumes as the materials are added to the collection. This bound volume of photographic copies of LC cards is referred to as the register. In order to find the photographic copy of the LC card in the register, one must first look the item up on the index, which refers one to the page number of the register on which the card in question will be found. There is no doubt that the patron who

desires to see a fuller citation than the one given in the index is inconvenienced, as is any member of the library staff who wants the same information. However, I think we ought very seriously to ask ourselves whether this inconvenience is not more than offset by the economy achieved in the printing of the index.

The next step in the production process, the division of the catalog, is again straightforward, and the major questions here are again those of catalog policy rather than production methodology. I would like to make one suggestion in this connection, however: if the catalog is to be divided into author, title, and subject catalogs, it seems that author entries ought to go into the author catalog and title entries into the title

Call No.	Author / Title	Location	Year	Reg.
R 016.371	FORRESTER, GERTRUDE OCCUPATIONAL LITERATURE	AI C	64	1010A
RQ 658.839	FORSTALL, RICHARD L., ED RAND MCNALLY CITY RATING GUIDE	C	64	673Q
329.006	FORSTER, ARNOLD, JT AUTH REPORT ON THE JOHN BIRCH SOCIETY, 1966	A C R	66	772K
	FORSTER, EDWARD MORGAN ETERNAL MOMENT, AND OTHER STORIES	C R	64	723O
	FORSTER, EDWARD MORGAN LONGEST JOURNEY	A C R	61	729M
	FORSTER, MARGARET BOGEYMAN	AI C	66	892F
M	FORSYTE, CHARLES DIVE INTO DANGER	R	62	888N
301.24	FORTUNE MYTHS OF AUTOMATION	A C R	66	968Q
390.09	FORTUNE, REO FRANKLIN SORCERERS OF DOBU	R	63	1010R
020.8	FOSKETT, D. J., ED LIBRARIES AND THE ORGANIZATION OF KNOWLEDGE	A C R	65	879F
821	FOSS, KENELM, ED SWINBURNE ANTHOLOGY	A	55	802H
973.81	FOSTER, G. ALLEN IMPEACHED THE PRESIDENT WHO ALMOST LOST HIS JOB	A C R	64	564V
635.7	FOSTER, GERTRUDE B. HERBS FOR EVERY GARDEN	A AI C R	66	981K
598.41	FOSTER, LAURA LOUISE KEER-LOO	A AI C	65	693L
540	FOSTER, LAURENCE STANDLEY, JT AUTH CHEMISTRY FOR OUR TIMES 3RD ED	A AI R	60	792E
913.2	FOUCHET, MAX POL RESCUED TREASURES OF EGYPT	A C R	65	684T
	FOULKES, DAVID SEE FOULKES, WILLIAM DAVID			
154.6	FOULKES, WILLIAM DAVID PSYCHOLOGY OF SLEEP	A C R	66	821K
Q 708.951	FOURCADE, FRANCOIS ART TREASURES OF THE PEKING MUSEUM	C R	65	741U
B SPOONER	FOWLER, DOROTHY CANFIELD JOHN COIT SPOONER, DEFENDER OF PRESIDENTS	C	61	825C
942.05	FOWLER, ELAINE W. ENGLISH SEA POWER IN THE EARLY TUDOR PERIOD. 1485-1558	C	65	888P

Sample 6. Author index.

Samples 6-7. East Bay (Calif.) Cooperative Library System. *Supplement to Basic Book Catalog.* February 1967. Methodology: Upper-case computer print-out. Full page size: 10 3/4 x 13 3/4 inches. 2 columns per page.

```
          MANAGEMENT - BIBL.

R         OLIVE, BETSY ANN, COMP                              C    65    901C
016.658     MANAGEMENT A SUBJECT LISTING OF RECOMMENDED BOOKS, PAMPHLETS ¤

          MANAGEMENT RIGHTS

658.315   FARMER, GUY                                    A C      65    654T
            MANAGEMENT RIGHTS AND UNION BARGAINING POWER

          MANCHUS

320.951   MICHAEL, FRANZ                                      C    65    973Q
            ORIGIN OF MANCHU RULE IN CHINA

          MANET, EDOUARD

Q         REY, ROBERT                                    A C R          985V
759.4       MANET

          MANN, THOMAS

830.      .GRAY, RONALD D.                                    R    65    705G
9009        GERMAN TRADITION IN LITERATURE

833.912   LUKACS, GYORGY                                 AI R      65    603C
            ESSAYS ON THOMAS MANN

833.912   THIRLWALL, JOHN CONNOP                         A C      66    918T
            IN ANOTHER LANGUAGE

838.      WHITE, ANDREW                                       R    65    682P
91209       THOMAS MANN

          MANN, WILLIAM DALTON

364.163   LOGAN, ANDY                                     C R      65    633S
            MAN WHO ROBBED THE ROBBER BARONS

          MANNED SPACE FLIGHT

629.47    FAGET, MAXIME ALLAN                            A C      65    816P
            MANNED SPACE FLIGHT

629.47    HILTON, WILLIAM F.                              C R     65    652H
            MANNED SATELLITES, THEIR ACHIEVEMENTS AND POTENTIALITIES

          MANNED UNDERSEA RESEARCH STATIONS

551.467   COUSTEAU, JACQUES YVES                     A AI C R     65    584C
            WORLD WITHOUT SUN

797.23    STENUIT, ROBERT                           A AI C R      66    747D
            DEEPEST DAYS

          MANNERISM /ART/

709.03    HAUSER, ARNOLD                                      C    65    564R
            MANNERISM

          MANNERS AND CUSTOMS

914.4     LACROIX, PAUL                                   C R     63    850E
            FRANCE IN THE EIGHTEENTH CENTURY
```

Sample 7. Subject index.

catalog. If this does not sound like a new or original idea, I will only say that I can mention several book catalogs supposedly divided in this manner, in which title main entries are placed in the *author catalog*. Usually they are placed in the title catalog also, which means that each title main entry appears twice. That costs money—money that is spent to no avail, in my opinion, since title entries serve no purpose whatsoever in an author catalog.

The next step in the sequence, filing, cannot be passed over so easily. Again, a whole panoply of professional questions arises here. No one, I believe, is completely satisfied with any set of filing rules that has been adopted. It is doubtful that this situation will change, since any method of arranging the complex data that are included in library catalogs is going to make some problems for some users. Since our purpose is to discuss production, we will pass over the question of what the filing rules ought to be, and discuss the problems of mechanizing an existing set of filing rules such as those of ALA or LC.

When it is given a set of rules to follow, the computer is a very fast and accurate tool to use for the filing of data such as those represented in catalog entries. That is, the computer will execute the rules given it with a speed and an accuracy which human filers cannot begin to match. This is not to say that your programmer will find it an easy task to program the ALA filing rules. One reason for this is that in filing catalog headings, the human filer makes use of much information that is either only implicit in the data in the heading or cannot be derived from the heading at all. The second reason is that the order of elements in a filing heading does not always correspond to the order in which we file them. For example, when we require someone to file a title in a certain place, it is not at all explicit, but only implicit, that the heading is in fact a title. Or when we require the filer to file "U.S.—Hist.—Civil War" in its proper chronological sequence, we do not provide him with the dates upon which this sequence is based. The filer may know all that because she may have been to high school and college, but I do not know any computers that have a BA. An example of a rule that requires us to file a text in a different order from that in which it appears on the card is the rule that provides for headings like "Louis XVI, King of France." The ALA rules require us to file it as if it were "Louis, King of France, XVI."

Some other problems that catalog data make for filing are abbreviations, numbers to be filed as if spelled out, words to be filed as if they were numbers, modified letters, Roman numerals, the various types of subdivisions under subject headings, etc. In some

```
CONTENTS IN ADVANCE. CURRENT CONTENTS OF LIBRARY +
    DOCUMENTATION LITERATURE.
    PHILADELPHIA. 1,1955-
        SUSPENDED PUBLICATION WITH 5,N.3 MR/AP 1959.
    KHAYF  1-5                                        RM

CONTEXT.
    CHICAGO. UNIVERSITY. OFFICE OF PUBLIC
    RELATIONS.
    CHICAGO. 1, SPRING 1961-
    KEMT   1-
    KHAYF  2-                                         RM
    KWIU   1-                                         2SS

CONTINENT MAGAZINE.
    SEE --
TA LU TSA CHIH.

CONTINENTAL MONTHLY. DEVOTED TO LITERATURE +
    NATIONAL POLICY.
    NEW YORK. 1-6, JA 1862-D 1864//
    KU     [4-6]                                      PERIOD

CONTINUING EDUCATION FOR ADULTS.
    CENTER FOR THE STUDY OF LIBERAL EDUCATION FOR
    ADULTS.
    CHICAGO. N.1, 1961-
    KHAYF  1-                                         RM

CONTINUING MEDICAL EDUCATION, MEDICAL SYMPOSIA.
    NEW YORK. 1, 1963-
    KU-M   1-

CONTINUOUS LEARNING.
    CANADIAN ASSOCIATION FOR ADULT EDUCATION.
    TORONTO. 1, JA/FE 1962-
    KMK    1-                                         LIBR

CONTRACT BRIDGE BULLETIN.
    AMERICAN CONTRACT BRIDGE LEAGUE, INC.
    NEW YORK.
        1-27 AS AMERICAN CONTRACT BRIDGE LEAGUE.
        BULLETIN.
    KHAYF  [28]-                                      RM

CONTRAT SOCIAL. REVUE HISTORIQUE ET CRITIQUE DES
    FAITS ET DES IDEES.
    PARIS. 1, MR 1957-
    KU     1-                                         PERIOD

CONTRIBUTIONS, ECONOMIC ANALYSIS.
    AMSTERDAM. 1, 1952-
    KU     1-                                         PERIOD

CONTRIBUTIONS IN HISTORY + POLITICAL SCIENCE.
    SEE --
OHIO
    STATE UNIVERSITY, COLUMBUS.
    -STUDIES. CONTRIBUTIONS IN HISTORY + POLITICAL
    SCIENCE.

CONTRIBUTIONS IN LANGUAGES + LITERATURES.
    SEE --
OHIO
    STATE UNIVERSITY, COLUMBUS.
    -CONTRIBUTIONS IN LANGUAGES + LITERATURES.

CONTRIBUTIONS TO BIBLIOGRAPHY IN JOURNALISM.
    SEE --
NEBRASKA
    UNIVERSITY.
    -SCHOOL OF JOURNALISM.
    --CONTRIBUTIONS TO BIBLIOGRAPHY IN JOURNALISM.

CONTRIBUTIONS TO CANADIAN PALAEONTOLOGY.
    SEE --
CANADA
    GEOLOGICAL SURVEY.
    -CONTRIBUTIONS TO CANADIAN PALAEONTOLOGY.
```

```
CONVEYANCER.
    SEE --
CONVEYANCER + PROPERTY LAWYER.

CONVEYANCER + PROPERTY LAWYER.
    LONDON. 1-21, D 1915-35/36, N.S.1, SE 1936-
        1-21 AS CONVEYANCER.
    KU-L   S.2,V.1-                                   LAW

CONVOY.
    LONDON. N.1, 1944-
    KU     1-2                                        PERIOD

COOK TECHNICAL REVIEW.
    COOK ELECTRICAL CO.
    SKOKIE, ILL. 1, 1954-
    KU     1-                                         ENGIN

CO-OP GRAIN QUARTERLY.
    NATIONAL FEDERATION OF GRAIN COOPERATIVES.
    ST. PAUL, MINN. 1, 1943-
    KMK    12-                                        LIBR

COOPER UNION FOR THE ADVANCEMENT OF SCIENCE
    AND ART, NEW YORK.
    COOPER UNION BULLETIN.
    -ENGINEERING + SCIENCE SERIES.
    NEW YORK. 1, 1930-
    KMK    24-                                        LIBR
    KU     1-                                         ENGIN

COOPERATIVAS.
    PAN AMERICAN UNION.
    WASHINGTON. 1, JA 1946-
    KU     N.14-                                      PERIOD

COOPERATIVE BULLETIN OF THE PROVIDENCE LIBRARIES.
    SEE --
PROVIDENCE, R.I.
    PROVIDENCE PUBLIC LIBRARY.
    -COOPERATIVE BULLETIN OF THE PROVIDENCE
    LIBRARIES.

CO-OPERATIVE CONFERENCE FOR ADMINISTRATIVE
    OFFICERS OF PUBLIC + PRIVATE SCHOOLS.
    PROCEEDINGS.
    CHICAGO. 1, 1938-
    KMK    4,9-10,14                                  LIBR

COOPERATIVE CONSUMER.
    CONSUMERS COOPERATIVE ASSOCIATION.
    NORTH KANSAS CITY, MO. 1, 1933-
    KHAYF  (24-29)-                                   RM
    KMK    17-20                                      LIBR

COOPERATIVE DIGEST. THE NATIONAL MAGAZINE OF FARM
    BUSINESS.
    ITHACA, N.Y. 1, 1940-
        ABSORBED FARM POWER.
    KHAYF  (17)-                                      RM
    KMK    (4)-(9-10,12-15)-(19)-(22)-               LIBR

COOPERATIVE FARMER.
    SEE --
SOUTHERN STATES COOPERATIVE FARMER.

COOPERATIVE JOURNAL.
    NATIONAL ASSOCIATION OF MARKETING OFFICIALS.
    WASHINGTON, D.C. 1-13, N.2, D 1926-MR 1939//
        1-8 1926-34 AS COOPERATIVE MARKETING
        JOURNAL.
    KMK    11-(13)                                    LIBR

CO-OPERATIVE MANAGER + FARMER.
    SEE --
GRAIN + FEED REVIEW.

COOPERATIVE MARKETING JOURNAL.
    SEE --
COOPERATIVE JOURNAL.
```

Sample 8. *Kansas Union List of Serials.* Lawrence, Kans.: the University of Kansas Libraries for the Kansas Library Council, 1965. Methodology: Upper-case computer print-out. Full page size: 8 1/2 x 11 inches. 3 columns per page.

```
'S EQUATION (NUMRANAL)= BOUNDS FOR DERIVATIVES IN THE ULRICH  6345 4641
ATORS (NUMRANAL)= ERROR BOUNDS FOR EIGENVECTORS OF SELF ADJO  6341 3717
AL)= CN ERROR BOUNDS FOR GAUSSIAN CUBATURE (NUMRAN  6234 2266
(NUMRANAL)= ON ERRCR BOUNDS FOR NUMERICAL DIFFERENTIATION  6123 0853
HEOREM OF CARR CN ERROR BOUNDS FOR RUNGE-KUTTA PROCEDURES (N  6012 C050
RANAL, FOREIGN-GERMAN)= BOUNDS FOR SOLUTIONS CF BOUNDARY VAL  6343 4259
BRANE (NUMRANAL)= LOWER BOUNDS FOR THE EIGENVALUES OF A FIXE  6342 4046
ICN AND UPPER AND LOWER BOUNDS FOR VARIATIONAL PROBLEMS (MAT  6234 2226
RANAL)= COMPUTING ERRCR BOUNDS IN SOLVING LINEAR SYSTEMS (NU  6342 4018
TY (NUMRANAL)= A-PRIORI BOUNDS IN THE FIRST BOUNDARY VALUE P  6341 3729
CTORS (NUMRANAL)= ERROR BOUNDS IN THE RAYLEIGH-RITZ APPRCXIM  6126 1296
(METATHRY)= LEAST UPPER BOUNDS ON MINIMAL TERMINAL STATE EXP  6232 1743
1 (INFTHRY)= SOME LOWER BOUNDS ON THE NUMBER OF CODE POINTS  6236 3257
2 (INFTHRY)= SCME LOWER BOUNDS ON THE NUMBER OF CODE POINTS  6236 3258
IATE PROBLEMS FCR LOWER BOUNDS TO EIGENVALUES (NUMRANAL)= TR  6126 1284
DESIGN FCR A BRAIN (ARTINT)=  6125 0982
THE COMPUTER AND THE BRAIN (SOCIMP)=  6122 0717
THE BRAIN AS A COMPUTER (ARTINT)=  6346 4695
BRAIN CURRENT TESTS (SOCLSCI)=  6123 0777
ELECTRONIC BRAIN TO OPERATE CANCU=  6343 4080
GIANT BRAIN, OR GIANT MORON (MGNTDP)=  6016 03C2
SIMULATION CF A BRAIN=  6343 4105
PLES OF THE WORK OF THE BRAIN= SOME PRINCI  6344 4459
CENTRAL CCNTRCL CF BRANCH INVENTORY=  6124 0897
BLEMS (NUMRANAL)= A BREAKPOINT TECHNIQUE FCR NETWORK PRO  6342 4014
ANATRAN', FIRST STEP IN BREEDING THE 'CIGINALOG' (ANLGDSGN)=  6235 2323
HE DETAILING OF AN ARCH BRICGE (ENGRING)= THE USE OF AN ELEC  6235 2446
YSTEM: A QUASI-BALANCED BRIDGE AS AN ELEMENT IN AN AUTOMATIC  6236 2929
LDSGN)= ON CONSTRUCTING BRIDGE CIRCUITS BY THE SHORT CIRCUIT  6231 1432
NETWORK COMES TO BRITAIN (MATHPROG)=  6344 4426
COMMERCIAL COMPUTERS IN BRITAIN, JUNE 1959 (MGNTDP)= THE STA  6013 C067
BRITISH BANKS MAKE READY (MGNTDP)=  6236 2984
= A SURVEY OF BRITISH DIGITAL COMPLTERS (PRCGLANG)  6121 0489
RCNICS, A REPORT ON THE BRITISH IRE SYMPOSIUM (ENGRING)= REC  6236 3012
NEW COMPUTERS REACHING BRITISH MARKET (PROGLANG)=  6121 C492
C COMPUTING SYSTEM= THE BRITISH PETROLEUM COMPANY ORDERS LAR  6125 1068
ED COMPUTERS TO RUN NEW BRITISH STEEL WORKS (REALTIME)= THRE  6235 2371
, (PART 2) COMPUTERS IN BRITISH UNIVERSITIES (EDUCATION)= TH  6013 0086
PEEK-A-BOO INDEX FOR A BROAD SUBJECT CCLLECTICN (INFRETR)=  6341 3651
MISSION= STOCK BROKER UTILIZES REAL-TIME CATA TRANS  6236 2989
ICN OF COORDINATES FROM BROUWER'S SCLUTION OF THE ARTIFICIAL  6235 2422
TOCHASTIC MODEL FCR THE BROWNING-BLECSGE PATTERN RECCGNITICN  6342 3763
DECAY CURVES (ENGRING)= BRUNHILDE, A CCDE FOR ANALYZING MULT  6345 4513
E AUTOMATIC SCANNING CF BUBBLE CHAMBER PHOTOGRAPHS (SCIENTIF  6235 2543
R ANALYSIS OF DATA FROM BUBBLE CHAMBERS, KINEMATIC ANALYSIS  6235 2548
R ANALYSIS CF DATA FROM BUBBLE-CHAMBERS (PART 4). THE KINEMA  6342 3822
R ANALYSIS CF DATA FROM BUBBLE-CHAMBERS, (PART 3) . THE KINE  6342 3823
AL DETERMINATION OF THE BUCKLING EIGENVALUES OF A THIN RECTA  6344 4342
LYTECHNICAL UNIVERSITY, BUDAPEST (DSGNGENL)= THE NEW DIGITAL  6016 0335
TICAL MODELS IN CAPITAL BUDGETING CAN PE CF GREAT AID IN MAN  6123 C839
ROCKETS, BUDGETS AND ECP (MGNTDP)=  6121 0441
BUDGETS AND HCME OFFICE EXPENSES=  6125 1016
NETWORKS (DSGNGENL)= A BUFFER MEMORY FOR SYNCHRONOUS DIGITA  6236 3177
REALTIME)= A BUFFER STCRE FCR DATA TRANSMISSICN (  6343 4078
' BUGS' IN AUTCMATION (MGNTDP)=  6126 1152
IED TO PUBLIC WORKS AND BUILDING (MGNTDP, FOREICN-FRENCH)= D  6341 3467
NG PRCCESSES IN MACHINE BUILDING (REALTIME)= MAIN TRENDS IN  6122 0585
EMES, ON THE PROBLEM CF BUILDING A READING DEVICE (ARTINT)=  6235 2330
RE FOR PARAMETRIC MODEL BUILDING AND BCUNDARY VALUE PROBLEMS  6234 2257
YSTEMS (DSGNGENL)= THE BUILDING BLOCK APPROACH TC CIGITAL S  6346 4785
COMPUTER WITH BUILDING BLCCK DESIGN (DSGNGENL)=  6015 0224
G CIRCUITRY, SECUENTIAL BUILDING BLOCKS FCR LCGICAL DESIGN (  6236 3270
RCCESSES IN THE MACHINE BUILDING INDUSTRY (MATHPROG, FOREIGN  6235 2787
BREAKTHROUGH FCR THE BUILDING INDUSTRY (MGNTDP)=  6341 3469
)= CN THE PRINCIPLES OF BUILDING READING MACHINES (ARTINT, F  6232 1531
STATE (MATHPRCG)= BUILDING THE ECP FUTURE IN NEW-YCRK-  6343 4218
T DIGITAL COMPUTER EVER BUILT (DSGNGENL)= FASTES  6234 2162
THEORY OF LOGICAL NETS, BUILT FROM ELEMENTS WITH THRESHOLDS=  6346 4831
PROCESSING, THE RW-530 BUILT IN LOGIC SYSTEM (REALTIME, FCR  6235 2671
CCER CF BINARY NUMBERS, BUILT WITH THE PCSITICN COMMUTATCRS  6346 4831
T (DSGNGENL)= A BUILT-IN TABLE LOOKUP ARITHMETIC UNI  6234 2154
LEX SYSTEMS (CCMPCCMP)= BUILT-IN TEST SYSTEM FCR AUTCMATIC F  6121 0474
HIGH-SPEED COMPUTER BULK STORAGE (LTILPRCG)=  6344 4368
```

Sample 9. *Permuted (KWIC) Index to Computing Reviews, 1960-1963:* Methodology: Upper-case computer print-out. Full page size: 8 1/2 x 11 inches. 2 columns per page.

cases, these problems exist because a specific filing rule is bad in the first place; some exist because when catalogers established the heading, they gave insufficient thought to how it was to file; and some exist only because the human being and the computer are dissimilar.

I believe the problem of machine filing rules should be solved for us by the Library of Congress, so that when the MARC tapes are distributed, the entries on them can be filed according to some set of filing rules. There are some principles which I think ought to guide the Library in devising this machine filing system. I will enumerate three.

First, it seems clear that LC cannot contemplate making extensive changes in the format of headings for the purpose of simplifying computer filing. The reason is that many libraries are going to be maintaining card catalogs for quite a long time, and we simply cannot make radical changes in LC cards because of the problems this would cause for such libraries. Second, the LC filing rules system must be capable of being operated locally, because no matter how much the quantity of LC cataloging increases, some cataloging will continue to be done locally. Third, I would hope that the LC filing system will allow us to experiment with various methods of arrangement. We have advocates of "straight alphabetical" arrangement, advocates of "classed" arrangement, and a lot of people in between; but we have no real evidence of the superiority of one system over another. It is to be hoped, therefore, that machine-readable cataloging will give us the capacity to experiment with alternate arrangements.

As in other systems, the merging of newly created entries into the existing files is a simple one, once the initial problem of sequencing the file has been solved.

In a computer system, page masters are usually created on the computer's line printer. This printer may have an upper-case character set only (see Samples 8 and 9), or it may have both upper- and lower-case letters (see Samples 10 and 11). In general, librarians have tended to prefer the upper- and lower-case print-out, in part because a larger character set, including diacritical marks and a wide range of punctuation symbols, is available. However, a quite attractive page layout is possible with a straight upper-case print chain.

An interesting technique which adds a bit of variety to a page of computer print-out is the "overstrike" technique, which is illustrated in the page from the Widener Library Shelflist (Sample 12). The headings on that page appear in bolder type because the computer printed each heading several times on the same line before going on to the next line.

Samples 13 through 18 from the Florida Atlantic University catalog illustrate the evolution of one computer-produced book catalog, from upper and lower case to straight upper case. Florida Atlantic made the change for reasons of economics: any particular computer-printer can operate nearly twice as fast when printing upper case only as when it is printing upper and lower case. The cost of printing, therefore, is cut approximately in half.

I would like to suggest that any library that is contemplating a computer-produced book catalog should probably encode its material in upper and lower case, even though it has decided to print in upper case only. Your programmer can write a program to give you an upper-case print-out from material encoded in this fashion; but if you have coded for upper case only, the program to convert to upper and lower case will be much more difficult to write, and the results will be considerably less accurate.

Another method of output printing from computers is photocomposition. The principal attraction of these

Horn, Paul V.
International trade principles and
practices, by Paul V. Horn and Henry Gomez.
4th ed. Prentice-Hall, 1961. 597 p.
HF1007.H63

Horn, Robert A.
Groups and the Constitution. Stanford
Univ. Press, 1956. 187 p. AS36.L54

Horn, Stanley F.
The Robert E. Lee reader. Edited by Stanley
F. Horn. Bobbs-Merrill, 1949. 542 p.
E467.1.L4H77

Horn, Stephen
The Cabinet and Congress. Columbia Univ.
Press, 1960. 310 p. JK616.H6

Hornbein, Thomas F.
Everest: the west ridge. Photographs from
the American Mount Everest Expedition and
by its leader, Norman G. Dyhrenfurth.
Introd. by William E. Siri. Edited by David
Brower. Sierra Club, 1965. 198 p., illus.
DS486.E8H54 Folio

Hornblow, Arthur
The captive, by Edouard Bourdet. Translated
by Arthur Hornblow, Jr. Introd. by J.
Brooks Atkinson. Brentano's, 1926. 255 p.
PQ2603.O77P72

The triumph of death, by Gabriele
d'Annunzio. Translated by Arthur Hornblow.
Introd. by Burton Rascoe. Boni and
Liveright, 1923. 412 p. PQ4803.Z3T7

Horne, Alistair
The price of glory: Verdun 1916. St.
Martin's Press, 1963. 371 p. D545.V3H6

Return to power; a report on the new
Germany. Praeger, 1956. 415 p.
DD259.4.H65

Horne, C. Silvester
Puritanism and art; an inquiry into a
popular fallacy. By Joseph Crouch. Introd.
by the Rev. C. Silvester Horne. Cassell,
1910. 381 p. N72.C8

Horned moon; an account of a journey through
Pakistan, Kashmir, and Afghanistan. By Ian
Stephens. Indiana Univ. Press, 1955. 288
p. DS377.S8

Sample 10. Author catalog.

CRUSADES--HISTORY
A history of the Crusades. Editor-in-chief,
Kenneth M. Setton. Univ. of Pennsylvania
Press, 1958-
Library has v.1-2. D157.S48

CRUSADES--FIRST, 1096-1099
The first crusade; the accounts of eye-
witnesses and participants. P. Smith,
1958. 299 p. D161.1.A3K7

Gesta Francorum et aliorum
Hierosolimitanorum. The deeds of the Franks
and the other pilgrims to Jerusalem. Edited
by Rosalind Hills; introd. by R.A.B.
Mynors. T. Nelson, 1962. 103, 103 p.
In Latin and English. D161.1.G4

CRUSADES--SECOND, 1147-1149
De profectione Ludovici VII in orientem,
edited, with an English translation by
Virginia Gingerick Berry. Columbia Univ.
Press, 1948. 154 p. D162.1.O3

CRUSADES--FOURTH, 1202-1204
Memoirs of the Crusades, by Geffroi de
Villehardouin and Jean de Joinville.
Translated by Frank T. Marzials. J.M.
Dent; E.P. Dutton, 1933. 340 p. D164.A3V4

CRUSADES--SEVENTH, 1248-1250
Memoirs of the Crusades, by Geffroi de
Villehardouin and Jean de Joinville.
Translated by Frank T. Marzials. J.M.
Dent; E.P. Dutton, 1933. 340 p. D164.A3V4

CRYOGENICS
See Low temperature research; Low
temperatures.

CRYSTAL OPTICS
The microscopical characters of artificial
inorganic solid substances: optical
properties of artificial minerals. By
Alexander Newton Winchell and Horace
Winchell. 3d ed. Academic Press, 1964.
439 p. QE367.W78

Optical crystallography, with particular
reference to the use and theory of the
polarizing microscope. By Ernest E.
Wahlstrom. 3d ed. J. Wiley, 1962. 365 p.
QD941.W28

Sample 11. Subject catalog.

Samples 10-11. Stanford University Undergraduate Library. *Catalog.* 1966. Methodology: Upper- and lower-
case computer print-out. Full page size: 8 1/2 x 11 inches. 2 columns per page.

CRUS   238   EXPEDITION UNDER WILLIAM OF AQUITAINE AND OTHERS, 1100-1102

    CRUS 238.1   RIANT, PAUL.   UN DERNIER TRIOMPHE D URBAIN.   PARIS, 1883.
    CRUS 238.2   RIANT, PAUL.   LE MARTYRE DE THIEMON DE SALZBOURG.   PARIS, 1886.

CRUS   240   KINGDOM OF JERUSALEM, 1099-1187 - LAWS AND ORGANIZATION - FOLIOS

    CRUS 24C.1   2V   ACADEMIE DES INSCRIPTIONS ET BELLES-LETTRES.   RECUEIL DES HISTORIENS DES CROISADES. LOIS.
                        ASSISES DE JERUSALEM...PUBLIEES PAR...A.A. BEUGNOT.   PARIS, 1841-43.
    CRUS 24C.2F   2P   JERUSALEM, KINGDOM OF.   ASSISES ET BONS USAGES DU ROYAUME DE JERUSALEM. 2 IN 1.   PARIS, 1690.
    CRUS 24C.3   2V   FOUCHER, VICTOR.   ASSISES DU ROYAUME DE JERUSALEM. PT. 1-2.   RENNES, 1839-41.
    CRUS 24C.4   ASSISES D ANTIOCHE.   VENICE, 1876.

CRUS   242   KINGDOM OF JERUSALEM, 1099-1187 - LAWS AND ORGANIZATION - OTHER WORKS

    CRUS 242.1   CROICTS, AUTORITEZ ET PREROGATIVES.   PARIS, 1586.
    CRUS 242.3   JERUSALEM (LATIN KINGDOM).   LES LIVRES DES ASSISES ET DES USAGES...JERUSALEM.   STUTTGARD..
                        1839.
    CRUS 242.5   THOMAS, G.M.   EINE ENCYCLICA AUS DEM 9. JAHRHUNDERT.   MUENCHEN, 1865.
    CRUS 242.6   MONNIER, FRANCIS.   GODEFROI DE BOUILLON ET LES ASSISES DE JERUSALEM.   PARIS, 1874.
    CRUS 242.7   GRANDCLAUDE, M.   ETUDE CRITIQUE SUR LES LIVRES DES ASSISES DE JERUSALEM.   PARIS, 1923.
    CRUS 242.9   REY, E.   LES COLONIES FRANQUES DE SYRIE AU XII ET XIII SIECLES.   PARIS, 1883.
    CRUS 242.11   PARDESSUS.   MEMOIRE SUR UN MONUMENT DE L ANCIEN DROIT.   PARIS, 1829.
    CRUS 242.12   DODU, G.   HISTOIRE DES INSTITUTIONS MONARCHIQUES.   PARIS, 1894.
    CRUS 242.13   LAMONTE, J.L.   FEUDAL MONARCHY IN THE LATIN KINGDOM OF JERUSALEM 1100 TO 1291.   CAMBRIDGE.
                        1932.
    CRUS 242.15   MAS LATRIE, L. DE.   LE FIEF DE LA CHAMBERLAINE ET LES CHAMBELLANS DE JERUSALEM.   1882.
    CRUS 242.17   MUNRO, C.C.   THE KINGDOM OF THE CRUSADERS.   STUDENTS ED. NY, 1935.

CRUS   245   KINGDOM OF JERUSALEM, 1099-1187 - TRACT VOLUMES

    CRUS 245.   PAMPHLET BOX.   KINGDOM OF JERUSALEM.

CRUS   250   KINGDOM OF JERUSALEM, 1099-1187 - HISTORY - GENERAL

    HOUGHTON CRUS 25C.1.10P*   CHRONIK DES KREUZFAHRER-KOENIGREICHES JERUSALEM...FACS. DER BURG.-FLAEMISCHEN MINIATUR
                               HANDSCHR.   MUENCHEN, 1924.
    HOUGHTON CRUS 25C.1.12F.   CHRONIK DES KREUZFAHRER-KOENIGREICHES JERUSALEM. GELEITWORT.   MUENCHEN, 1924.
    CRUS 25C.3   RESOLD, CHRISTOPH.   HISTORIAE URBIS ET REGNI HIEROSOLYMITANI...   ARGENTORATI, 1636.
    CRUS 25C.4   HAGENMEYER, H.   FULCHERI CARNOTENSIS HIST. HIEROSOLYMITANA, 1095-1127.   HEIDELBERG, 1913.
    CRUS 25C.4.5   FULCHERIUS CARNOTENSIS.   FULCHER OF CHARTRES, CHRONICLE OF THE FIRST CRUSADE.   PHILADELPHIA,
                        1941.

Sample 12. Harvard University Library. *Widener Library Shelflist: Crusades.* 1965. Methodology: Upper-
case computer print-out. Full page size: 8 1/2 x 11 inches. 1 column per page.

CHAMBERLAIN, Lawrence Henry, 1906-
Loyalty and legislative action; a su-
rvey and activity by the New York State
Legislature, 1919-1949.
Ithaca, Cornell University Press,
1951. 254 p. (Cornell studies in civil
liberty)
JC599.U52N52

CHAMBERLIN, Edward, 1899-
The theory of monopolistic competition; a re-orientation of the theory of
value. 8th ed.
Cambridge, Harvard University Press,
1962. 396 p. (Harvard economic studies,
v. 38)
HB201.C5 1962

CHAMBERLIN, Edward, 1899-
Towards a more general theory of
value.
New York, Oxford University Press,
1957. 318 p.
HB201.C52

Chamberlin, Edward Hastings, 1899-
see
CHAMBERLIN, Edward, 1899-

Chamberlin, Edward Hastings, 1899-
see
CHAMBERLIN, Edward, 1899-

CHAMBERLIN, Mary W
Guide to art reference books.
Chicago, American Library Association,
1959. 418 p.
Z5931.C45

CHAMBERLIN, Waldo, 1905-
A chronology and fact book of the
United Nations, 1941-1961 [by] ** [and]
Thomas Hovet. With a pref. by Andrew
W. Cordier.
New York, Oceana Publications, 1961.
64 p.
JX1977.C482

CHAMBERLIN, William Henry, 1897-
America's second crusade.
Chicago, Regnery, 1950. 372 p.
D753.C55

CHAMBERLIN, William Henry, 1897-
The evolution of a conservative.
Chicago, Regnery, 1959. 295 p.
PN4874.C37A32

CHAMBERLIN, William Henry, 1897-
A false Utopia: collectivism in
theory and practice.
London, Duckworth [1937] 264 p.
Also published as Collectivism, a
false Utopia.
HX86.C36 1937a

CHAMBERS, Whittaker.
Witness.
New York, Random House [1952] 808 p.
E743.5C47

Chamblain de Marivaux, Pierre Carlet de,
1688-1763.
see
MARIVAUX, Pierre Carlet de Chamblain de
1688-1763.

CHAMPNEYS, Mrs. Mary C.
An English bibliography of examina-
tions (1900-1932); with a foreword by
Sir Michael Sadler and Sir Philip
Hartog.
London, Macmillan and co., limited,
1934. 140 p.
Z5814.E9C4

CHAN, Edmund Nathaniel, 1906-
The predicament of democratic man.
New York, Macmillan, 1961. 194 p.
JC423.C23

CHANAL, Hubert, joint author
STARCHUK, Orest.
Essentials of scientific Russian, by
** and H. Chanal.
Reading, Mass., Addison-Wesley Pub.
Co. [1963] 300 p.
PG2120.S3S7

CHANDLER, Albert Richard, 1884- ed.
The clash of political ideals; a source book on democracy and the totalitar-
ian state, selected and annotated by **
. 3d ed., with annotated bibliography.
New York, Appleton-Century-Crofts
[1957] 374 p.
JA36.C48 1957

CHANDLER, Bobby Joe, 1925- g.d.
Education in urban society. Ed. by
**, Lindley J. Stiles [and] John I. Kit-
suse.
New York, Dodd, Mead, 1962. 279 p.
LC5015.C45

CHANDLER, Bobby Joe, 1925-
Personnel management in school admin-
istration; [by] ** [and] Paul V. Petty.
Yonkers-on-Hudson, N.Y., World Book
Co. [1955] 598 p.
LB2831.5.C45

CHANDLER, Frank Wadleigh, 1873-1947.
The literature of roguery.
New York, B. Franklin, 1958 [1907]
2 v. (The Types of English literature)
Burt Franklin bibliographical series
no. 9)
PN3430.G6C5 1958

Sample 13. Author catalog, 1964.

Samples 13-18. Florida Atlantic University Library. *Catalog.* Methodology: Samples 13-15, upper- and lower-case computer print-out; Samples 16-18, upper-case computer print-out. Full page size: 8 1/2 x 11 inches. 3 columns per page.

ABRAHAM,   Gerald Ernest Heal, 1904–
    A hundred years of music. [3d ed.]
Chicago, Aldine [1964] 325 p.
ML196.A3 1964

ADAMS,   Mark Hancock, 1912– 1956.
    Bacteriophages. With chapters by
E.S. Anderson [and others] Electron
micrographs by E. Kellenberger. New
York, Interscience, 1959. 592 p.
QR185.B4A3

AHMAD,   Zahiruddin.
    China and Tibet, 1708–1959, a résumé
of facts. [Oxford] Oxford U.P.,
1960. 31 p.
    Chatham House memoranda.
DS786.A3

AMERICAN   Council on Education.
EDUCATIONAL   Conference, New York.
    Report. 1st– , 1932– . Washington,
American Council on Education. For
holdings, see Serials holdings list.
L13.A3825

AMERICAN   Council on Education.
    Studies. Series 1: Reports of
Committees and Conferences, no. 35
[etc.]
EDUCATIONAL   Conference, New York.
    Report. 1st– , 1932– . Washington,
American Council on Education. For
holdings, see Serials holdings list.
L13.A3825

AMERICAN   Universities Field Staff.
    A select bibliography: Asia, Africa,
Eastern Europe, Latin America. New
York 1960–. For holdings, see serials
holdings list.
CB357.A4

ANDREWS,   David H.
    Latin America; a bibliography of
paperback books, compiled by **. Ed. by
T.J. Hillimon. Washington, Hispanic
Foundation, Reference Dept., Library
of Congress, 1964. 38 p. (Hispanic
Foundation bibliographical series,
no. 9)
F1401.H5 no. 9

ANDREWS,   William George, 1930– ed.
    Constitutions and constitutionalism.
2d ed. Princeton, N.J., Van Nostrand
[1963] 201 p. (Comparative government
books)
JF95.A5

AZAÑA,   Manuel, 1880– 1940, ed.
VALERA   y Alcalá Galiano, Juan,
    1824– 1905.
    Pepita Jiménez. Edición y prólogo
de Manuel Azaña. Madrid, Espasa-Calpe
[c1963] 229 p. (Clásicos castellanos)
PQ6573.P4 1963

BAUM,   Bernard Helmut, 1926–
    Decentralization of authority in a
bureaucracy. Englewood Cliffs, N.J.,
Prentice-Hall, 1961. 173 p.
    Ford Foundation doctoral disserta-
tion series.
JK691.B35 1961

BECKHART,   Benjamin Haggott, 1898–
    ed.
    Business loans of American commercial
banks. New York, Ronald [1959] 453 p.
HG1641.B418

BENGTSON,   Hermann, 1909–
    Einführung in die alte Geschicte.
4., durchgesehene Aufl. Munchen, C.
H. Beck, 1962 [c1959] 205 p.
    IN REFERENCE
D56.B4 1959

BHARATIYA   Itihasa Samiti.
    The HISTORY and culture of the Indian
        People. General ed.: R.C. Majumdar;
        assistant ed.: A.D. Pusalkar.
        London, Allen and Unwin [1951–
    Vols. 2+ have imprint: Bombay,
Bharatiya Vidya Bhavan.
DS436.A1H5

BHARATIYA   Vidya Bhavan.
    The HISTORY and culture of the Indian
        People. General ed.: R.C. Majumdar;
        assistant ed.: A.D. Pusalkar.
        London, Allen and Unwin [1951–
    Vols. 2+ have imprint: Bombay,
Bharatiya Vidya Bhavan.
DS436.A1H5

BLIXEN,   Karen, 1885–
    Winter's tales [by] Isak Dinesen.
New York, Vintage [c1942] 312 p.
PZ3.B62026Wi

BOSWORTH,   William.
    Catholicism and crisis in modern
France; French Catholic groups at the
threshold of the Fifth Republic.
Princeton, N.J., Princeton U.P., 1962.
407 p.
BX1530.2.B6

BOULDING,   Kenneth Ewart, 1910–
    Conflict and defense; a general
theory. New York, Harper [1962] 349 p.
HM136.B6

BOUQUET,   Alan Coates, 1884–
    Comparative religion, a short outline.
[6th ed.] Baltimore, Penguin [1962]
320 p.
BL80.B625 1962

BREWER,   Clifton Hartwell, 1876–
    A history of religious education in
the Episcopal Church to 1835. New
Haven, Yale U.P., 1924. 362 p.
BX5850.B8

Sample 14. Author catalog—proposed revised format.

```
---------------------------------------
Theology, Doctrinal
---------------------------------------
BRUNNER,  Heinrich Emil, 1889-
   The Christian doctrine of creation
and redemption. Tr. by Olive Wyon.
Philadelphia, Westminster Press [1952]
386 p. ( His Dogmatics, v. 2)
BT75.B842 vol. 2
           ------------------------
BRUNNER,  Heinrich Emil, 1889-
   The Christian doctrine of god.
Tr. by Olive Wyon. Philadelphia,
Westminster Press [1950] 361 p.
( His Dogmatics, v. 1)
BT75.B842 vol. 1
---------------------------------------
Theology--20th cent.
---------------------------------------
BARTH,  Karl, 1886-
   [Works. Selections. English. McNab ]
   God, grace and the gospel, tr. by
James Strathearn McNab. Edinburgh,
Oliver and Boyd [1959] 74 p.
   Tr. of Evangelium und Gesetz, Die
Menschlichkeit Gottes, and Evangelische
Theologie im 19. Jahrhundert.
   Scottish journal of theology. Occa-
sional papers, no. 8.
BR85.B3 1959
---------------------------------------
Thompson, Francis, 1859- 1907 Hound
of heaven.
---------------------------------------
Le BUFFE,  Francis Peter, 1885-
   The hound of heaven; an interpreta-
tion. New York, Macmillan [c1921] 89 p.
   Text of poem included.
PR5650.H6L4 1921
---------------------------------------
Thomson, James, 1700-1748. The seasons.
---------------------------------------
COHEN,  Ralph, 1917-
   The art of discrimination: Thomson's
The seasons, and the language of criti-
cism. Berkeley, U. of California P.,
1964. 529 p.
PN99.G7C6 1964
---------------------------------------
Tibet--For. rel.--China.
---------------------------------------
AHMAD,  Zahiruddin.
   China and Tibet, 1708-1959, a résumé
of facts. [Oxford] Oxford U.P.,
1960. 31 p.
   Chatham House memoranda.
DS786.A3
---------------------------------------
```

```
---------------------------------------
U.S.--For. rel.--1945- --Addresses,
   essays, lectures.
   lectures.
---------------------------------------
IRISH,  Marian Doris,  ed.
   World pressures on American foreign
policy [by] Henry B. Mayo [and others]
Englewood Cliffs, N.J., Prentice-Hall
[1964] 172 p.
E744.I68
---------------------------------------
U.S.--For. rel.--1953-1961.
---------------------------------------
ROSENAU,  James N.
   National leadership and foreign pol-
icy; a case study in the mobilization of
public support. Princeton, N.J.,
Princeton U.P., 1963. 409 p.
E835.R596
---------------------------------------
U.S.--For. rel.--20th cent.
---------------------------------------
MILLIS,  Walter, 1899-
   Arms and the state; civil-military
elements in national policy, by **, with
Harvey C. Mansfield and Harold Stein.
New York, Twentieth Century Fund,
1958. 436 p.
E744.M56
           ------------------------
MURPHY,  Robert Daniel, 1894-
   Diplomat among warriors. [1st ed.]
Garden City, N.Y., Doubleday, 1964.
470 p.
E744.M87
---------------------------------------
U.S.--Hist.--Civil War--Fiction.
---------------------------------------
KANTOR,  Mackinlay, 1904-
   If the South had won the Civil
War. New York, Bantam [c1961] 112 p.
PZ3.K3If
---------------------------------------
U.S.--Hist.--Civil War--Personal
   narratives--Bibl.
---------------------------------------
DORNBUSCH,  Charles Emil, 1907-
   Regimental publications and personal
narratives of the Civil War; a check-
list. New York, New York Public
Library, 1961-
E464.D6
---------------------------------------
```

Sample 15. Subject catalog—proposed revised format.

SEEGER, RUTH PORTER (CRAWFORD) 1901
  JOINT ARR.
  *LOMAX, JOHN AVERY, 1872-1948. ARR.
  FOLK SONG U.S.A., THE 111 BEST AM-
  ERICAN BALLADS. COLL., ADAPTED AND ARR.
  BY ** AND ALAN LOMAX.
  NEW YORK, DUELL, SLOAN AND PEARCE
  (C1947) 407 P.
  M1629.L85F6

SEELEY, JOHN R.
  *KELLER, MARK, 1907-
  THE ALCOHOL LANGUAGE. WITH A SELECT-
  ED VOCABULARY (BY) ** (AND) JOHN R.
  SELLEY.
  (TORONTO) UNIVERSITY OF TORONTO PRESS
  (1958) 82 P.
  HV5017.K4
----
*SEELEY, JOHN R
  CRESTWOOD HEIGHTS, A STUDY OF THE
  CULTURE OF SUBURBAN LIFE (BY) **, R.
  ALEXANDER SIM (AND) ELIZABETH W. LOO-
  SLEY. INTROD. BY DAVID RIESMAN (1ST ED.)
  NEW YORK, BASIC BOOKS (1956) 505 P.
  HT351.S3
----
*SEELIG, ERNST, 1895- 1955.
  LEHRBUCH DER KRIMINOLOGIE. NEUBEARB.
  UND ERGANZT VON HANNS BELLAVIC.
  3. AUFL. GRAZ, KIENREICH (1963) 406 P.
  HV6025.S4 1963
----
*SEERS, DUDLEY, ED.
  CUBA, THE ECONOMIC AND SOCIAL REVOLU-
  TION. BY ** (AND OTHERS)
  CHAPEL HILL, U. OF NORTH CAROLINA
  P. (1964) 432 P.
  HC157.C9S4

SEGAL, CHARLES M., ED.
  *LINCOLN, ABRAHAM, PRES. U.S.
  1809-1865.
  CONVERSATIONS WITH LINCOLN. COMP. ED.,
  AND ANNOT. BY CHARLES M. SEGAL.
  NEW YORK, PUTNAM (1961) 448 P.
  E457.15.L5
----
*SEGAL, LOUIS, 1887-
  NEW COMPLETE RUSSIAN-ENGLISH DIC-
  TIONARY (NEW ORTHOGRAPHY) (POCKET ED)
  NEW YORK, PRAEGER (1959) 2 V. IN 1.
  PG2640.S42
----
*SEGAL, RONALD, 1932-
  POLITICAL AFRICA, A WHO'S WHO OF PER-
  SONALITIES AND PARTIES.
  NEW YORK, PRAEGER (1961) 475 P.
  DT18.S4
----
*SEGHERS, ANNA, 1900-
  DIE RETTUNG, ROMAN. BERLIN, AUFBAU-
  VERLAG, 1947 (C1937) 479 P.
  PT2639.E29R4 1947

SEGHERS, PIERRE, JOINT ED.
  *CHARPIER, JACQUES, ED.
  THE ART OF PAINTING, FROM PREHISTORY
  THROUGH THE RENAISSANCE. EDITED BY
  PIERRE SEGHERS IN COLLABORATION WITH **.
  EXCERPTS TRANSLATED BY SALLY T. ABELES.
  (1ST AMERICAN ED.) NEW YORK, HAWTHORN
  (1964) 345 P.
  ND1135.C463 1964
----
*SEGRE, EMILIO, ED.
  EXPERIMENTAL NUCLEAR PHYSICS.
  NEW YORK, WILEY (1953-59) 3 V.
  QC173.S313
----
*SEGY, LADISLAS.
  AFRICAN SCULPTURE SPEAKS.
  N.Y., HILL + WANG (1952) 264 P.
  NB1090.S4
----

*SEIDMAN, JEROME M ED.
  THE ADOLESCENT, A BOOK OF READINGS.
  REV. ED.
  NEW YORK, HOLT, RINEHART AND WINSTON
  (1960) 870 P.
  HQ796.S424 1960
----
*SEIDMAN, JEROME M ED.
  THE CHILD, A BOOK OF READINGS.
  NEW YORK, RINEHART (1958) 674 P.
  BF721.S455
----
*SEIDMAN, JEROME M ED.
  READINGS IN EDUCATIONAL PSYCHOLOGY.
  BOSTON, HOUGHTON MIFFLIN (1955) 402 P.
  LB1051.S4
----
*SEIFERT, WILLIAM W. ED.
  CONTROL SYSTEMS ENGINEERING. EDITED BY
  ** AND CARL W. STEEG, JR. CONTRIBUTORS,
  WILLIAM W. SEIFERT (AND OTHERS)
  NEW YORK, MCGRAW-HILL, 1960. 964 P.
  TJ213.S4
----
*SEIGLIANO, ROBERT.
  SOUTH VIETNAM, NATION UNDER STRESS.
  BOSTON, HOUGHTON (C1963) 227 P.
  DS557.A6S22
----
*SEITZ, FREDERICK, 1911-
  THE PHYSICS OF METALS. 1ST ED.
  NEW YORK AND LONDON, MCGRAW-HILL,
  1943. 330 P.
  TA459.S47
----
*SEITZ, WILLIAM CHAPIN.
  THE ART OF ASSEMBLAGE.
  NEW YORK, MUSEUM OF MODERN ART, DIST-
  RIBUTED BY DOUBLEDAY, GARDEN CITY, N.Y.
  (1961) 176 P.
  N6490.S35

SEITZ, WILLIAM CHAPIN
  *NEW YORK. MUSEUM OF MODERN ART.
  CLAUDE MONET. SEASONS AND MOMENTS.
  BY WILLIAM C. SEITZ.
  GARDEN CITY, N. Y. (1960) 64 P.
  ND553.M7N4

SELBIE, JOHN ALEXANDER, 1856- 1931,
  JOINT ED.
  *ENCYCLOPAEDIA OF RELIGION AND ETHICS,
  ED. BY JAMES HASTINGS, WITH THE
  ASSISTANCE OF JOHN A. SELBIE (AND)
  OTHERS)
  NEW YORK, SCRIBNER'S, (1951) 13 V.
  BL31.E4 1924

SELBIN, JOEL, 1931- JOINT AUTHOR
  *DAY, MARION CLYDE, 1927-
  THEORETICAL INORGANIC CHEMISTRY (BY)
  ** (AND) JOEL SELBIN.
  NEW YORK, REINHOLD (1962) 413 P.
  QD475.D3

SELBY, BIGGE, LEWIS AMHERST,
  BART., 1860 ED.
  *HUME, DAVID, 1711-1776.
  (AN ENQUIRY CONCERNING HUMAN UNDER-
  STANDING.' ENGLISH. DELBY-BIGGE'
  ENQUIRIES CONCERNING THE HUMAN UNDER-
  STANDING AND CONCERNING THE PRINCIPLES
  OF MORALS. ANALYT. INDEX BY L.A. SEL-
  BY-BIGGE. 2D ED.
  OXFORD, CLARENDON PRESS (1902) 371 P.
  B1455.A5 1902

SELBY, BIGGE, LEWIS AMHERST,
  BART., 1860 ED.
  *HUME, DAVID, 1711-1776.
  A TREATISE OF HUMAN NATURE. REPRINTED
  FROM THE ORIGINAL ED. IN THREE VOLUMES
  AND ED., WITH AN ANALYTICAL INDEX, BY
  L.A. SELBY-BIGGE.
  OXFORD, CLARENDON PRESS (1888) 709 P.
  B1485.S4 1888

Sample 16. Author catalog, May 1966.

EDUCATION, HIGHER--ADDRESSES, ESSAYS,
   LECTURES

AMERICAN COUNCIL ON EDUCATION.
   HIGHER EDUCATION AND THE SOCIETY IT
   SERVES. STATEMENTS PRESENTED AT THE ANNU
   AL MEETING OF THE **, 1956, CHICAGO (BY)
   DAVID D. HENRY (AND OTHERS) ED. BY
   RAYMOND F. HOWES.
   WASHINGTON (1957) 103 P.
   LC191.A6

FRANKEL, CHARLES, 1917- ED.
   ISSUES IN UNIVERSITY EDUCATION, ESSAYS
   BY TEN AMERICAN SCHOLARS.
   NEW YORK, HARPER (1959) 175P.
   LB2325.F7

GOULD, SAMUEL B
   KNOWLEDGE IS NOT ENOUGH.
   (YELLOW SPRINGS, OHIO) ANTIOCH PRESS,
   1959. 232 P.
   LB2325.G66

GRISWOLD, ALFRED WHITNEY, 1906-
   ESSAYS ON EDUCATION.
   NEW HAVEN, YALE UNIVERSITY PRESS
   (1954) 164 P.
   LD6330 1950.A5

GRISWOLD, ALFRED WHITNEY, 1906-
   IN THE UNIVERSITY TRADITION.
   NEW HAVEN, YALE U.P. (C1957) 161 P.
   LD6330 1950.A52

HOFSTADTER, RICHARD, 1916- ED.
   AMERICAN HIGHER EDUCATION, A DOCUMENT-
   ARY HISTORY. ED. BY ** AND WILSON SMITH
   (CHICAGO) UNIVERSITY OF CHICAGO PRESS
   (1961) 2 V.
   LA226.H53 1961

HOFSTADTER,RICHARD, 1916- ED.
   AMERICAN HIGHER EDUCATION, A DOCUMENT-
   ARY HISTORY. ED. BY ** AND WILSON SMITH.
   (CHICAGO) UNIVERSITY OF CHICAGO PRESS
   (1961) 2 V.
   LA226.H53 1961

HOPKINS, ERNEST MARTIN, 1877-
   THIS OUR PURPOSE.
   HANOVER (N.H.) DARTMOUTH PUBLICA-
   TIONS, 1950. 428 P.
   LD1436 1916

KERR, CLARK, 1911-
   THE USES OF THE UNIVERSITY.
   CAMBRIDGE, MASS., HARVARD UNIVERSITY
   PRESS, 1963. 140 P. =(THE GODKIN
   LECTURES AT HARVARD UNIVERSITY,1963)
   LB2325.K43

NEWSOM, CARROLL VINCENT, 1904-
   A UNIVERSITY PRESIDENT SPEAKS OUT, ON
   CURRENT EDUCATION. (1ST ED.)
   NEW YORK, HARPER (1961) 118 P.
   LB2325.N45

PUSEY, NATHAN MARSH, 1907-
   THE AGE OF THE SCHOLAR, OBSERVATIONS ON
   EDUCATION IN A TROUBLED DECADE.
   CAMBRIDGE, MASS., BELKNAP PRESS OF
   HARVARD UNIVERSITY PRESS, 1963. 210 P.
   LB2325.P8

WEATHERFORD,WILLIS DUKE, 1916- ED.
   THE GOALS OF HIGHER EDUCATION.
   CAMBRIDGE, HARVARD UNIVERSITY PRESS,
   1960. 122 P.
   LB2325.W38

WHAT IS A COLLEGE FOR.(BY) JOHN D.
   MILLETT (AND OTHERS)
   WASHINGTON, PUBLIC AFFAIRS PRESS
   (1961) 48 P.
   LB2325.W455

EDUCATION, HIGHER--CONGRESSES.

GEORGIA.UNIVERSITY.
   HIGHER EDUCATION IN A WORLD OF CONF-
   LICT. ED. BY GEORGE S. PARTHENOS.
   ATHENS, UNIVERSITY OF GEORGIA PRESS
   (1962) 175 P.
   LB2301.G45 1961C

EDUCATION, HIGHER--CURRICALA

MCGRATH, EARL JAMES, 1902-
   MEMO TO A COLLEGE FACULTY MEMBER.
   (N.Y.) PUBLISHED FOR THE INSTITUTE OF
   HIGHER EDUC. BY THE BUREAU OF PUBLICA-
   TIONS, (1961) 54 P.
   LB2361.M33

EDUCATION, HIGHER--CURRICULA

HUNGATE, THAD LEWIS.
   A NEW TRIMESTER THREE-YEAR PROGRAM
   (BY) ** AND EARL J. MCGRATH.
   (NEW YORK) TEACHERS COLLEGE, COLUM-
   BIA UNIVERSITY (1963) 31 P.
   LB2361.H8

EDUCATION, HIGHER--RESEARCH

PRICE, DANIEL O
   UNIVERSITY RESEARCH ADMINISTRATION
   POLICIES.
   ATLANTA, SOUTHERN REGIONAL EDUCATION
   BOARD, 1962. 35 P.
   LB2341.P68

EDUCATION, HIGHER--THE WEST

MCNICKLE, ROMA K.
   FOR A GROWING WEST, THE UNIVERSITY AS
   A RESOURCE, THE ROLE OF WESTERN UNIVER-
   SITIES AND COLLEGES IN THE ECONOMIC DE-
   VELOPMENT OF THE WEST.
   BOULDER, COLO., THE WESTERN INTER-
   STATE COMMISSION FOR HIGHER EDUCATION
   (1961) 36 P.
   LB2321.M5

EDUCATION, HIGHER--1945-

RADCLIFFE COLLEGE. COMMITTEE ON GRAD-
   UATE EDUCATION FOR WOMEN.
   GRADUATE EDUCATION FOR WOMEN, THE RAD-
   CLIFFE PH. D.
   CAMBRIDGE, HARVARD UNIVERSITY PRESS,
   1956. 135 P.
   LB1567.R3

ROYAL SOCIETY OF CANADA.
   CANADIAN UNIVERSITIES TODAY, SYMPOSIUM
   PRESENTED TO THE ** IN 1960. LES UNIVER-
   SITES CANADIENNES AUJOURD'HUI, COLLOQUE
   PRESENTE A LA ** EN 1960. ED. BY
   GEORGE STANLEY + GUY SYLVESTRE.
   (TORONTO) PUBL. FOR THE SOCIETY BY U.
   OF TORONTO P., 1961. 97 P.
   LB2325.R65 1960

TEAD, ORDWAY, 1891-
   THE CLIMATE OF LEARNING, A CONSTRUC-
   TIVE ATTACK ON COMPLACENCY IN HIGHER EDU
   CATION.
   NEW YORK, HARPER (1958) 62 P.
   LB2325.T38

EDUCATION, HIGHER-1945-

BROWN, KENNETH IRVING, 1896-
   SUBSTANCE AND SPIRIT IN EDUCATION.
   NASHVILLE, DIVISION OF HIGHER EDUCA-
   TION, METHODIST CHURCH, 1969. 117 P.
   LC383.B7

Sample 17. Subject catalog, May 1966.

THE NATURAL HISTORY OF RELIGION.
  *HUME, DAVID, 1711-1776.
   THE NATURAL HISTORY OF RELIGION. ED.
   WITH AN INTROD. BY H. E. ROOT.
   STANFORD, CALIF., STANFORD UNIVERSIT-
   Y PRESS (1957) 76 P.
   BL51.H963 1957

THE NATURAL HISTORY OF SELBORNE IN
   THE COUNTY OF SOUTHAMPTON.
   LONDON, OXFORD UNIVERSITY PRESS, H.
   MILFORD (1937) 300 P.
  *WHITE, GILBERT, 1720-1793.
   THE NATURAL HISTORY OF SELBORNE IN
   THE COUNTY OF SOUTHAMPTON.
   LONDON, OXFORD UNIVERSITY PRESS, H.
   MILFORD (1937) 300 P.
   QH138.S4W5 1937B

THE NATURAL HISTORY OF SENSIBILITY.
   DETROIT, WAYNE STATE U.P., 1962.
   104 P.
  *BREDVOLD, LOUIS IGNATIUS, 1888-
   THE NATURAL HISTORY OF SENSIBILITY.
   DETROIT, WAYNE STATE U.P., 1962.
   104 P.
   PR448.S4B7

THE NATURAL HISTORY OF THE LEWIS AND
   CLARK EXPEDITION.
  *BURROUGHS, RAYMOND DARWIN, 1889- ED.
   THE NATURAL HISTORY OF THE LEWIS AND
   CLARK EXPEDITION. (EAST LANSING)
   MICHIGAN STATE U.P. (1961) 340 P.
   CHIEFLY EXCERPTS, DEALING WITH NATURAL
   HISTORY, FROM THE JOURNALS OF LEWIS AND
   CLARK.
   QL155.B8

NATURAL HISTORY OF THE WEST INDIES.
  *OVIEDO Y VALDES, GONZALO FERNANDEZ
   DE, 1478-1557.
   NATURAL HISTORY OF THE WEST INDIES.
   TR. AND ED. BY STERLING A. STOUDEMIRE.
   CHAPEL HILL, U. OF NORTH CAROLINA
   P. (1959) 140 P.
   PC13.N67 NO. 32

A NATURAL HISTORY OF WESTERN TREES.
  *PEATTIE, DONALD CULROSS, 1898-
   A NATURAL HISTORY OF WESTERN TREES.
   ILLUSTRATED BY PAUL LANDACRE.
   BOSTON, HOUGHTON MIFFLIN, 1953. 751 P.
   QK481.P42

THE NATURAL HOUSE.
   NEW YORK, HORIZON, 1954. 223 P.
  *WRIGHT, FRANK LLOYD, 1869- 1959.
   THE NATURAL HOUSE.
   NEW YORK, HORIZON, 1954. 223 P.
   NA7208.W68

NATURAL LAW.
  *PASSERIN D'ENTEVES, ALESSANDRO,
   1902-
   NATURAL LAW, AN INTROD. TO LEGAL
   PHILOSOPHY.
   LONDON, HUTCHINSON (1951) 126 P.
   (HUTCHINSON'S UNIVERSITY LIBRARY)
   BJ55.P3

NATURAL ORGANIC MACROMOLECULES.
  *JIRGENSONS, BRUNO, 1904-
   NATURAL ORGANIC MACROMOLECULES.
   OXFORD, NEW YORK, PERGAMON PRESS,
   1962. 464 P.
   QD471.J5 1962
----
*THE NATURAL PHILOSOPHER. V. 1-
   NEW YORK, BLAISDELL PUB. CO., 1963-
   1 V.
   QC1.N35

THE NATURAL SUPERIORITY OF WOMEN.
   NEW YORK, MACMILLAN. 1953. 205 P.
  *MONTAGU, ASHLEY, 1905-
   THE NATURAL SUPERIORITY OF WOMEN.
   NEW YORK, MACMILLAN. 1953. 205 P.
   HQ1206.M65

THE NATURAL WAY TO DRAW.
  *NICOLAIDES, KIMON, 1892- 1938.
   THE NATURAL WAY TO DRAW, A WORKING
   PLAN FOR ART STUDY.
   BOSTON, HOUGHTON MIFFLIN, 1941. 221 P.
   NC650.N5

NATURALISM AND SUBJECTIVISM.
  *FARBER, MARVIN, 1901-
   NATURALISM AND SUBJECTIVISM.
   SPRINGFIELD, ILL., C.C. THOMAS (1959)
   389 P.
   B828.2.F3 1959

NATURALISM AND THE HUMAN SPIRIT.
  *KRIKORIAN, YERVANT HOVHANNES, 1892-
   ED.
   NATURALISM AND THE HUMAN SPIRIT.
   NEW YORK, COLUMBIA UNIV. PRESS
   (C1944) 397 P.
   B828.2.K7

NATURALLY OCCURRING OXYGEN RING
   COMPOUNDS.
  *DEAN, FRANCIS MEDCALF.
   NATURALLY OCCURRING OXYGEN RING
   COMPOUNDS. LONDON, BUTTERWORTHS (1963)
   661 P..
   QK865.D4

NATURALLY OCCURRING QUINONES.
  *THOMSON, RONALD HUNTER.
   NATURALLY OCCURRING QUINONES.
   NEW YORK, ACADEMIC PRESS, 1957.
   302 P.
   (ORGANIC CHEMISTRY MONOGRAPHS)
   QD341.Q4T5

NATURE, MIND, AND MODERN SCIENCE.
  *HARRIS, ERROL E.
   NATURE, MIND, AND MODERN SCIENCE.
   LONDON, ALLEN + UNWIN, NEW YORK,
   MACMILLAN (1954) 455 P.
   B72.H33

NATURE + SIGNIFICANCE OF ECONOMIC SCIEN
   CE
  *ROBBINS, LIONEL CHARLES, 1898-
   AN ESSAY ON THE NATURE + SIGNIFICANCE
   OF ECONOMIC SCIENCE. 2D ED., REV. AND
   EXTENDED.
   LONDON, MACMILLAN, 1935. 160 P.
   HB171.R6 1935

NATURE ADRIFT.
  *FRASER, JAMES, 1909-
   NATURE ADRIFT, THE STORY OF MARINE
   PLANKTON.
   LONDON, FOULIS (1962) 178 P.
   QH91.F66 1962

THE NATURE AND CONDITIONS OF LEARNI-
   NG.
  *KINGSLEY, HOWARD L. 1892- 1948.
   THE NATURE AND CONDITIONS OF LEARNI-
   NG. REV. BY RALPH GARRY. 2D ED.
   ENGLEWOOD CLIFFS, N.J., PRENTICE-
   HALL (1957) 565 P.
   LB1051.K58 1957

THE NATURE AND DESTINY OF MAN.
  *NIEBUHR, REINHOLD, 1892-
   THE NATURE AND DESTINY OF MAN, A CH-
   RISTIAN INTERPRETATION.
   NEW YORK, C. SCRIBNER'S SONS (1949)
   2 V. IN 1.
   BT701.N5214

Sample 18. Title catalog, May 1966.

ECLAMPSIA (C6)

-Post-partum eclampsia. Jackson L, et al.
   J Nat Med Ass 56:71-2, Jan 64
-Nutritional status and liver function in toxemia of
   pregnancy. Maqueo M, et al.
   Obstet Gynec 23:222-6, Feb 64
-Preliminary experiences with the intravenous
   administration of hydrochlorothiazide (Lyo-Hydro
   Diuril) in the management of eclamptogenic toxemia
   and of hydramnios. Tatum HJ, et al.
   Western J Surg 72:25-9, Jan-Feb 54
-(Severe eclampsia. Tracheotomy and assisted
   respiration. Recovery) Magnin P, et al.
   Bull Fed Gynec Obstet Franc 15:514-5, Sep-Oct 63 (Fr)
-(Placental changes and their relation to late toxicosis
   and perinatal infant mortality) Budliger H.
   Bibl Gynaec 28:86-110, 1964 (34 ref.)   (Ger)
-(Evaluation of collective eclampsia statistics of the
   years 1957 to 1960 from 72 German gynecologic clinics.
   A comparison with the Hungarian collective statistics
   from 97 clinics of the years 1959 to 1961) Kyank H, et
   al. Geburtsh Frauenheilk 23:961-9, Nov 63 (Ger)

ECOLOGY (G1)

-Ecological factors in nutritional disease. Scrimshaw NS.
   Amer J Clin Nutr 14:112-22, Feb 64 (30 ref.)
-Pesticides: a hazard to nature s equilibrium. Cole LC.
   Amer J Public Health 54:Suppl24-31, Jan 64
-Environmental health and human ecology. Lee DH.
   Amer J Public Health 54:Suppl7-10, Jan 64
-(The relations of the surface water bacteria to a few
   ecological factors of the biotope) Daubner I.
   J Hyg Epidem (Praha) 7:436-43, 1963   (Ger)
-(Human ecology in Easter Island) Cruz-Coke R.
   Rev Med Chile 91:773-9, Oct 63   (Sp)

ECONOMICS (I)

-Support for research, training and education in medical
   electronics.
   Amer J Med Electronics 3:57-61, Jan-Mar 64
-Sex, socio-economic status, and secular increase in
   stature, a family study. Acheson RM, et al.
   Brit J Prev Soc Med 18:25-34, Jan 64
-(Mortality according to economic levels in Mexico City)
   Flores R, et al.
   Salud Publica Mex 5:865-8, Nov-Dec 63   (Sp)
-(The public health programs and the economic
   development in Cuba) Pereda Chavez R.
   Salud Publica Mex 5:869-73, Nov-Dec 63   (Sp)
-(The nature of the Mexican and economic
   development) Torres Manzo C.
   Salud Publica Mex 5:875-9, Nov-Dec 63   (Sp)

ECONOMICS, HOSPITAL (G3, I)

-The anatomy of autonomy. Dick WW.
   Canad Hosp 41:51, Feb 64
-Autonomy s strong men. Law J.
   Canad Hosp 41:39-40, Feb 64
-Administrative audit service.
   Canad Hosp 41:52-3, Feb 64
-New skills will be needed for managing tomorrow s
   hospitals. Johnson EA. Hospitals 38:67-9, 16 Feb 54
-Budgetary practices and their defects.
   Ment Hosp 15:108-9, Feb 64

Sample 19. *Index Medicus* (National Library of Medicine). Methodology: Upper- and lower-case computer print-out. (Note: Sample taken from *Electronic Composing System: A Guide for Its Utilization* [Washington: Govt. Print. Off., 1966].)

76   KELLEY L. CARTWRIGHT

[Epilepsy with features of myoclonus] Zouhar A.
Cesk Neurol 27:48-52, Jan 64 (Cz)
[Relation of vitamin B6 to epilepsy] Nádvorník P, et al.
Sborn Ved Prac Lek Fak Karlov Univ 6:569-71, 1963 (Cz)
[Electroencephalographic changes in congenital and acquired toxoplasmosis] Lalisse A, et al.
Ann Pediat (Paris) 11:41-6, 10 Jan 64 (Fr)
[Influence of ACTH on the electroencephalographic tracings of children with phenylketonuria] Tamir A, et al.
Electroenceph Clin Neurophysiol 15:1036-8, Dec 63 (Fr)
[Rheoencephalography. III. Study of various parameters; introduction to a systematic analysis of rheoencephalographic curves] Martin F, et al.
Schweiz Arch Neurol Psychiat 93:14-25, 1964 (Fr)
[On EEG changes in comparison with intraoperative determination of brain tissue conductivity] Schwarz HJ, et al. Zbl Neurochir 24:14-23, 1963 (Ger)
[On physiopathologic cerebral conditions after uni- and bilateral laterocervical dissections] Bartalena G, et al.
Boll Mal Orecch 81:491-501, Sep-Oct 63 (It)
[Effect of selective unilateral lesions of "specific" and "aspecific" STRUCTURES OF THE PONS ON THE ELECTROENCEPHALOGRAPHIC ACTIVITY OF DEEP SLEEP] Candia O, et al.
Boll Soc Ital Biol Sper 39:1566-8, 15 Dec 63 (It)
[Electroencephalographic determination of the "anxiety threshold" in patients with Parkinson's disease] Paolozzi C, et al.
Boll Soc Ital Biol Sper 39:1619-21, 31 Dec 63 (It)
[Electro- encephalographic changes in subjects with systemic vascular diseases and normal arterial blood pressure] Barbagallo Sangiorgi G, et al.
Boll Soc Ital Cardiol 8:593-7, 1963 (It)
[Electro- encephalographic changes in subjects with arterial hypertension] Barbagallo Sangiorgi G, et al.
Boll Soc Ital Cardiol 8:578-85, 1963 (It)
[The electroencephalogram in newborn infants] Di Gruttola G. Pediatria (Napoli) 71:871-96, 1963 (It)
[Electroencephalography findings in children with whooping cough, with or without neurological complications] Fanuele G.
Pediatria (Napoli) 71:968-79, 1963 (It)
[Electroencephalographic changes caused by experimental intraspinal introduction of the subject's own blood in man] Spadetta V, et al.
Rass Med Sarda 65:699-700, Nov-Dec 63 (It)
[Bilateral chronic subdural hematomas: clinical and radiological contribution] Invernizzi G, et al.
Riv Sper Freniat 87:1362-83, 31 Dec 63 (It)
[Studies on the basic pattern of EEG in epilepsy, with relation to age and clinical findings] Mori A.
Brain Nerve (Tokyo) 16:311-9, Apr 64 (Jap)
[On the EEG activities of the cerebral sensory area and thalamus in the cat] Teramoto S.
Brain Nerve (Tokyo) 16:129-38, Feb 64 (Jap)
[Studies on the seasonal changes in minor tremor] Yamauchi I, et al.
Brain Nerve (Tokyo) 16:101-7, Feb 64 (Jap)
[Study of electroencephalography in newborn infants] Shirahashi K, et al.
Obstet Gynec Ther (Osaka) 8:185-94, Feb 64 (Jap)
[The problem of epileptic seizures and EEG hypersyndronism in cerebral palsy in children (Little's disease)] Horyd W, et al.
Neurol Neurochir Psychiat Pol 13:829-34, Nov-Dec 63 (Pol)
[Clinical and electroencephalographic evaluation of the treatment of epilepsy with 2-ethyl-2-methylsuccinimide] Jus K.
Neurol Neurochir Psychiat Pol 13:915-20, Nov-Dec 63 (Pol)
[Pathological EEG picture and epilepsy in children] Michalski T
Neurol Neurochir Psychiat Pol 13:777-83, Nov-Dec 63 (Pol)
[The effect of peripheral vestibular afferentation on the synchronization of slow cortical rhythms] Gil'man IM. Biull Eksp Biol Med 56:8-13, Sep 63 (Rus)
[The effect of nanophyne, pachycarpine and ganglerone on the activating and convulsive effects of nicotine] Il'uchenok RIu, et al.
Biull Eksp Biol Med 56:85-9, Oct 63 (Rus)
[On changes in the electrical activity of the rabbit cerebral cortex during the action of an ultra-high-frequency electromagnetic field. II. On the direct action of the ultra-high-frequency field on the central nervous system] Kholodov IuA.
Biull Eksp Biol Med 56:42-6, Sep 63 (Rus)
[Studies on the effect of adreno- and cholinolytic drugs in trigeminal section of the brain stem] Il'uchenok RIu, et al.
Farmakol Toksik 26:525-31, Sep-Oct 63 (Rus)
[Bioelectrical activity of the brain in thrombosis of the internal carotid artery in the neck] Ginzburg SE.
Vop Neirokhir 27:22-9, Sep-Oct 63 (Rus)
[EEG peculiarities in tumoral lesions of subcortical nodes] Grindel' OM, et al.
Vop Neirokhir 27:34-9, Sep-Oct 63 (Rus)
[Electrophysiological research in schizophrenic patients in the terminal stage] Belen'kaia NIa.
Zh Nevropat Psikhiat Korsakov 63:1223-8, 1963 (Rus)

[Results of the use of a nonparametric statistical procedure in electroencephalogram analysis in cerebrovascular diseases] Moiseeva NI, et al.
Zh Nevropat Psikhiat Korsakov 63:1147-52, 1963 (Rus)
[Electroencephalographic changes in hydrocephalus of non-neoplastic origin] Hajnšek F, et al.
Neuropsihijatrija 11:39-47, 1963 (Ser)
[Value of electroencephalography in clinical medicine] Guija JA. Hispalis Med 21:5-20, Jan 64 (Sp)

ELECTROLYSIS (H)

Electrolysis--a factor in cardiac pacemaker electrode failure. Rowley BA.
IEEE Trans Biomed Electronics 10:176, Oct 63
Research on solid-phosphorus pentoxide electrolytes in electrolysis cell for production of breathing oxygen. Techn Docum Rep AMRL-TDR-63-95. Beach JG, et al.
US Air Force 6570 Aerospace Med Res Lab 1-37, Oct 63

ELECTROLYTES (D1)

Electrolyte content and distribution in human myometrium. I. Postmenopausal age group. Cibils LA, et al. Amer J Obstet Gynec 88:715-20, 15 Mar 64
Electric impedance and rectification of fused anion-cation membranes in solution. Schwartz M, et al. Biophys J 4:137-49, Mar 64
Osmolarity. Hicks JB.
Med Rec Ann (Houston) 57:329 passim, Mar 64
Research on solid-phosphorus pentoxide electrolytes in electrolysis cell for production of breathing oxygen. Techn Docum Rep AMRL-TDR-63-95. Beach JG, et al.
US Air Force 6570 Aerospace Med Res Lab 1-37, Oct 63
[Influence of digitalis on the active transport of electrolytes] Mattioli G, et al.
Arch Pat Clin Med 40:252-6, Jan 64 (It)
[Changes of the aldosterone effect induced by spironolactone and triamterene. Study of the possible mechanism of action] Amerio A, et al.
Boll Soc Ital Biol Sper 39:1404-7, 30 Nov 63 (It)
[Changes in renal plasmatic flow, in diuresis, in the urinary Na/K ratio, in the hemodynamics of the greater and lesser circulation and in pulmonary ventilation induced by distention of a rubber balloon in the right atrial cavity] Migliau G, et al.
Boll Soc Ital Cardiol 8:654-62, 1963 (It)
[On the water and electrolyte content of cells of various bacterial species] Galdiero F, et al.
Riv Ist Sieroter Ital 38:257-62, Nov-Dec 63 (It)
[Effect of serotonin and of anti-serotonin preparations on the electrolyte diuresis] Chodera A, et al.
Postepy Hig Med Dosw 17:815-8, Nov-Dec 63 (Pol)
[Role of electrolytes in the pathogenesis, clinical course and treatment of cardiac insufficiency] Mezhebovskii RG. Ter Arkh 35:68-76, Aug 63 (Rus)

ELECTROMYOGRAPHY (E1)

Myoelectric servo control. Sullivan GH, et al.
Aerospace Med 35:243-8, Mar 64
Electromyography of laryngeal and respiratory muscles: correlation with phonation and respiration. Buchthal F, et al. Ann Otol 73:118-23, Mar 64
Electromyography of extrinsic laryngeal muscles during phonation of different vowels. Faaborg-Andersen K, et al. Ann Otol 73:248-54, Mar 64
Technic for insulating monopolar electromyographic needles with teflon. Lawrence RS.
Arch Phys Med 45:95-8, Feb 64
Electromyogram in muscular dystrophy. With particular reference to differential diagnosis between this disease and other neuromuscular disorders. Marinacci AA.
Bull Los Angeles Neurol Soc 29:7-16, Mar 64
Intracellular stimulation myography in man. Beránek R. Electroenceph Clin Neurophysiol 16:301-4, Mar 64
Phasic activity of intrinsic muscles of the foot. Mann R, et al. J Bone Joint Surg (Amer) 46:469-81, Apr 64
Physiological effects of performing a difficult task in patients with anxiety states. Wing L.

[The remainder of the third column is printed in a shaded/hatched pattern representing the space saved, and includes the following section headings, which remain partly legible:]

ELECTRONARCOSIS (E3)

ELECTRONICS (H)

ELECTROPHORESIS (E1, E5, H)

ELECTROPHYSIOLOGY (G1)

SPACE SAVED

Sample 20. *Index Medicus* (National Library of Medicine). Methodology: Computer-driven phototypesetting. The shaded area represents the amount of space saved by this method of production. (Note: Sample taken from *Electronic Composing System: A Guide for Its Utilization* [Washington: Govt. Print. Off., 1966]. It is not clear what the size of the original was; as printed in *Electronic Composing System*, it was 8-1/2 inches by 11. Sample 20 is a reduction of a full page, made in order to demonstrate the amount of space saved with photocomposition equipment.)

machines is the high quality of their product. One such machine can automatically mix from 16 different type fonts of 90 characters each, or a total of 1440 different characters in each of twelve different type sizes ranging from 5 to 95 point.[3] One by one, the characters of the text are photographically copied at very high speeds. The page master, in this case, is a photographic negative ready to be sent to the printer for reproduction.

Such machines produce a very attractive product, but they are also very expensive. In fact, I know of no library which has used photocomposition techniques to print its catalog. *Index Medicus* (see Samples 19 and 20) is produced by this method, of course, as is the National Library of Medicine's *Current Catalog*. In this case, the greater costs of production are to a large degree offset by the fact that these costs can be distributed over many more copies than the couple of hundred copies which a library usually makes of its catalog.[4]

An interesting aspect of computer output through a photocomposition device is that while the cost of creating page masters is much higher than it is on a computer-printer, the number of pages is lower. The reason is that this system, with its multiple type fonts and variable-width characters, allows us to pack more entries onto a page without losing legibility. Consequently, the cost of reproducing multiple copies, binding and so forth, is reduced. Nevertheless, the information I have been able to procure indicates that the total cost of printing a catalog with photocomposition equipment is still considerably higher than the cost of computer print-outs. I hope this situation will change, because there is no question that photocomposition devices can produce a very attractive product.

Sample 20 illustrates how much space can be saved when a photocomposition device is used. The portion that is not shaded is the portion that could be printed on the same page using a print-out on the computer's line printer.

These, then, are the major steps in producing a book catalog by computer. In most of them, there are unsolved problems and unanswered questions—some major, some minor. In general, however, the methods of producing a book catalog by computer are tested and work well. I should like to close by reiterating what I believe are some of the major advantages of this system of book catalog production.

One of the greatest advantages is the flexible manner in which the data can be manipulated. The unit card that is input can be regarded as a protean body of data consisting of a number of identified elements, which can be utilized in a wide variety of ways, limited principally by the precision with which the various elements that constitute the entry have been identified. For example, the data can be used to print book catalogs, in which each entry contains that portion of the information from a catalog record which is appropriate to the purpose of the entry. These entries may be printed out in a variety of formats designed to make the catalog as useful as possible. The entries themselves may be divided into a number of groupings, depending upon the purpose of the particular printing; for example, this facility can be taken advantage of in dividing the catalog, in printing catalogs of special collections within the library, and in producing various recurring and special bibliographies.

Another important advantage of this approach is that when the catalog data are captured in machine-readable form; one is not irrevocably tied to a specific physical output format or a specific output technology. When the catalog is produced initially, it will be subjected to use both within and outside the library, and the experience gained may indicate the desirability of certain changes in form and content of the entries or of the catalog structure. Such changes can be effected with greater facility than would be the case with any other method of catalog production.

Finally, in considering production methods, it is important to consider certain probable future developments in the library environment. One such development has already been mentioned, the availability of Library of Congress catalog data in machine-readable form. Another such change will surely be the development of on-line technologies which are feasible for libraries. Another may be the reduction of the cost of photocomposition methods. A library whose catalog information is in machine-readable form will be in an excellent position to take advantage of these future developments.

---

[3]David E. Sparks, Lawrence H. Berul, and David P. Waite, "Output and Printing for Library Mechanization," in *Libraries and Automation:* Proceedings of the Conference on Libraries and Automation held at Airlie Foundation...1963; ed. by Barbara Evans Markuson (Washington: Library of Congress, 1964), p.155-89.

[4]Since writing the above, I have been informed of two libraries that have produced book catalogs using photocomposition equipment. These libraries are the Chester County Library in Pennsylvania and the Oregon State Library. I am unable to judge at this time whether the costs encountered by these libraries are competitive with print-out on a computer's line printer. My own fairly recent check of the prices obtained for this service indicates that it is still not competitive.

DISCUSSION

ROLAND MARGNIS, Dearborn, Michigan, Public Library: For a book catalog running around 100,000 titles, how frequently is it feasible to produce a new edition, completely revised and cumulated.

JOHN KOUNTZ, Orange County Public Library: In response to the gentleman's question, we have just undergone quite an extensive study on a computer-supplemented catalog, and it works out something like 26 cents per entry on 15,000 titles added to a basic collection of 115,000 titles. We run supplements up to 8-month cycles and reprint the entire catalog once every two years.

Moderator MacQUARRIE: Could I ask one question on that? Does 26 cents per entry mean per title, or each time it appears in the catalog?

MR. KOUNTZ: No, we are capturing our data from an acquisition system and repeating it into a catalog or master inventory file system, and then manipulating the data so that we can have any sort of a printout we want. The 26 cents also includes the amortization of our initial master inventory file input as well as capturing the data in an acquisition system. It is per entry, but one time only.

EVERETT WALLACE, Systems Development Corporation: I wanted to comment on the film output of a computer, because there are two things that look rather promising here. For one, speed; the printers onto film have a potential of about 9000 lines a minute, and that's a considerable step ahead of any of the line printers that are available now.

Secondly, you could duplicate catalogs on microfilm or microfiche much more inexpensively than in hard copy, and in many, many copies, so that exchanges in this kind of format might be much more useful and within reach.

MRS. MacQUARRIE: Do you know whether these catalogs lose any of their sharpness or their legibility when they have to be reduced and then blown up again?

MR. WALLACE: This depends on the resolution of the film and on the printer and the speed at which it is run, of course. But I see no inherent reason why you cannot get as much resolution as you need for clarity.

JOHN HARRISON, Yale: Have you found that people are limiting their data base just for the printed catalog? There's a very good chance that we are going to want a good many more subject headings and more intensive subject work. Are the systems that we are developing to turn out a book catalog flexible enough or dynamic enough to have the possibility of adding these subjects later?

MRS. MacQUARRIE: I think that's one of the things that we should not lose sight of; we mustn't limit our catalogs in any way. We must keep them flexible, and we mustn't limit the length of the entry. We must make the catalog as usable as possible, and it must be kept flexible so that information can be added when needed.

GUENTER JANSEN, Suffolk Cooperative Library System: Is there a maximum size that book catalogs should be in order to be efficient?

MR. CARTWRIGHT: I don't think there is a maximum. The question should be answered in terms of the individual situation, in terms of what you are trying to do and how much it's worth to you.

LEON KARPEL, Mid-Hudson Libraries: You described one type of book catalog with a random register and an index to it, which is an author-subject-title index approach. It should be pointed out that the cost of that random register is cut down tremendously because it does not have to be reprinted, although the indexes are reprinted; therefore, that cost is immediately eliminated. The register continues to be added to.

Implications of Project MARC

Henriette D. Avram

Senior Systems Analyst
Library of Congress

The MARC [Machine-Readable Cataloging] Pilot Project and the next phase referred to as Project MARC reflect the basic philosophy of the Information Systems Office of the Library of Congress. It is our conviction that evidence gained from experience is a constructive means to set the criteria for an operational system. Many efforts to date have conceptualized the design of systems in terms of the future. This speculation carries the seeds of implementation to a distant, undefined environment and uncertain fruition. We decided that we should develop tomorrow's system in terms of the evolving present. The premise is that the operational system will uncover new paths for expansion and improvement. It is now especially timely to discuss MARC since we are concluding the pilot project on June 30, 1967, and are concentrating our efforts on the development of Project MARC, beginning July 1, 1967.

Before moving ahead to discuss the implications of MARC, it is appropriate to provide some background and original definitions for those who may not be familiar with the project.

BACKGROUND

A conference on Machine-Readable Catalog Copy was held at the Library of Congress in January 1965 under the joint sponsorship of the Library and the Committee on Automation of the Association of Research Libraries. The conference was stimulated by the increased interest in the computer as a tool in the library environment. The conversion of bibliographic material to machine-readable form is an expensive burden for individual libraries, and capturing data at a centralized cataloging source so that it could be used by other libraries was attractive. As a result of this conference, a report entitled *A Proposed Format for a Standardized Machine Readable Catalog Record* was written by staff members of the Library of Congress and circulated to the library community. The report was widely discussed. There was general agreement that the Library of Congress, as the major source of bibliographic data for American libraries, should conduct an experiment to produce and distribute catalog records in a machine-readable format which could be manipulated by recipients to serve their local needs.

In December 1965, the Library received a grant from the Council on Library Resources for design and implementation of the experiment. In February 1966, the effort which became known as the MARC Pilot Project was initiated.

The original concept of MARC was that of a model system to demonstrate, through an actual test, the problems incurred and the benefits derived from a distribution service for machine-readable catalog data. Since the data elements that make up the unit of information called cataloging data are used in many ways and for many purposes, an evaluation of the MARC machine-readable format was considered a significant part of the test.

The experiment included the Library of Congress, participants, a time frame in which to conduct the test, and an evaluation of the results. The model system had two severe constraints: time and funds. The constraint of time was self-imposed. Since MARC was but a building block, we wished to evaluate the results and modify the machine-readable format as early as possible. Funds influenced our choice of hardware and placed limitations on the number of participants which we could include.

Sixteen libraries were selected (see Table I) from a larger number which had expressed interest. The libraries were chosen to represent different types, i.e., research libraries, public school libraries, state and county libraries, special libraries, and other government libraries. The objective was to reflect unique needs of different kinds of libraries in a test environment. Participating libraries received computer programs to print catalog cards and other listings, and they were asked to develop local programs to meet their individual requirements. The use made of the machine-readable records and an evaluation of

TABLE I

MARC PARTICIPANTS

Primary	Secondary
Argonne National Laboratory, Argonne, Ill.	Hershey Medical Center Library, Hershey, Pa. Cleveland (Ohio) Public Library Sandia Corporation, Albuquerque, N.M. Oak Park Regional Processing Center, Oak Park, Ill. Rensselaer Polytechnic Institute, Troy, N.Y.
University of Florida, Gainesville	Florida Atlantic University, Boca Raton
Harvard University, Cambridge, Mass.	Cornell University, Ithaca, N.Y. Columbia University, New York, N.Y.
Montgomery County (Md.) Public Schools	United States Naval Academy, Annapolis, Md.
Nassau Library System, Garden City, N.Y.	SUNY [State University of New York]-Stony Brook Curriculum and Enrichment Center, Guilford, New York
Rice University, Houston, Tex.	Texas A & M, College Station
University of California, Los Angeles	Institute of Library Research, Berkeley, Calif. SUNY-Buffalo University of California, Santa Cruz and Irvine
Washington State Library, Olympia	Washington State University, Pullman Department of Public Instruction, Olympia
Yale University, New Haven, Conn.	University of New Mexico, Library of the Medical Sciences, Albuquerque
Indiana University, Bloomington	Purdue University, Lafayette University of Wisconsin, Madison
Georgia Institute of Technology, Atlanta	_____
National Agricultural Library, Washington, D.C.	_____
Redstone Arsenal, Huntsville, Ala.	_____
University of Chicago, Chicago, Ill.	_____
University of Missouri, Columbia	_____
University of Toronto, Toronto, Ont.	_____

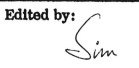

Edited by: Sim

900

Description	Tag
Main Entry	100
Filing Title	150
Statements	
Title	200
Edition	250
Imprint	300
Collation	400
Notes	
Series-Add	500
Series-No	510
Notes	600
Tracings	
Subject	700
Pers Auth	710
Corp Auth:	
Govt Body	72B
Soc or Inst	72C
Relig Body	72D
Miscell	72E
Uniform	730
Title	740
Series	750
Copy Stmt	800
Nat Bib No	830
NBN (over 15)	831
LC Call No	900
DDC No	920
LC Card No	940

PH6480 .M6 1967   MARC

100 Morford, M. P. O.#
200 The poet Lucan:# studies in rhetorical epic,# by M. P. O. Morford. 300 Oxford,# Blackwell,# 1967.# □

400 [1], xi, 93 p. 22 1/2 cm. -/25/-

830 (B67-8807)

600/1 "Substantially a revision of a doctoral thesis presented in 1963 at the University of London under the title Some aspects of Lucan's rhetoric."
600/2 Bibliography: p. 89-90.

DO NOT SET

700 Lucanus, Marcus Annaeus.

740 T
I. Title. e

	920 873.01	940 67- 91001

Library of Congress

FIXED FIELD INPUTS:

TAG	Type of Entry	Form of Work	Biblio	Illus	Map	Supp No.	Conf or Meet	Juvenile
000	A		X					
	1	2	3	4	5	6	7	8

Language Data | | | Publication Data

Class	Lang. 1	Lang. 2		Key	Date 1	Date 2	Place	Name	Height
S	ENG			S	1967		ENOX	BLKW	23
10	11	12		13	14	15	16	17	18

Figure 1. Example of an edited MARC Input Worksheet

THE MARC PROJECT RECORD
MARC DIAGNOSTIC LISTING

							RECORD BATCH NO.	66-008987 CM00076

TYPE OF ENTRY(1)	FORM OF WORK(2)	BIBLIO(3)	ILLUS(4)	MAPS(5)	SUPPLEMENT NUMBER(6)	CONFERENCE OR MEETING(7)	JUVENILE WORK(8)	RECORD INDICATOR(9)
PERSONAL AUTHOR	MONOGRAPH	NO	YES	YES	NO	NO	NO	NEW THIS WK

LANGUAGE DATA

CLASS(10)	LANG 1(11)	LANG 2(12)	KEY(13)	DATE 1(14)	DATE 2(15)	PLACE(16)	NAME(17)	HEIGHT(18)
SINGLE	ENG		MULTIVOLUME	1966		MSED	SBDY	25 CM

PUBLICATION DATA

TYPE OF SECONDARY ENTRY------GS   SERIES-NO   LENGTH OF RECORD-0672
VARIABLE FIELDS-

L. C. CALL NUMBER	90	F72.M5B22
DEWEY CLASS. NUMBER	92	974.494
MAIN ENTRY	10	Banks, Charles Edward,# 1854#-1931.
TITLE STATEMENT	20	The history of Martha's Vineyard,# Dukes County, Massachusetts.
IMPRINT STATEMENT	30	Edgartown,# Dukes County Historical Society [Mass.]# 1966.#
COLLATION STATEMENT	40	3 v., illus., facsims., maps, ports. 25 cm.
NOTES	60	On label mounted on t.p.: Distributed by Regional Pub. Co., Baltimore, Md.
NOTES	60	Reprint of the 1911-25 ed.
NOTES	60	Contents.--v. 1. General history.--v. 2. Town annals.--v. 3. Family genealogies, 1641-1800.
SUBJECT TRACING	70	Martha's Vineyard, Mass.--Hist.
SUBJECT TRACING	70	Martha's Vineyard, Mass.--Geneal.
SUBJECT TRACING	70	Dukes Co., Mass.--Hist.
TITLE TRACING	74	T

Figure 2. Example of a Computer-Produced MARC Diagnostic Listing

the content and structure of the record were to be reported to the Library of Congress for appraisal.

At the Library of Congress, the data base selected for the project was the English-language monograph cataloging. Procedures were designed to use the available equipment in the Library and to minimize disruption of the on-going production of LC printed cards.

MARC PRODUCTION CYCLE

The MARC cycle begins with the manuscript card, which is used to produce the printed Library of Congress card, borrowed from its normal flow and reproduced onto an input worksheet. The input worksheet then becomes the source data for MARC and is passed to a MARC editor who tags or codes each item of information for recognition by the machine. The edited worksheet (see Figure 1) is then typed on a typewriter which simultaneously produces a punched paper tape. The paper tape is read into the computer; records are organized into an efficient form for machine processing and assembled onto a daily work tape. A diagnostic listing (Figure 2), produced by the computer, is used for proofing and correction. Verified records are transferred from the daily work tape to a master tape containing only records declared error free. At the end of each week, current material is merged with a cumulated tape, i.e., this week's data is recorded with the data of all prior weeks. This updated tape is duplicated for distribution to the participants along with bibliographic listings. Figure 3 illustrates the production flow of the MARC Pilot System Operation.

Summarized, the description of the MARC Pilot Project seems quite simple. As a point of fact, the detailed exposition of the effort required 4000 pages to document.

THE MARC EXPERIENCE

The first tapes were distributed in November 1966, ten months after original planning had begun. The MARC Pilot Project has therefore been in operation for seven months. To date, 17,000 records have been distributed. With the present complement of people, the production rate is stabilizing at approximately 800 titles a week. The type of personnel required, the rate per person, and methods for training and pacing people can now be defined. Much has been learned from the pilot experience. Data are being collected and analyzed, and the extension of MARC will have the benefit of such analysis. As time permits, the Information Systems Office will publish its findings so the entire library community may gain from the pilot program.

Since the application of computer technology to the library problem is relatively new, some participants were handicapped in contributing to the project due to insufficient lead time for preparation. The announcement of LC intent to extend MARC into fiscal 1968 has provided the necessary stimulus for continued activity. It is still too early to draw conclusions. The evaluation will be an uninterrupted effort carried over into Project MARC.

The MARC record is already being exploited in many ways. In conjunction with other conventional media, it is being used for book selection and to handle the processes required by the purchase of a book, i.e., order forms, acquisitions records, etc. The MARC record is also used to prepare book cards, book pockets, spine labels, and, in fact, to do all of the housekeeping operations required to put a book on the shelf or into circulation. Most of the interest in MARC, however, will undoubtedly center around its use as a cataloging tool, either in producing the traditional records such as catalog cards or book catalogs or in developing new on-line systems. The flexibility of the MARC record is also demonstrated by special Selective Dissemination of Information (SDI) projects undertaken at various participating libraries. A list of some of the uses made of MARC records by the participants is presented below:

1. As a tool for book selection. This is usually in conjunction with other conventional media of awareness of new books, such as publishers' announcements and LC depository cards for those libraries participating in the National Program for Acquisitions and Cataloging (Title II-C of the Higher Education Act of 1965)
2. To print book order forms, lists of books "in process," etc. This is accomplished by a special machine file of MARC records reformatted for acquisitions use. The record contains information about the status of an item to be ordered, on order, received, etc.
3. In the cataloging process. A print-out of the record is supplied to the cataloger with the book. The cataloger edits the print-out and this is used as input to a local cataloging conversion project to produce one or more output records
4. To produce 3-by-5 catalog cards automatically
5. To produce book catalogs using MARC records in conjunction with local catalog records. In some cases, these book catalogs will show holdings by more than one library, thus providing the beginnings of experimental union catalogs based in whole or in part on MARC records
6. To produce printed library products, such as book cards for circulation control, book pockets, spine labels, etc.
7. To test the use of MARC records for printing bibliographies, subject listings, special indexes, etc.
8. To test the use of the cross reference tracing records supplied in Files 3 and 4 of the MARC tape for experimental authority file maintenance
9. As the source data for an experimental project

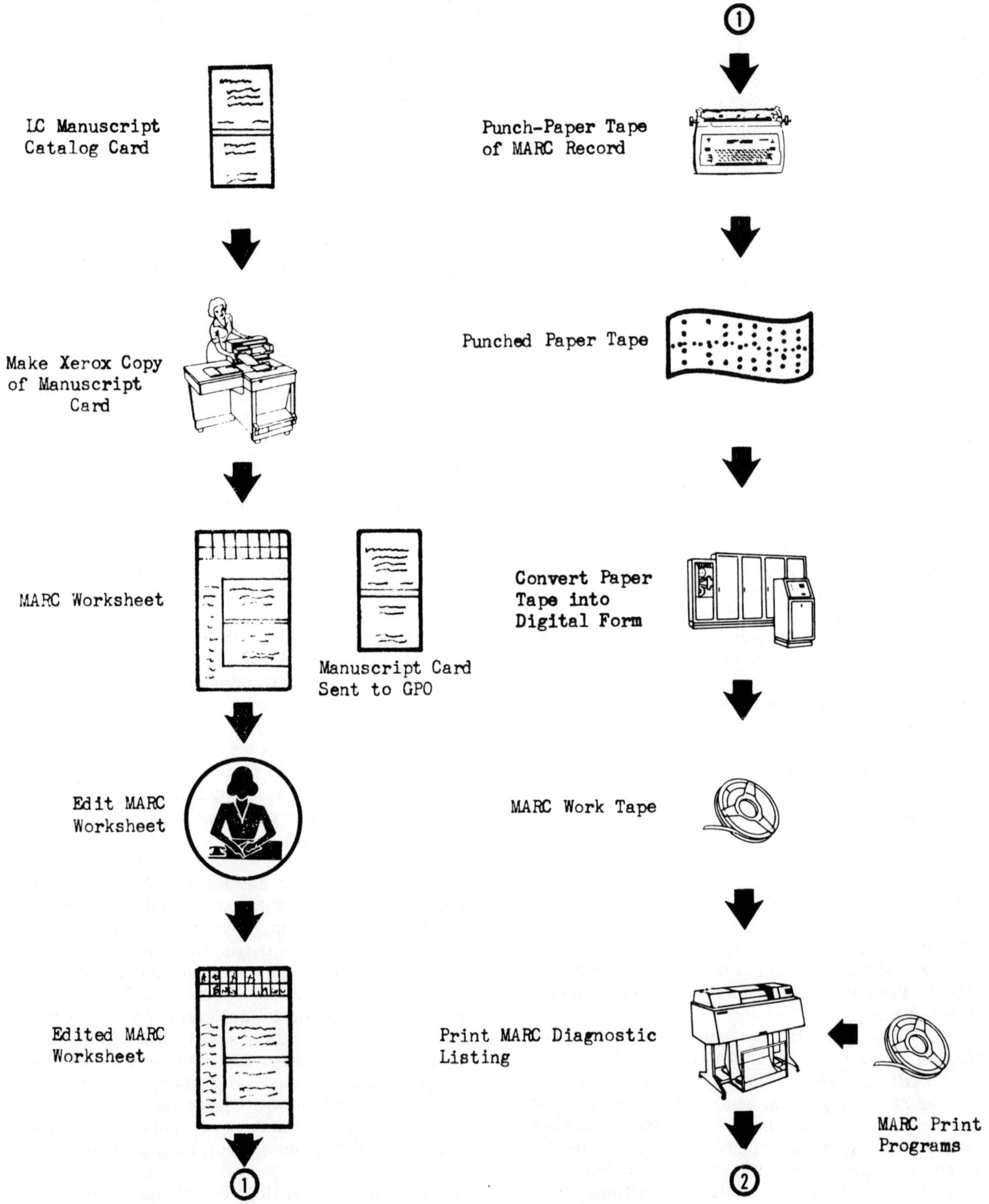

LC Manuscript
Catalog Card

Make Xerox Copy
of Manuscript
Card

MARC Worksheet

Manuscript Card
Sent to GPO

Edit MARC
Worksheet

Edited MARC
Worksheet

Punch-Paper Tape
of MARC Record

Punched Paper Tape

Convert Paper
Tape into
Digital Form

MARC Work Tape

Print MARC Diagnostic
Listing

MARC Print
Programs

Figure 3. MARC Pilot System —

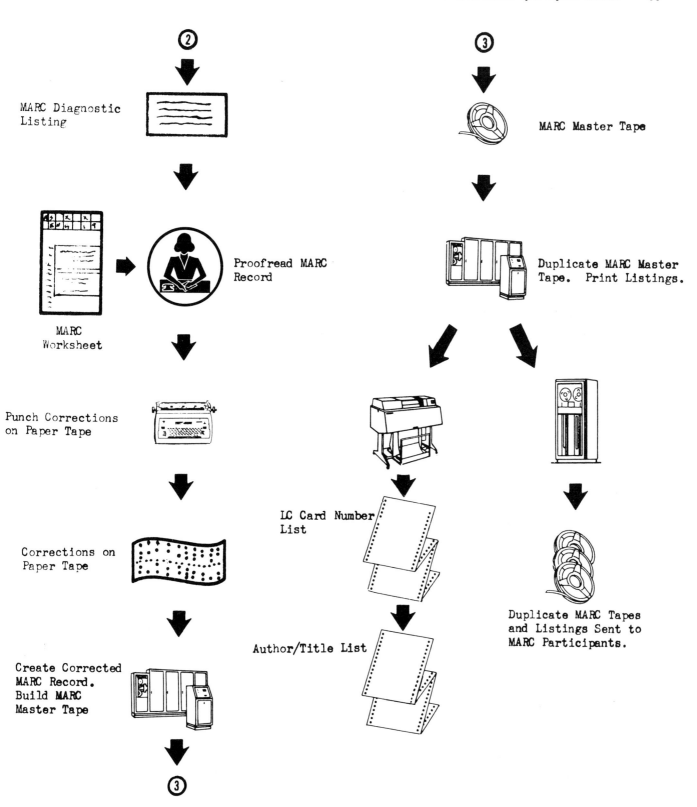

MARC Diagnostic
Listing

MARC Master Tape

MARC
Worksheet

Proofread MARC
Record

Duplicate MARC Master
Tape. Print Listings.

Punch Corrections
on Paper Tape

LC Card Number
List

Corrections on
Paper Tape

Author/Title List

Duplicate MARC Tapes
and Listings Sent to
MARC Participants.

Create Corrected
MARC Record.
Build MARC
Master Tape

Operation Flow Chart

to disseminate records concerning new books to university faculty members according to subject interests (an SDI program)

10. As the source data for an experimental project to create and maintain university course syllabi and bibliography lists by computer, using both MARC records and locally produced records in MARC format

11. As an experimental vehicle for automatic search-ing of machine files. Some of the uses planned are: matching machine-readable faculty book requests, matching machine-readable book purchase orders to find matching catalog records, etc.

12. As an experimental vehicle for on-line computer-aided editing and reformatting of MARC records to adapt the cataloging data for local library use

13. To design local projects to convert records of li-brary materials to machine form.

The most important result of the project is that an operational system exists. It has its deficiencies, but awareness of these defines our next tasks and leaves a firm foundation upon which to build. In addi-tion to providing guidelines for ourselves, we are in a position to help other libraries avoid the pitfalls of a first attempt.

MARC BUILDS A NETWORK

The sixteen primary participants were encour-aged to reproduce their MARC tapes to accommodate those libraries that were interested but unable to be included in the test (the secondary participants listed in Table I). Thus, as an outgrowth of the experimental project, embryonic networks have been formed, some on a regional basis.

The "in" topic today is information networks and studies for their development. As a word of caution, it must be realized that there is a sizable gap, both in time and technology, between now and the day of im-plementation. Complex problems must be solved if we are to design effective information networks. Indi-viduals across the many disciplines that contribute to information science must cooperate in the develop-ment and use of common data forms and procedures, despite the requirements of their special interests. Also, effective logistics must be developed for the distribution of data to core centers and the transmis-sion of data from centers to satellites.

MARC has forced primitive resolutions of these human and logistic problems resulting in an unplanned bonus, the outline of a network. The flow of MARC data moves in one direction, i.e., from the Library of Congress core to participating library to the secon-dary participant. This type of network may be referred to as simplex, i.e., in one direction. Inter-estingly, the development of duplex networks, charac-terized by the two-way flow of data between core centers, is implied by events outside of the MARC project. The Harvard University Library has re-ceived a grant from the National Science Foundation to produce bibliographic data in the MARC format. In the United Kingdom the British National Bibliography will soon be producing MARC formatted data for itself and participating libraries. The exchange of machine-readable data between LC and other domestic and in-ternational producers thus becomes both feasible and probable. The importance of shared cataloging under Title II-C of the Higher Education Act of 1965 is fully appreciated. Recognition that we may be on the thresh-old of a machine-oriented cooperative system is an ex-citing thought. The evolution from the original concept of distribution to that of exchange has influenced our thinking and is affecting our future plans. As the num-ber of project users increases, the significance of this presently uncontrolled network development will be better understood and should provide experience for the future implementation of major networks.

MARC STANDARDS

A by-product of MARC is the evolution of stan-dards from the increased usage and acceptance of its data forms. Early in the project, a character set was established through the joint efforts of the Library Typewriter Keyboard Committee, Resources and Technical Services Division of the American Library Association and the MARC staff of the Library of Con-gress. This character set accommodated the specifi-cations and design of an input keyboard for a manual typewriter as well as a paper-tape typewriter. A computer print train with expanded upper and lower case and diacriticals was developed to be compatible with the keyboard.

Libraries began to use the MARC sets for input and output. This use motivated us to analyze the sets to define their present coverage of Roman-alphabet languages. Table II lists the languages covered by the MARC keyboard and the MARC print train.

Study was also made to determine which additional characters would accommodate the highest percentage of typographic requirements. Feedback from libraries cooperating in this task is augmenting the effort. An important result will be the specification from the li-brary community to the manufacturer for the design of character sets for on-line devices. It is already evident that libraries working together toward common objectives will influence advancing technology.

The development and adoption of a format stan-dard for monographs was fundamental to the imple-mentation of the MARC pilot. Based on comments from participants and nonparticipants, our own expe-rience, many on-site visits, telephone surveys, and, recently, informal working groups, we are recasting the pilot format into a more effective standard to sup-port the exchange of bibliographic data. It is recog-nized that each participating institution may wish to employ a local variant of the exchange format in its internal processing. Therefore, ease of conversion

TABLE II

LANGUAGES COVERED BY THE MARC KEYBOARD
AND THE MARC PRINT TRAIN

ROMAN ALPHABET LANGUAGES

MARC Keyboard	MARC Print Train
Albanian	Albanian
Dutch	Dutch
English	English
Esperanto	Esperanto
Estonian	Estonian
Finnish	Finnish
French	French
German	German
Italian	Italian
Latin	Latin
Portuguese	Portuguese
Spanish	Slovene
Swedish	Spanish
Welsh	Swedish
	Welsh
(with improvisation)[1]	
	(with improvisation)[1]
Afrikaans	
Danish	Afrikaans
Norwegian	Czech
Rumanian	Danish
	Latvian
	Norwegian
	Rumanian
	Slovak
	Wendic

NON-ROMAN ALPHABET LANGUAGES (ROMANIZED FORM)

MARC Keyboard	MARC Print Train
Greek	Greek
(with improvisation)[1]	(with improvisation)[1]
Chinese	Chinese
Japanese	Japanese
Korean	Korean

[1]Special characters and diacriticals could be manufactured by using combinations of characters already in the character set or by symbols to represent missing diacriticals, i.e., by using the cedilla instead of the Rumanian "hook."

between the exchange and a local format is a primary concern. Although magnetic tape will probably continue to be the mode of transmission for some time, it is anticipated that in the future other media, such as common carrier lines, will be used. The exchange format should be hospitable to either mode.

The new format should support at least the following library functions:

1. Printing of bibliographic information in a variety of forms
2. Production of divided catalogs
3. Filing
4. Data retrieval.

Format design which optimizes support for any one function risks degradation of one or more of the others. Therefore, the design of the exchange format should take into account all of these library activities and must include the concomitant trade-offs necessary to satisfy all of them.

Redesign of the MARC format is still principally oriented toward monographs. Because of our prior work, this is the medium best understood at present. However, monographs do not exhaust a library's resources or interests. It is anticipated that libraries will broaden their data bases to include authority files, serials, and collections of other physical forms found in library collections such as maps, audiovisual material, microforms, etc.

No format can accommodate such diverse data bases. However, a format concept has been conceived to tie records from all source data bases into a common search and retrieval file. The approach is to tag each record with a prefix code which will *identify* the type of record and *describe* the characteristics of the record in detail. The identification will contain labels at the generic level such as bibliographic, authority, etc. Associated with each generic level will be labels providing further identification. For example, *bibliographic* might have the associated term *monograph* or *serial*; *authority* could be more uniquely characterized as *subject* or *descriptive*. The record description will include length of record, format style (e.g., MARC) character set employed, (e.g., ASCII [American Standard Code for Information Interchange] or BCD [Binary Coded Decimal]) and record history (original or revised).

Advanced planning of this type will have major implications for future software design. The consistency of format used in file and record definition should make it possible to design a common software package for part of the processing cycle with specific program modules written to handle categories of records with unique characteristics. Successful implementation of these concepts will facilitate the exchange of computer programs and the development of productive library user groups.

The new MARC format focuses on exchange rather than processing. It aims at both convertibility and compatibility. This signifies that a library, upon receipt of a record, may convert to a local processing format or elect to process directly with the new format. Input procedures and processing procedures will remain a local option, but only one conversion will be necessary to receive and one conversion to transmit information.

FUTURE EXTENSIONS AND MODIFICATIONS OF MARC

Those of us responsible for working toward the systems of the future have the obligation not only to learn from our mistakes but also to act to correct and expand our original nucleus as experience warrants. Because procedures were installed and programs written for the pilot to meet very strict deadlines, it was necessary to implement an interim MARC system at the Library of Congress. Procedures and programs are now being upgraded to increase the efficiency of the present operation.

MARC is one of the two major automation programs of the Library of Congress. The system study of the Central Bibliographic System seeks to discover how to apply man-machine techniques to LC functions. Empirical data from MARC influence the system study, while, conversely, system concepts from the study guide the development of MARC. Because each LC project complements the other, it was natural that our efforts be expanded to provide some service to the Library of Congress in the next MARC model. Processes necessary to produce such output products as book catalogs, bibliographies, etc., for LC have been analyzed in parallel with the processes necessary to distribute MARC records.

A new structure is being designed and implemented. The new model will be more adaptable to prospective changes, achieving the flexibility required of a dynamic system. The necessary steps to satisfy a product have been defined as a series of functions. Programs will be written for each function and will be designed to be modular so that they can be altered to conform to a particular need. Consequently, the system can be expanded or contracted by an assembly of the modules.

In some cases, operating efficiency will be sacrificed, but this loss can be justified by the expansion of system capabilities. Concurrent with the analysis of the internal LC functions, we are making plans to expand the present MARC data base. During fiscal 1969, the goal is to distribute all English cataloging and some foreign material.

The pilot project included the distribution of subject and name cross-reference tracing records. The objective was to stimulate experimentation with the use of this data in a local environment. Feedback from the participants indicated this file of information would be useful if a method could be found to associate the cross reference with the MARC record that had generated the tracing. The Technical

Processes Research Office in the Processing Department and the Information Systems Office are jointly investigating the problems associated with the mechanization of authority files. Statistical measures based on a sample of the file have been specified. Plans are underway to study the techniques for the identification of variant names by machine. One of our principal goals is to make the cross-reference material more useful through the next generation of MARC. Another joint effort is the study of the filing rules and their aplication in computer-produced bibliographic listings.

We intend to use the MARC data base as a research vehicle to test the potential for new uses for the catalog record in the library technical processes environment. Accesses to the record in ways which are not now practical will be available. The future adoption during this fiscal year of on-line devices to input MARC data will also allow experimentation with on-line cataloging.

CONCLUSION

The pilot project must be observed in context. It has been exactly what is was described to be: an experiment, limited in time, limited in participants, and limited in scope. The interest expressed in the project by the library community has been encouraging to the staff of the Library of Congress. It is difficult to measure the value of a product when there is uncertainty about its use. The new uses and services resulting from a MARC system cannot yet be clearly perceived. The worth of MARC will be evident as many libraries, both here and abroad, increase their services through imaginative local design of MARC products. The cost benefits to be derived have not yet been determined. In the final analysis, the economics must be weighted against the total value of improved information functions in a highly complex community. There will be new dimensions of service, with an enormously enlarged capacity for future utilization. We are looking forward to a nation-wide bibliographic system. The future of such a system will depend on the coordination of two disciplines. Librarians and systems personnel must communicate with each other and work together to achieve the best understanding of the potentialities and limitations of this new communications media.

PUBLICATIONS ABOUT THE MARC PILOT PROJECT

1967

Avram, Henriette D.; Guiles, Kay D.; and Meade,

Guthrie T. "Fields of Information on Library of Congress Catalog Cards: Analysis of a Random Sample, 1950-1964," *The Library Quarterly*, 37: 180-92 (April 1967).

Avram, Henriette D., and Markuson, Barbara Evans. "Library Automation and Project MARC: An Experiment in the Distribution of Machine-Readable Cataloging Data," in John Harrison and Peter Laslett, ed. *Brasenose Conference on the Automation of Libraries:* Proceedings of the Anglo-American Conference on the Mechanization of Library Services, p.97-127. London and Chicago: Mansell, 1967.

1966

Avram, Henriette D. "The Philosophy behind the Proposed Format for a Library of Congress Machine-Readable Record," in Institute on Information Storage and Retrieval, 2d, University of Minnesota, 1965. *Information Retrieval with Special Reference to the Biomedical Sciences*, p.155-74. Minneapolis, Minn., 1966.

"CLR Grant," in U.S. Library of Congress. *Information Bulletin*, 25:122-24 (Mar. 4, 1966).

Shuart, Rodney A. "Application of Information Processing Techniques to Library Systems" (MARC Pilot Project), in American Institute of Aeronautics and Astronautics, Annual Meeting, 3d, Boston. *Papers*. New York, 1966.

"Test Tapes for MARC Project Shipped," in U.S. Library of Congress. *Information Bulletin*, 25:683-85 (Nov. 3, 1966).

"The Third Conference on Machine-Readable Catalog Copy," in U.S. Library of Congress. *Information Bulletin*, 25:122-24 (Mar. 4, 1966).

U.S. Library of Congress. Conference on Machine-Readable Catalog Copy, 3d, 1965. *Proceedings:* Discussion of the MARC Pilot Project. Washington, 1966. 30p.

1965

U.S. Library of Congress. Conference on Machine-Readable Catalog Copy, 2d. *Proceedings*. Washington, 1965. 35p.

U.S. Library of Congress. Information Systems Office. "A Proposed Format for a Standardized Machine-Readable Catalog Record": A preliminary draft prepared by Henriette D. Avram, Ruth S. Freitag, and Kay D. Guiles. (Planning Memorandum Number 3) Washington, 1965. 110p.

The Library of Congress Systems Study and Its Implications for Automation of Library Processes

Barbara Evans Markuson

Assistant Coordinator
Library of Congress Information Systems Office

The history of events leading up to the Library of Congress' present effort to automate its Central Bibliographic System has been described in a number of articles.[1] None of these papers, however, provides much information about the problems encountered and the planning required in the preparation, negotiation, and management of such a system effort. These topics and a discussion of the actual work done to date will form the major part of this paper.

The Preconference Institute papers by Chapman and St. Pierre discuss systems concepts in general; this paper will serve, in effect, as a companion piece, since it will discuss the application of such concepts to a system analysis and design project at a specific library. Principles will be enumerated and illustrated. That the library happens to be the largest in the world complicates the analysis and makes it necessary for the analysts to spend relatively more time in data gathering and analysis before the design phase begins.

Furthermore, the complexities of operations and the size of the organization make it impossible for one analyst to perform the job; when a large team of analysts is therefore required, it becomes important to document work procedures and results. Thus, what might be done by fairly informal techniques becomes far more organized and formalized. Libraries should be cautioned, however, against allowing any analysis team, however small, to become too informal; to the extent that the results are understood only by a few people and to the extent that documentation is nonexistent or extremely informal, the program is jeopardized if the team should be unable to continue with the project for any reason.

The Library's system program will be described in four sections: Planning the Systems Study; Conducting the Systems Study; Results of the Study to Date; and Implications for the Future.

PLANNING THE SYSTEMS STUDY

Background

The Library of Congress began its early, informal excursions into the area of computer applications in the late 1950's. These first ventures generally resulted from the interest and initiative of individual staff members, but they were undertaken with the encouragement and support of top Library management. By 1958, this activity warranted the appointment of a committee. This group, called the Committee on Mechanized Information Retrieval, conducted informal studies and asked a number of experts—including Mortimer Taube, Calvin Mooers, and Robert A. Fairthorne—to speak to them about the applications of computers to library problems. By 1960, there was, thus, a cadre at the management level who had been exposed to computer concepts. This group conceived of and formulated the plans for a feasibility study to determine where, when, and how the Library could apply computer techniques with the least risk and the greatest promise of successful achievement. The results of this study, undertaken for the Library by a survey team headed by Dr. Gilbert W. King, were published in a project report, *Automation and the Library of Congress*, which has been widely discussed and reviewed.[2]

The published report reflects only a portion of the total work done by the team. In numerous communications, individual studies, supporting contract work, and meetings, the problems facing the Library of Congress and other large research libraries were thoroughly aired, and the possibilities of ameliorating these problems with computers and related equipment

---

[1] Barbara Evans Markuson, "The Library of Congress Automation Program: A Progress Report to the Stockholders," *ALA Bulletin*, 61:647-55 (June 1967); "The United States Library of Congress Automation Survey," *Unesco Bulletin for Libraries*, 19:24-34 (Jan.-Feb. 1965).

[2] Gilbert W. King and others, *Automation and the Library of Congress* (Washington: Library of Congress, 1963).

were discussed many times and from many different viewpoints.

The team recognized the many problems that automation would bring to libraries. For example, libraries lacked experience in managing large-scale system design efforts and negotiating the kinds of contracts that would be required. However, if a library did not manage its system design and development work itself, there would be still another set of problems. In such cases, librarians would have to place tremendous faith in some other management group to look after their interests.

Developing the Systems Staff

After many such discussions, the team finally recommended to the Librarian of Congress that contractors should be utilized for systems work, but that it would be essential to monitor such contracts from within the Library by a group expert in library problems, computer technology, systems design, and contract management. This advice has been followed by the Librarian, and the talents represented in the Information Systems Office reflect the recommended skills.

Building such a staff takes time. Librarians do not, in general, have contacts in the computer field, and they cannot find a programmer, as they might a circulation librarian, by calling a few friends. When they do find programmers and systems analysts, they may find it difficult to assess both the work experience and the competence of these specialists. The salaries demanded are almost always far in excess of those paid to comparable staff members with library skills. The isolation which computer people will face as library employees presents problems, and a relatively high turnover may result.

Notwithstanding all these problems, it is possible to find competent people and to attract them to the library field. One must not minimize the initial effort required to recruit systems people and the subsequent work required to orient these new kinds of staff members to the library community. Successful automation projects depend on this foundation.

It is also possible to develop the required staff by training existing library staff members in programming and various other skills. This approach is generally the most desirable, but it requires an even longer lead time. The library must be willing to absorb the cost of the training, and it still runs the risk of losing the trained employee to another institution.

In the future, there will be increasing numbers of college graduates who will have been trained in basic computer skills, but this gain may be offset by the increasing demand for these skills. Recent projections show that more than one-half-million new programmers will be needed in the early 1970's, if future computer development and application are to grow even at present levels.

Developing a Statement of the Problem

After the staff is familiar with the library and its problems, an overall system study should be prepared showing the long-range problems and goals of the institution with respect to automation. In the larger library, it may be desirable, for a number of reasons, to have this study done by an outside group; it is important, however, that such a group be thoroughly grounded in library matters to avert recommendations which would be inimical to future programs. Such a survey or feasibility study would be comparable to the King survey team report—a document that has proven useful in explaining the goals and objectives of the LC automation program to funding agencies, to the staff of the Library, and to interested private citizens. Having an overall blueprint in hand, one can develop an orderly schedule, identify tasks to be undertaken, and request funds.

The King report took a rather broad view of the Library of Congress, and the resulting conceptual system (even with the exclusion of unique activities such as the Copyright Office) was extremely large and complex. Under the guidance of Library management, the Information Systems Office narrowed the area for system design study still further and identified a core of operations to be included in what has been termed the Central Bibliographic System (CBS). CBS operations include: acquisitions, cataloging, serial control, catalog maintenance and searching, and selected inventory control activities.

A seven-phase program to accomplish the automation of the Central Bibliographic System was developed. Each phase was defined and estimates of time and manpower required to accomplish stated objectives were projected. Table I shows the phases to be accomplished, the purpose of each phase, and the expected results of each phase. Table II indicates the areas to be covered, methods to be used, and related studies underway in the Information Systems Office.

Preparing and Planning for Contract Assistance

When the overall program schedule was developed, tasks for which contract labor would be required were identified. Contract manpower can be used effectively for projects in which: (1) needed skills are not available or would be hard to develop in the Library staff; (2) large numbers of people are needed for relatively short periods of time; and (3) analysts with highly specialized skills need to be applied to a particular problem.

The utilization of computers, or the planning for such utilization, has brought many libraries face to face with the problems of contracting for professional labor and of dealing with companies whose clientele is largely nonlibrary. In the past, most library contracts have involved fairly tangible products, e.g., binding or buildings. Contracts for systems design,

TABLE I

PHASES IN DEVELOPMENT OF LC CENTRAL BIBLIOGRAPHIC SYSTEM

Phase	Estimated Calendar Time	Estimated Man Years	Purpose	Expected Product
I. Survey of present system	Feb. '65– Dec. '66 (completed)	9	To describe and analyze the present operation	Detailed description of present system: flow charts, statistical studies of files, analysis of use of files, identification of needed changes and improvements
II. System requirements analysis	Oct. '66–Apr. '67 (completed)	5	To identify the objectives of the Library's bibliographic functions and to identify specific operational requirements	Detailed description of major functional requirements, interfaces with other libraries, projections of requirements into 1970's, functional flow chart of system, showing magnitude of operations, identification of data elements needed in overall system operation
III. Functional description of new system	Apr. '67–Jan. '68	6–10	To create a sound conceptual model for system development and one or more alternative systems meeting requirements developed in Task II and encompassing various degrees of automation	Recommended system indicating operations to be performed, personnel requirements, files to be converted, indication of new or eliminated functions
IV. System specifications	Spring '68[1]	—	To specify types and capabilities of needed equipment to fulfill functional requirements and to specify operating and computer program requirements	Report of specifications in detail for submission to equipment manufacturers, with cost estimates
V. System design	—	—	To specify exact equipment, operating procedures, computer programs, documentation, etc., required to implement the new system	Statement of specific equipment required; detailed presentation of conversion methods, phasing of new system modules, and training programs planned; specification of building changes required
VI. Implementation	—	—	To bring the "paper" system to reality	Procurement and installation of equipment, writing of programs, debugging of programs, conversion of files, and training of staff
VII. Operation of new system	—	—	To put LC staff in charge of operating the new system	Completely operational system

[1] Until further details about the new system are available, projections of time schedule and manpower for Phases IV–VII are not possible.

TABLE II

THE LIBRARY OF CONGRESS SYSTEM DEVELOPMENT STUDY

Areas of Study	Methods of Study	Related Studies at LC
Acquisitions	Flow charts	MARC Project (catalog data analysis)
Cataloging	Interview	National serials
Reference	Statistical analysis	Data Project (serial data analysis)
Serial Control	Function and data analysis	Filing rules study
Circulation	Modeling	Classification and subject heading studies
Management data	Questionnaire	

programming, and related activities require different evaluation guidelines and perhaps a stronger emphasis on monitoring by the library staff than is generally realized.

The Library obtained the services of a consultant to aid in laying out the ground rules to follow in planning for contract assistance, in preparing procedures for evaluation of proposal submitted, and in alerting the Library to some of the problems which could arise. There are several approaches which can be taken in contracting, but the approach taken by the Library included the following steps:

1. Preparation and distribution of a "Request for Proposal" which stated the tasks for which contract assistance was sought
2. Conduct of a bidders' meeting to provide interested companies with an opportunity to ask questions about the "Request for Proposal"
3. Submission of proposals by potential contractors
4. Review and evaluation of proposals
5. Submission of evaluation report; notice of elimination of unsatisfactory proposals
6. Interview of proposed system teams
7. Submission of cost bids by those companies submitting satisfactory proposals
8. Evaluation of cost bids and selection of winning bidder
9. Negotiation of final contract
10. Announcement of contract.

Each of these steps requires careful planning, and, in each, unforeseen problems can arise. Certain points are worth emphasizing. Ample time should be allowed to plan for, execute, and complete each phase in an orderly manner. If the library has a budget cycle and monies must be committed before the fiscal year ends, then this cycle becomes an important factor in scheduling the precontract work.

Companies put a lot of manpower into preparing proposals, and while they do not expect to have them all accepted, they do expect, and should receive, objective treatment. Every effort should be made to be scrupulously fair; no contractor should receive information which is not available to all. When proposals include proprietary information, libraries should re-

spect the confidentiality of this information. In general, all proposals should be treated as confidential documents, and the winning company should not be allowed to have access to the ideas and plans submitted by its competitors. If a library intends to distribute the proposal outside its own staff for comments, this should be so stated in the "Request for Proposal." Our experience has been that thorough contract evaluation is time consuming and extremely difficult.

The proposals received by the Library were evaluated on the points listed below. The order of the criteria does not reflect the weighting assigned for our evaluation. These are general criteria for evaluating proposals, and the weighting would vary depending upon the type of tasks for which contract assistance is sought:

1. Offerers' understanding of the Library's automation program as a whole and of the specific work of the proposed contract
2. Feasibility and desirability of technical approach and plan
3. Backgrounds and caliber of personnel to be assigned to the task
4. Availability of replacement personnel
5. Organization and management of the project team
6. Backup resources of the contractor
7. Relevant past experience of the offerer
8. Suitability of facilities needed to perform the work
9. Capability of the offerer to absorb the additional work load of the library contract
10. Time schedule for achieving contract milestones.

Several problems were encountered during the precontract phase at the Library of Congress. For one thing, requests were submitted by a number of companies who wanted to observe library operations in action. This, we felt, should not be permitted for one company unless a library is willing to do it for all; the Library of Congress then solved this request by scheduling four tours open to all. Requests were also received from companies who wanted to inspect previous system work done by the Library staff. Generally, it is not feasible to permit this sort of access to a library's working files, but some effort should be made to provide samples of existing documentation for all contractors. The Library included these samples in its "Request for Proposal" and permitted no further access to its survey data during the proposal stage.

CONDUCTING THE SYSTEMS STUDY

Task I, Survey of the Present System

The Information Systems Office had undertaken to do a major portion of Phase I, the description of the present Library of Congress Central Bibliographic System, with its own staff. A group of recent library school graduates was assigned to the Information Systems Office to undertake this task under the supervision of a senior library analyst. This group prepared flow charts of the twenty-nine divisions to be included in the system study and gathered other pertinent documentation as required. For each division or section studies, the following information was obtained:

1. A narrative report on the administrative unit under study (see Appendix 1, page 103)
2. A flow chart of pertinent operations
3. Special studies: questionnaires, file use studies, etc., as manpower permitted.

At the end of this effort, the Library had an extensive data base with which the contractors could begin their work and a group of junior analysts with some knowledge of system techniques and an extensive knowledge of the Library. Some members of this group of analysts continue to serve with the contractor as a liaison with the library staff and as a resource group familiar with library operations.

The flow chart project may be of interest because of its extensive and complex nature. The work was begun with two objects in mind: (1) to prepare a description of the Library's operations which would be uniform as well as accurate and (2) to provide the description in such a manner that it could be read and understood by nonlibrarians. The symbols chosen for the flow charts were not different from those suggested by Chapman and St. Pierre and appear to be almost identical to those proposed by the United States of America Standards Institute. Accompanying each page of flow chart was a facing page of text, which supplied additional explanation and amplification where necessary to explain the flow chart. An appendix provided examples of documents referred to in the flow charts to aid those unfamiliar with the nature of library records. Types of documents included interlibrary loan forms, authority cards, and purchase orders. In general, an attempt was made to gather both a blank and a completed form to allow the analyst to see how the data are actually gathered and recorded in the system. For example, he can note data elements which are usually typed, handwritten, stamped, etc. (See Appendix 2, pages 104-106, for illustrations and explanations of flow charts.)

At about the time the final flow charts were being completed, the contract had been signed and the contractor's team joined the system team at the Library. A three-week orientation period permitted the contractor an opportunity to become acquainted with the Library, thus forestalling misunderstandings about the present system which might lead to naïve suggestions for future improvements. The orientation consisted of morning sessions, during which flow charts were reviewed and explained in general detail, and afternoon sessions devoted to meeting key staff members and observing operations in the working environment.

At the end of the orientation, work was begun on tasks which would complete the documentation of the existing system. These tasks included:

1. A census of all files in, or relevant to, the Central Bibliographic System (see Appendix 3, page 107)
2. A study of the file census to determine the files of most importance, and a more intensive study of these files (see Appendix 4 and 4A, pages 112-17)
3. A sampling of the Official Catalog of LC to determine its composition and condition
4. A study of the gross number of users approaching the major file cluster during a one-hour period
5. Identification of major functions (based on a study of the flow charts) and analysis of their characteristics (see Appendix 5 and 5A, pages 118-26).

These studies, together with the existing documentation prepared by the Information Systems Office and reports, studies, etc., undertaken by staff in other units of the Library, comprise the corpus of data concerning the existing system.

Task II, System Requirements Analysis

The purpose of Task II was to identify the requirements of the Library system from a number of viewpoints. These included: (1) identification of the mission and objectives of the Library's bibliographic services; (2) determination of operational changes and improvements required to enhance present services and to add new services needed to meet the identified missions and objectives; and (3) analysis of bibliographic and operational data required to support Library operations. Another project of Task II was to provide a statistical description of the Library system in 1972 and 1980 if no changes were made in present operating procedures. This projection, termed the baseline system, provides a vehicle for comparison of proposed automated systems with manual systems.

Task II projects included:

1. Preparation of higher-level (i.e., summary) flow charts which indicate the basic functions being performed and the magnitude of the inputs, outputs, and operations for each function (This work

was based on an analysis of the detailed flow charts. An example of the higher-level flow chart appears in Appendix 6, page 127. This effort reduced the detailed flow charts from more than 1000 pages to 70 pages, thus providing a more manipulatable system description. The summary charts are, however, keyed to the original, detailed charts)

2. Identification of missions and objectives of the Library of Congress by reviewing statements issued by the administration, by examining the basic legislative documents concerning the Library, and by conferences with Library administrators
3. Brainstorming sessions with LC operating staff to determine: (a) ideas for improvement of existing operations, (b) ideas and comments about new services which could be provided, and (c) areas of dissatisfaction with present operation and services
4. Definition of boundaries for the Central Bibliographic System and identification of major inputs to and outputs from it (see Figure 1)
5. Projection of statistical data to 1972 and 1980 to indicate system loads at these points in time.

Task III, Development of Recommended and Alternative Systems

The Central Bibliographic System of the Library of Congress is without doubt the best-documented research library system in existence. However, the main purpose of systems analysis is not just data gathering, no matter how fascinated the analyst gets with different methods of describing complex organizations. At some point, the decision has to be made to begin the development of at least initial systems on the basis of the data at hand. As the system design process proceeds, there is a constant cycling back to gather specific data in answer to specific design problems or concepts.

The process of formulation of alternative computer-based systems for the CBS has only just begun, and it is too early to predict the specific kind of system or systems which will be recommended. A final report on the project will be published in 1968 so that the library community may become familiar with the kinds of systems under consideration at the Library of Congress.

RESULTS OF THE STUDY TO DATE

The flow charts of the CBS confirmed the complexity and interrelatedness of the library operations. Many processes, even in the large library, depend on the skill and knowledge of one particular person or are habitually performed by one person. Even in the large library, most procedures are not documented, and existing manuals are inadequate or completely out of date. The paths which an incoming item may take throughout the system are based on a series of

complex decisions. The result is that an item does not move through the processing operation in a fixed order like an automobile assembly line. Paths are based on the physical condition of the item (e.g., bound versus unbound), value, type of material, language, date, subject content, previous cataloging status (e.g., added copy or edition), origin of request (e.g., items purchased for special purposes), and so on. Most of these decisions depend on the ability of staff members to remember these criteria, recognize the conditions, and respond accordingly. To the extent that such recognition criteria cannot be specified in advance, they pose difficult conditions for computer systems. It is, of course, not the intent of the analyst to copy such a system using machines. The task is to recognize, underneath the complex patterns, the essential operations and to determine whether or not a computer can assist the basic process.

In general, manual library routines produce many records for the processing of a single item. These records are required to provide the needed traces and controls in case of malfunction. For example, in the order process, one needs to be able to trace by dealer, by title, by order number, and so forth, and appropriate records are so maintained.

Thus, the library is a file-centered organization. This may seem obvious, but generally librarians talk about only two kinds of files—the card catalog of holdings and the serial record. These files may represent the largest complex of data in the system, but concentration on them masks the characteristic of the library as a system based on a multitude of single- and multipurpose files. A file census of the Library of Congress determined that 1260 files of potential importance to the Central Bibliographic System are in existence. The distribution of these files is shown in Table III. (Note that this survey does not include all files in LC but only those of concern to this study.) Table IV indicates that these files contain more than 220 million records and illustrates the distribution of the records among the files. The curve in Figure 2 shows that the majority of records are found in a few files (75 percent of all records are concentrated in about 11 percent of the files) whereas 25 percent of the records are dispersed throughout some 1124 files, each of which numbers less than 100,000 items each. The data cited here refer specifically to the Library of Congress, but the characteristic is probably found in most library systems. What is not yet well understood is the relationship of these satellite files to the overall work flow and to the large central catalogs.

One other comment concerning the file-oriented library should be made. That the Library of Congress, or any library, has a large number of files is not necessarily an indictment of the manual system. Rather, it may be taken as graphic proof that people want data in a form convenient to them and to the operation at hand. The present manual card catalog may be considered to be a monumental bibliography in an edition of one, two, or at the most three copies. In addition

2. INPUT DATA:
2.1 Preliminary Cataloging Data from LC Overseas Offices
2.2 Shared Cataloging Copy
2.3 Preliminary Catalog Data (e.g., from Publishers)
2.4 Lists of Possible Acquisitions (e.g., National Bibliographies)
2.5 Purchase Data from Other Libraries
2.6 Holdings Data from Other Libraries
2.7 Status or Location Data
2.8 Recommendations
2.9 Other Inputs

1. INCOMING MONOGRAPHS AND SERIALS:
1.1 Unprocessed
1.2 Partially Processed
1.3 Fully Processed

7. OUTGOING MONOGRAPHS AND SERIALS:
7.1 Fully Processed
7.2 Partially Processed

3. OUTPUT DATA (ROUTINE):
3.1 Messages in Support of Acquisitions Activities
3.2 Messages in Support of Materials Preparation Collection Maintenance and Circulation
3.3 Bibliographic Data for Preparation of LC Products
3.4 Selected Authority Data
3.5 Other Outputs

4. DEMANDS FOR BIBLIOGRAPHIC DATA:
4.1 In Support of Congress
4.2 In Support of Reference Activities
4.3 In Support of Circulation Activities (Outside Loans and Use within LC)
4.4 In Support of Acquisitions Activities
4.5 In Support of Sale of LC Products
4.6 In Support of Other LC Activities (e.g., Copyright)

5. DEMANDS FOR CONTROL DATA:
5.1 In Support of Circulation Activities
5.2 In Support of Other LC Activities

6. DEMANDS FOR MATERIALS:
6.1 Circulation Requests (Outside Loans and Use within LC)

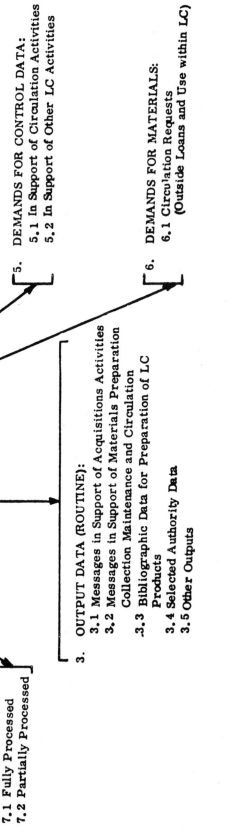

CBS

Figure 1. CBS Inputs and Outputs

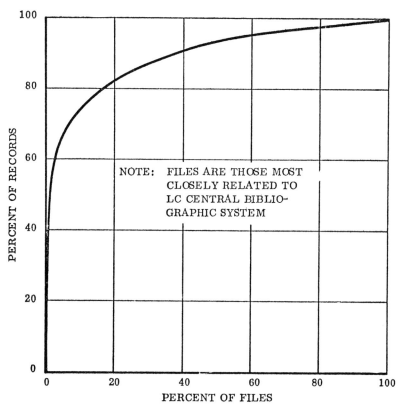

Figure 2. Relationship of Percentage of Files and Records

(A record is any file medium such as a catalog card, visible file entry, invoice, etc.)

TABLE III

SUMMARY OF CENSUS OF LIBRARY FILES

Administrative Department	Copyright Office	Law Library	Legislative Reference Service	Processing Department		Reference Department	
Photo Dupl 10	72	61	Amer Law 10 Libr Serv 23	Cyrillic Biblio	10	Off of Dir	1
				PL 480	4	Blind	29
				Binding	13	Gen Ref & Bib	150
				Card	36	Hispanic	17
				Cat Maint	53	Loan	11
				Decimal Clas	17	Manuscript	39
				Desc Cat	61	Map	31
				Exch & Gift	75	Music	38
				Order	31	Nat Ref Cntr	17
				Serial Record	16	Orientalia	91
				Sub Catalog	32	Prints & Photo	67
				Union Cat	15	Rare Book	7
				Shared Cat	5	Sci & Tech	132
				Children's	4	Serial	44
						Slavic & Ce	32
						Stack & Reader	6
$\overline{10}$	$\overline{72}$	$\overline{61}$	$\overline{33}$	$\overline{372}$		$\overline{712}$	
						1260	

TABLE IV

DISTRIBUTION OF FILES BY SIZE INCREMENT

File Size Category (Millions)	In File Category	Estimated No. of Records[1] in File Category (Millions)	Cumulative Data			
			No. of Files	Est. No. of File Items	% of File Items	% of Records
14-15	1	14.5	1	14.5	.1	6.6
13-14	1	13.5	2	28	.2	12.7
12-13	2	25	4	53	.3	24.0
11-12	0	0	4	53	.3	24.0
10-11	0	0	4	53	.3	24.0
9-10	0	0	4	53	.3	24.0
8-9	1	8	5	61	.4	27.6
7-8	0	0	5	61	.4	27.6
6-7	2	13	7	74	.6	33.5
5-6	1	5.5	8	79.5	.6	36.0
4-5	2	9	10	88.5	.8	40.0
3-4	2	7	12	95.5	1.0	43.2
2-3	5	12.5	17	108	1.4	48.9
1-2	9	13.5	26	121.5	2.1	55.0
.5-1	23	17.5	49	139	3.9	63.0
.1-.5	87	26	136	165	10.8	74.7
.1	1124	56	1260	221	100.0	100.0
Totals	1260	221				

[1]A record is any file medium such as a catalog card, visible file entry, invoice, etc.

to being in a fixed location, it also presents a very fixed access to the collection—by authors, titles, and subjects. If data are needed in another arrangement, the staff member or user must maintain his own file. Thus, we find that many rare book collections—for which access by date and publisher is essential—have catalogs which are rearrangements of the basic card catalog. In LC, the Serial Division has a card catalog of serials arranged by language and a card catalog arranged by country of publication, thus providing approaches to the collection essential to the support of reference service to Congress and to the public. The Card Division arranges its stock of printed cards by card number, since this approach is essential to the filling of card orders and to the maintenance of a master file of printed cards.

The task of the systems analyst is to determine the approaches to data which are needed and used in the system and to determine the extent to which they can be supported by enriching the initial input record so that such searches can be provided. The MARC format, for example, would provide access to the collection by date, by LC card number, by type of material, by language, by country of origin, etc.[3]

_____
[3] "The Request for Proposal: System Development Study for Library of Congress Automation Program" is reprinted, with only minor omissions, in *Library Quarterly*, 36:197-273 (July 1966).

Files

The basic file census was followed by an analysis of the core files, of which the most important was the Official Catalog. This file contains in a single alphabetic sequence a number of different types of records: cards for titles cataloged, name and subject authority cards, series treatment cards, etc. A statistical study of this file was formulated, and a random sample of 1369 cards was drawn. These cards were analyzed and their characteristics were coded. Table V summarized some of the results of this statistical analysis.

When the detailed flow charts were summarized, some 358 library functions were identified, defined, and analyzed (see Appendix 5). Functions were studied to determine whether or not they depended on data; e.g., pasting book labels would not depend on data, whereas assignment of call numbers would. Data-dependent operations have been analyzed to determine the specific elements of data used from the records accessed. For example, a complete, printed catalog card may be accessed when only a check of a call number is required. The list of data elements was analyzed, and a standardized list of 116 elements prepared. Of these, 106 could be considered as discrete data elements, e.g., title or purchase price. These data elements were defined and divided into two categories. One category included bibliographic elements,

TABLE V

DISTRIBUTION OF RECORD TYPES IN STATISTICAL SAMPLES OF THE OFFICIAL CATALOG

Records	Number of Sampling Units (Complete Records)	Estimated Proportion of Catalog	Estimated Number of Cards in Official Catalog	Tolerance of Estimate	Estimated[1] Number of Records
Master record[2]	1114	0.814	11,450,000	± 320,000	9,750,000[3]
Authority cards, nonsubject	139	0.102	1,429,000	± 230,000	1,402,802
Cross references, nonsubject	75	0.055	771,000	± 174,000	771,000
Cross references, subject	22	0.016	226,000	± 96,000	226,000
Cataloging treatment cards	12	0.009	123,000	± 70,000	123,000
Authority cards, subject	4	0.003	41,000	[4]	[4]
Information and other cards	3	0.002	31,000	[4]	[4]
TOTALS	1369		14,071,000		

[1]The number of records is lower than the number of cards to account for those records that required two or more cards.

[2]A master record is the entry for a work cataloged. Master records were defined to include two kinds of cards, main entries and added entries.

[3]The number of unique master records (or titles) is estimated at 3,780,000.

[4]Proportion too low for a reliable estimate.

that is, information which specifically relates to a book, serial, or article, such as an author. This kind of data would be of interest to users outside LC. The second category included nonbibliographic information generally of use for control and processing purposes, such as custodial assignments. Such data would, in general, be of interest only within LC. These data elements are listed in Appendix 7 (pages 128-29). Through the development of a detailed matrix, a portion of which is shown in Appendix 8 (page 133), we are now able to identify the basic set of data elements associated with any CBS function.

File Use

Although a great deal is known about the composition of the CBS files, their use still remains an area for intensive investigation. A study of the major files containing printed cards for cataloged titles revealed that, during a brief survey period, as many as 638 *different* people were accessing this file complex per hour.[4] The study also revealed that, for the period

sampled, the use of the files by LC staff was 3 to 4 times as great as that by nonstaff (see Table VI). These results are based on a very small sample and are useful only as an indication of gross trends in file use.

We do not yet know the purposes for which these users accessed the files, the methods by which they searched, the number of searches per file use, and the satisfaction received. These questions need to be investigated, and preliminary analyses of file usage by LC staff members have been undertaken. These studies have led us to believe that indepth analysis of file use will be extremely complex and time consuming.

Projections

We have obtained a rather frightening picture of the magnitude of operations in the manual library

[4] These files were the Official Catalog, Main Catalog, Annex Catalog, Card Division Search files, the Shelflist, the National Union Catalog, Music Catalog, Law Catalog, and the Process Information File. These catalogs may all be considered as duplicates or rearrangements of data in the Official Catalog in that they essentially consist of printed catalog cards. It was assumed that in an automated system this complex of files might be replaced by a single digital file with multiple indexes. This brief survey was taken to provide an estimate of the use of such a centralized file.

TABLE VI

SUMMARY OF SURVEY OF GROSS USE OF MAJOR CATALOGS[1]

Name of Catalog	Sample 1			Sample 2			Sample 3			Sample 4			Grand Total per File
	LC User	Non-LC User	Total	LC User	Non-LC User	Total	LC User	Non-LC User	Total	LC User	Non-LC User	Total	
Official	176	1	177	135	2	137	148	0	148	155	0	155	617
Main	49	126	175	56	102	158	53	80	133	42	74	116	582
Shelflist	78	0	78	56	0	56	62	0	62	58	0	58	254
Author File Card Division	74	0	74	37	0	37	34	0	34	24	0	24	169
PIF	37	0	37	37	0	37	40	0	40	53	0	53	167
NUC	16	3	19	39	5	44	41	6	47	40	6	46	156
Annex	12	28	40	12	18	30	16	17	33	14	18	32	135
Law	17	3	20	12	2	14	17	4	21	13	6	19	74
Series File Card Division	13	0	13	5	0	5	0	0	0	6	0	6	24
Music	4	1	5	0	0	0	0	0	0	5	1	6	11
TOTALS	476	162	638	389	129	518	411	107	518	410	105	515	2189

[1]The four samples were taken on October 18, 19, 20, and 21, 1966, respectively.

system in 1980. How much credence can be given to such projections? In a recent book, *The Great Leap*,[5] John Brooks notes that the projections made for the World's Fair of 1939, whose theme was "The World of Tomorrow," consistently underestimated the changes which the future would bring—the "reality of change over the preceding quarter century had outstripped the vision." For example, it was predicted that 38 million automobiles would be in use in 1960; and when 1960 rolled around, the real figure was 74 million, almost twice the prediction. The Census Bureau, in the same year, predicted a peak population of 136 million and a long decline to a leveling off of 126 million by 1980. The decline never came, and assuming a continuation of the current birth rate, our estimated 1980 population will be 260 million, or more than twice the estimate made by the Census Bureau in 1939.

In the Library of Congress in 1980, it is predicted that:

1. The filing load for the major LC catalogs will be equal to filing one present Official Catalog (about 14 million cards) a year. At present staff levels, filing will have to proceed at a rate of two cards a

[5]John Brooks, *The Great Leap: The Past Twenty-Five Years in America* (New York: Harper and Row, 1966).

second (7200 cards an hour for each 8-hour work day); at present production levels, this increase could be met only by the addition of 125 to 170 filers. More than 2240 incoming pieces will be received for processing every hour, 24 hours a day and 365 days a year.
2. At current production rates, LC will need a 500 percent increase in staff in its cataloging divisions by 1980.

Table VII presents 11 out of the approximately 150 system parameters for which projections were made. Computer projections were used in each case, but where data were discontinuous, manual methods were also applied. In every case, the final data were reviewed and modified, where necessary, based on the judgment of division administrators.

IMPLICATIONS FOR THE FUTURE

Background

In the early 1900's, Frederick W. Taylor was doing classic studies at Bethlehem Steel Company. His approaches and those of the men who succeeded him are largely discredited now, but it is important to remember that their work represented a management breakthrough in that, for the first time, men were not *performing* operations, but *analyzing* them. In the library field, only within the last few years—some sixty years later—are we getting such people. Therefore, we have come relatively late into the field and, as a result, do not have the background of experience and data which would be desirable. Time and motion studies, micromotion studies, quality control, cost accounting, aptitude testing, and logistical analysis have been approached occasionally and cautiously. As a result, articles on these subjects may be found sprinkled through the library literature, but no cohesive and substantial body of data exists on the application of such techniques to libraries.

Our problem, then, is that although we now have corrected some of the basic inadequacies—for example, we now have a vast amount of data about the Library of Congress—we still have not advanced too far in our understanding of the basic needs of people who approach libraries for information. In this conference, as in others, we will spend much more time talking about the characteristics of library records than about the characteristics of their use or their users.

We therefore fall back on broad concepts and guidelines to aid us in developing the future system. We assume that: (1) present services to readers and other libraries must be continued or equivalent services provided; (2) new services must be provided and

new demands met; that is, the library must solve both the problems of influx of more materials and of the shortage of skilled, trained staff; (3) speed of processing and speed of response to requests for information must be improved; (4) libraries cannot assume that their costs can grow as fast as their rate of accretion of new materials and as the rate of increase of demands for service; and (5) libraries should reflect the technical achievements of the society of which they are a part by utilizing that technology as quickly and as skillfully as possible.

Goals

Our goal in system design is to make it appear to the user that the CBS is one immense data file. We would like to generalize and standardize, as nearly as possible, the techniques, computer formats and programs, and the equipment used in the system so that it is transferable, as appropriate, to other parts of the Library of Congress and to other libraries.

We are not overly optimistic that we can achieve all of these goals, but by building a variety of model systems, we can decide where we can begin to apply computers to the greatest benefit. The goals of the Library of Congress as well as any other library are complex and subtle. For example, the oft-stated goal of "the right book to the right reader at the right time" provides little that the systems analyst can get

TABLE VII

COMPARISON OF PRESENT SYSTEM WITH FUTURE LOADS AND DEMANDS

PARAMETER	FY 1965	FY 1972	FY 1980
Total receipts (pieces)	8.7 M[1]	9.7-11.5 M	13.2-19.6 M
Monographic titles for regular cataloging (duplicates excluded)	102 T[2]	157-300 T	253-629 T
Data on holdings of other libraries submitted to NUC	1.7 M	3.4 M	6.5 M
Total printed catalog cards sold	61 M	110-126 M	197-308 M
Total serial pieces processed	1.7 M	2.3-2.7 M	3.1-4.6 M
Descriptive cataloging authority cards established	50 T	157 T	335 T
Subject cataloging subject headings established	4 T	11 T	23 T
Filing Section (total cards filed all catalogs)	2 M	5.4-6.4 M	10.6-13.4 M
Growth of Official Catalog (total cards)	13.7 M	17.8 M	23.9 M
Total cards	40.3 M	54 M	71 M
Staff (total all funds)	3.4 T	5.7 T	7.2 T

[1] M = Million
[2] T = Thousand

his teeth into compared, for example, to a good clean statement such as, "We want to produce product **X** for this cost **Y**, and our long range goal is to drive the cost down to **Z**." Libraries do not want to lower cost if it means poorer data, bad service, and fewer books. However, they also do not want to provide services (for example, detailed analyses of their collections) if these services require an extremely high cost. All this really means is that the systems analyst can measure, quantify, and gather data, but the real choice in systems design will be made on the basis of this system information coupled with the librarians' knowledge of and judgment about the system, since the things which cannot be measured are equally important.

LC as a Total System

Although only the Central Bibliographic System has been described, that is not our only concern in Information Systems Office systems studies. We need to understand how the CBS system fits into the total information processes of the library. The CBS is considered to be a complex of certain manual and machine operations, but there could be several other systems in operation, e.g., a man/machine copyright system. These relationships are, however, only part of the total picture, because we need also to understand how the Library of Congress would function as the center of a national man/machine library system. This leads us to the still larger problems of how the Library system would relate to the broader national information system and to its role within international library networks.

Our attitude at this point might be considered that of a pessimistic optimist. Some things, we believe, can be greatly improved in library operations. We are beginning to understand not only the constraints of the computer system, but the constraints which manual operations force on us as well. We also recognize those problems which are probably beyond our control and know we must determine how best to come to terms with them. For example, librarians cannot really control the data entering the system—we do not allow catalogers to reject materials because they do not like the title page—and we must find a way to work any bibliographic entry, however incomplete or absurd, into the system. We recognize that the librarian and the patron are often in competition for file access and, in many cases, for the materials in the collection. Assignment of priorities may become difficult.

The solution of many of these problems may resist rigorous analysis and may rest on empirical evidence. However, there are many library operations to which the scientific method can be applied and, to the extent that time and money are available for such an analysis, the Library of Congress, as well as other libraries, should profit. It is quite clear that the benefits of the LC automation program will not be felt immediately since implementation of certain system modules may take years to accomplish. It is equally clear that the application of a systems approach—that

is, the persistent use of logic in the analysis of library operations, policies, and data bases—will yield results.

SUMMARY

From the developments noted in this paper, it is clear that automation has a major role in current Library of Congress programs. Work is under way, the results of which may influence each and every working librarian.

Many of the developments which may result from the LC system study may be transferable to other libraries, but many smaller libraries will find them too sophisticated or too costly to use directly. These libraries may have to develop their own systems, use service bureaus, or join regional groups. The experiences within the Library of Congress and in the field, however, should contribute to an increased understanding of the role automation will play during the next few decades.

These experiences will also be enhanced if each librarian will accept responsibility for keeping abreast of developments and offering comments and advice when he approves or disapproves of proposed features of the new Library of Congress system. Many improvements in existing operations and services have resulted from unsolicited as well as solicited comments, and librarians in the field are encouraged to view LC automation projects as something about which they have a right and duty to comment. Obviously, not all suggestions can be assimilated into the new system, but they might provide additional insight for the system designer and in some manner influence developments.

John Donne's statement that "no man is an island, entire of itself" is equally applicable to libraries. Even the largest library in the world is not self-sufficient; it has neither all the materials, the financial resources, nor the human talent required to solve all of the important library problems of our time. This lack of self-sufficiency among libraries will become more and more apparent as we try to provide enriched service to an increasingly educated and sophisticated clientele. The need for financial and human resources will be even more evident as librarians acquire and use complex machinery such as computers, on-line consoles, and photocomposers, and as they begin to convert huge data files. Cooperation among libraries in both the planning and execution of automation programs is mandatory. The Library of Congress is pursuing its own program in this light; progress may be slower, but the benefits will be surer.

DISCUSSION

FRED BELLAMY, the University of California, Santa Barbara: With over a thousand files at the Library of Congress, I can't help but suspect that you found one or two useless files. Was there any conscious attempt to try and clean up the existing systems during your studies?

MRS. MARKUSON: Not at this point. I think our goal would be to try to determine which ones are redundant information and to eliminate this duplication as speedily as possible, but this would be done as part of the total systems study and not on a piecemeal basis.

I'd like to make a plea to all of you to remember that, when we talk about cooperation—what other libraries want—and standardization, one of the first things that we do in the Information Systems Office is to try to find out what's going on, who knows what, who is working on a project. Today, sitting here, I heard many projects described, some of which I had not heard of, and I don't think we have a documentation about them in the LOCATE [Library of Congress Automation Techniques Exchange] file. This is an extremely useful file and I would like to invite all of you to spread the word around. You don't have to wait for an elaborate, pretty document from us to be interested in it; we would like working notes, formats, code sheets. If you don't want them shown to anyone else except us, we will honor any restriction you put on us. But this file is important both for historical reasons and for enabling us to locate libraries that would be interested in cooperating with us on a particular project. If you don't keep us aware, it's hard for us to know what you might be interested in.

APPENDIX 1
OUTLINE FOR DIVISIONAL REPORTS

I. Administrative Framework

> Where division fits into department and total library

II. Brief History

> Concentrate on reorganizations or major changes in scope, responsibilities, mode of operation, etc.

III. Present Administrative Structure of Division

> A. Organizational
> B. Functional

> Describe under A the sections, etc., and size of present staff
> Describe under B the functional responsibilities

IV. Products or Services Provided

> Describe products and attach samples
> Describe services and gather any pertinent reports, etc.

V. Problems

> A. In what respects does the division function well at the present time?
> B. What aspects of current operations provide difficulties?
> C. What are the crucial operations? How do bottlenecks arise?
> D. Will the next 10 years bring any major (unforeseen) changes?
> E. Are selection and training of staff crucial to operation?
> F. Has increased cost of staff and/or materials influenced operations?

VI. Legal Framework or Other Operating Constraints

VII. Suggestions for Improvements

> What does present administration see as areas needing most improvement?
> Where would money or talent be spent?

> Survey group comments

VIII. Areas for Further Study

IX. Appendixes

> Statistics   Flow Charts   Bibliography of any special
> Job Rolls   Studies   reports, studies, etc.
> Etc.

APPENDIX 2

DRAFT—POST-1951 IMPRINTS SECTION SEARCHING UNIT PROCEDURES FOR NEWLY RECEIVED OUTSIDE-LIBRARY REPORTS

Notes

<u>Block</u>

4-7   The supervisor or assistant of the Searching Unit examines each pack of outside-library reports which has been searched. The following basic operations may occur: The reviser may transfer a slip that the searcher has placed in the "not found" category to the "exclude" category due to oversight, unfamiliarity with some of the intricacies of catalog data, level of training attained, etc., on the part of the searcher. Some of the "excludes" may have been excluded by mistake and should be searched. These sorts of decisions are made for each slip by the reviser as a control on the work of the searchers. Mistakes that recur are corrected with the searchers to give them feedback and increase their competence. Items which matched an entry in the file ("founds") are revised only for trainees.

13   The searcher's accuracy and completeness in annotating the outside-library report data is carefully checked by the reviser for consistency and compliance with instructions. (The symbols to be used to annotate the slips in the search process are listed on page 3 of Appendix IV to this flow chart.) [Not part of this paper.]

14   The added entries and cross references that may have been traced on the outside-library report slip are not all searched by the searchers in the Control File. Subject added entries are never searched, as the Control File does not contain subject entries. Other secondary entries (added entries for editors, joint authors, title added entries, etc.) are not searched unless there is no match found under the outside-library's main entry heading. If the added-entry headings recorded on the outside-library slip have been used as search leads, they must be properly marked with the annotation symbols stipulated in Appendix IV of the flow chart. [Not part of this paper.]

15   The reviser also checks the cross references recommended by the searcher or that he has flagged as containing conflicts. The reviser may direct a repeat search if the problem is not clear or if an obvious mistake has been made. Otherwise, the conflict will have to be resolved by the Catalog Editorial Group (Section Head) staff.

(Appendix 2)

SAMPLE OF FLOW CHART, SEARCH UNIT,
CATALOG MAINTENANCE AND CATALOG PUBLICATION DIVISION

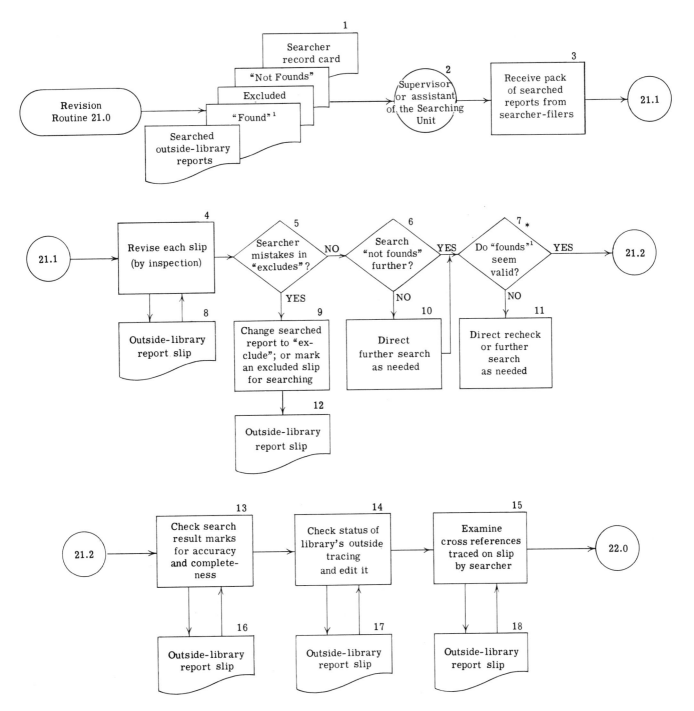

¹"Found" items are reviewed only for trainee-searchers. Normally, they are sent directly
to the NUC Unit.

(Appendix 2)

```
987
B68Z
A69      Arias, Juan de Dios.
            Simón Bolívar.  Bucaramanga, Colombia,
         Imprenta del Departamento, 1964.
            272 p.  21cm.




            1. Bolívar, Simón, 1783-1830

FARMINGTON • AzU
```

```
            Arias, Juan de Dios
CF2235.3    Simón Bolívar.  Bucaramanga [Colombia] Impr.
A73         del Departamento, 1964.
               272 p.  22 cm.



               1. Bolívar, Simón, 1783-1830.
            CDU  LA
```

12-1-65

Arias, Juan de Dios.
Simón Bolívar.
Bucaramanga [Colombia]
1964   272p

CLU

Example of outside-library report slips (top two cards) which Searching Unit of Post-1951 Imprints Section has treated as "founds"; that is, the two top entries are a bibliographic match of the blue-colored temporary card, which had arrived first in the Control File. In accordance with searcher's procedure, the top two cards are clipped to the temporary card, in anticipation of the "refile" of the original outside-library report slip which the temporary card represents.

APPENDIX 3

SAMPLE DATA-COLLECTION FORM FOR FILE CENSUS

LIBRARY OF CONGRESS

FILES CENSUS

Division where located: Exchange and Gift   Processing Dept.

No.	Section/Unit	Name of file	Cds.	Corres.	Visi. File	Other (flex)	Purpose; comments (stress type of card); gross size
	All Exch's	Files contained in each Exchange Section (AFR./Asian, Hispanic, British, European (3), American, Intl. Org. Sections					
1		Correspondence (8 files)		X			By exchange agreement No., within No. by date (exception for American in that filing is alphabetical by correspondent (Total: 193 Drawers)
2		Country File (6 files)					Used for corres. with agencies with which no exchange has been established. Filed alphabetically by country; then by institution and individual (Total: 7 Drawers)
3		Chronological Correspondence (4 files)					Used when correspondence does not give exchange No. Kept for five years. American and British together with I/O. (Total: 7 Drawers)
4		Card File (7 files)	X				Index to correspondence file exchange agreement address card. Alphabetically by country, then by city or province. Ordered by exchange agreement No. (None for American section) (Total: 46 trays)
5		Outstanding Request File (8 files)	X			3x5 slip	Carbon copy of exchange request. Two parts: one by date, one by exchange No. (American is alphabetically by institution and date) used for claiming materials. (1-2 trays) Several types of slip, cards, etc. (Total: 9 trays)
6		Mailing List (4 files)	X				Filed by title sent, then by country, city, county, institutions, (single file for American-British) also duplicated and ordered geographically first (Total: 8 trays)

(Appendix 3)

FILES SELECTED FOR CORE GROUP (Sheet 1 of 4)

File Groupings in RFP	Primary Files	Secondary Files
1. Acquisitions Control Files – Monographs	**Order Division** a. Outstanding P. R. File b. Cancelled P. R. File c. Paid P. R. File d. Blanket Order File **E & G Division** a. Outstanding Post – Confer. File b. Distribution Record c. Committee Report Distribution Record d. Priced Exchange Card File e. Outstanding Request File – Gift f. Outstanding Request Files – (All Sections) g. Correspondence Card File	**Order Division** Dealer Address File **E & G Division** a. Exchange Mailing List File b. Active Deposits Index c. Preprinting File for Yearly Index d. Card Index to Inactive Corresp. File **Shared Cataloging Division** a. English Language Master Control File b. English Language Acquisition Control File c. French Language Master Control File d. French Language Acquisition Control File e. German Language Master Control File f. German Language Acquisition Control File g. Scandinavian Languages "Merged Master Acquisition Control Files"
2. Acquisitions Control Files –Serials	**Order Division** a. Outstanding Continuations P. R. b. Continuations Master File for P. R.'s	**Order Division** a. Index to Continuations Orders

(Appendix 3)

FILES SELECTED FOR CORE GROUP (Sheet 2 of 4)

File Groupings in RFP	Primary Files	Secondary Files
	E & G Division	**E & G Division**
	Serials and Groups of Publications Received File	a. Catalog of Monographs and Serial Entries (1952 –) b. Mailing List (Serials) **Shared Cataloging Division** a. Series Files b. Serial Record Files
3. Central Serial Record	Serial Record (Visible File and 3 x 5 File and Sheaf Shelf List)*	
4. Process Information File	Process Information File	a. Title File (Prelim. Cat. Section) b. Subject Suspense File (Shared Cat. Div.)
5. Central Card Catalogs a. Official and Main Catalogs b. National Union Catalog	a. Official Catalog b. Main Catalog c. NUC Pre-1952 (Main) d. NUC Pre-1952 (Supplement) e. NUC 52-55 Supplement f. NUC Post 56 Control File g. Register of Additional Locations	a. NUC Post 56 Printing File b. Searching Catalog (Card Div.) c. Rare Book Div. Dictionary Catalog d. Serial Division Reading Room Catalog(s)
6. Card Catalog Authority File-Names	Included in Official Catalog (5. a. above)	
7. Card Catalog Authority File Subjects	Included in Official Catalog (5. a. above)	

(Appendix 3)

FILES SELECTED FOR CORE GROUP (Sheet 3 of 4)

File Groupings in RFP	Primary Files	Secondary Files
8. Subject Classification Authority Schedules	Subject Classification Authority Schedules (i.e., Official copies of Library classification schedules)	
9. Card Catalog (Shelflist)	Shelflist (cards and sheafs)	Rare Books Division Shelflist
10. Binding Files (Permanent)	a. Permanent Binding File b. Block Number File c. Block Assignment Record File d. Music C Quad File e. Russian Quarter – Bind File f. Permanent Blue Slip File g. Quarter – Binding File h. Russian Gaylord File i. Rebinding File j. Miscellaneous Blue Slip File k. Miscellaneous Binding Work (Blue Slips) File l. Block Summary Record (Special) File m. Current Special File n. Block Assignment List, GPO File o. Periodicals Bindings File (Serials Division)	

(Appendix 3)

FILES SELECTED FOR CORE GROUP (Sheet 4 of 4)

File Groupings in RFP	Primary Files	Secondary Files
	p. Government Publications Binding File (Serials Division)	
11. Central Charge File (Not-On-Shelf Record)	a. Central Charge File b. Library Employees and Special Borrowers Account	
12. Loan Files (Out-Of-Building Control)	a. Interlibrary Loan File b. Government Borrowers Account c. Congressional Borrowers Account	

(Appendix 4)

SAMPLE DATA FORM

ANALYSIS OF FILES

_____
Organizational Unit (Section/Unit)

_____
Name of File

1. Description
   a. Contents and organization

NAME OF RECORD (eg. Prelim. Card)	ORG. OF FILE	RECORD ORIGINATOR	DETAILED ANAL REQD(x)

   b. Purpose:

   c. Type of record: Card___, Corresp.___, Visifile___, Other_____
   d. Physical location:

2. Size
   a. Tray-count:
   b. Estimated total number of records:
   c. Record length in characters(range:ave)
   d. Approx space currently used: Floor area _____, Height _____

(Appendix 4)

3. Activity
    a. File Maintenance
        (1) Responsibility
        (2) No. of personnel
    b. Annual activity rates: No. entries added_____
                               No. entries deleted_____
                               No. entries corrected or revised_____

    _____

    c. Use of files (include other groups)
        TYPE OF USER   HOURLY   DAILY   WEEKLY

4. Problems in file use or maintenance:

5. Problems in conversion to machine readable form:
    a. Est. of percentage of records in non Roman alphabet
        Small_____, Significant _____, Large _____
    b. Other problems:

6. Should file be changed?
    a. What items added
    b. What items deleted
    c. Other changes

Continued on following page

(Appendix 4)

7. Relationship of file to other files

8. Remarks

FILE CONTENT ANALYSIS

Organization Unit (Section/Unit)
_____

Name of File
_____

NAME OF RECORD	LIST OF DATA ELEMENTS	LANGUAGE	ELEMENTS USED (x)	SEARCH ENTRY

APPENDIX 4A

SAMPLE COMPLETED FORM, SHELF LIST

SUBJECT CATALOGING DIVISION
BOOK CONTROL AND PREPARATION SECTION
CLASSIFICATION RECORD UNIT
           Organizational Unit (Section/Unit)

SHELF LIST
     Name of File

1. Description

    a. Contents and organization

NAME OF RECORD (eg. Prelim. Card)	ORG. OF FILE	RECORD ORIGINATOR	DETAILED ANAL. REQD(X)
(1) Preliminary cards	Shelf list order	Shelflister	
(2) L.C. printed cards	(Some sub series	(trainee GS-5;	
(3) Typewritten cards	arranged alpha-	GS-6,7,8)	
(4) Manuscript cards (hand written)	betically by author within		
(5) Photocopied manuscript cards	one classification number: example,		
(6) Mimeographed cards	JX 1977.A2)		
(7) Guide cards (pasted sections of classified schedules)			
(8) Call number change cards			
(9) Form cards			
(10) Classification numbers cross references			
(11) Continuation cards (from L.C. 68-1a)			
(12) Priority 4 entries (multilithed)			
(13) Handwritten entries on sheets			

    b. Purpose: (1) Classified arrangement
                  (2) Complete inventory of holdings
                  (3) Records all copies including duplicates
                  (4) Records Assignments
                  (5) Shows holdings for open entries
    c. Type of record: Card X, Corresp._____, Visifile _____, Other Sheets
    d. Physical location:
            Deck 7 S.W.

2. Size
    a. Tray-count: 4,440 card trays; 2,400 volumes of sheets
    b. Estimated total number of records: 4,440,000 cards; 1,440,000 entries on sheets
                                estimated on basis of 3 entries on page, 200 pages
                                per volume.
        Record length in characters (range: avg) 82-270; average 156
        Approx. space currently used: Floor area 296 sq. ft.   Height 5'5" (cards)
                                                   128 "   "   6'6" (sheets)

Continued on following page

(Appendix 4A)

SUBJECT CATALOGING DIVISION
SHELF LIST

3. Activity
    a. File Maintenance
        (1) Responsibility Shelflisters
        (2) No. of personnel 51 total (Shelflisters grades 5-8,44; reviewers & super-
                 visors grades 9-11,7)
    b. Annual activity rates: No. entries added   127.8K (FY 1966)
                               No. entries deleted
     volumes re-shelflisting: No. entries corrected or revised 18.9K$^+$
             13K   Conversion from sheet shelf list: 16K
                             + adapting prelim cards to L C printed cards

    c. Use of files (include other groups)
        TYPE OF USER   HOURLY   DAILY   WEEKLY
        Almost any member of   Used
        library staff may have   extremely
        occasion to consult this   frequently.
        file, and many use it
        very frequently.

4. Problems in file use or maintenance:
    (1) Average of cards to be adapt to L.C. printed cards: 812.7K (FY 1966)
    (2) Human error (misfiling)

5. Problems in conversion to machine readable form:
    a. Est. of percentage of records in non Roman alphabet
        Small_____, Significant__X *__, Large_____
    b. Other problems: Roman numerals

6. Should file be changed:
    a   What items added
    b. What items deleted - no particular reason to delete unnecessary date on L.C. card
    c. Other changes   if contained in automated file.

7. Relationship of file to other files
    Duplicates information in official and public catalogs, but has different
        arrangement (other access) and includes unique information (holdings, etc.)

8. Remarks
        Many items of data on preliminary cards and L.C. printed cards are not essential
        for shelflisting# , but are nevertheless helpful if already available. Items
        needed are: author, title, edition statement, place and date of publication,
        pagination, size, series note, "imperfect", "bound with", thesis statement,
        "errata slip". (all of these from printed card).

* and increasing as a result of title II and P. L. 480; presently about 25% non-Roman.

e.g., tracings; publisher

(Appendix 4A)

Subject Cataloging Division
Book Control and Preparation Section
Classification Record Unit
Organizational Unit   (Section/Unit)

Shelf List
Name of File

NAME OF RECORD	LIST OF DATA ELEMENTS	LANGUAGE	ELEMENTS USED (X)	SEARCH ENTRY
Shelf list entry	unbound, date of shelflisting, added copies, holdings for open entries, assignments, filing titles,	can be any language, but filing words always Romanized		Classification Number **or** **Call Number**

"bound with",   ")
"imperfect",   } *
edition statement   }

on lower left hand
of preliminary card
source: e.g.   Cpf = foreign copyright
               ad -= acquisition donation (gift)
               adco =   "   "   copyright copy
                                                 expected
               apco =   "   purchase "   "   } #
               ag =   "   government
               ax   "   exchange

date typed & typist's initials "unbound"

* Elements necessary for shelflisting
\# elements useful to shelflisting

APPENDIX 5

ANALYSIS OF FUNCTIONS

1. Data Concerning Functions (No. transactions per year)

Organizational Unit _____

Item No.	Function	No. pers perf funct	Title and Av GS Level	Capacity per person	Input(s) Type	Load (items/yr)	Funct Trans items/yr	Output(s) Type	Load (items/yr)
50	51	52	53	54	55	56	57			

2. Size of Arrearage

Size of Arrearage [specify units (e.g. uncataloged monographs) |

Item No.	Function	Arrearage Prior to 1949	58	59	60	61	62	63	64	65	66

(Appendix 5)

3. Growth Information

   a. No. people (by GS rating)

      _____
      _____
      _____
      _____

   b. Space (square ft)

   c. Facilities – dollars
      (other than office)

   d. Activity Statistics

4. Effect of Title II on Function   (List other significant programs if applicable)

5. Critical skills needed

6. Output Products

   a. Publications
      (1) Name
      (2) Identification Number
      (3) No. copies per printing
      (4) Frequency of publication
      (5) Est size: No. pages _____, Av No. records per page _____
      (6) Growth rate: Est increase per year

Continued on following page

(Appendix 5)

b. Reports
   (1) Type
   (2) Purpose
   (3) Frequency
   (4) General Content
   (5) Sources of information
   (6) Distribution
   (7) No. pages per report

c. Other

7. <u>Function – File Relationships</u>

			Est File Use per Transaction		Response Time Required					
Item No.	Function	File Used	No. Accesses	Av No. records access	Immed	Hrly	Overnight	Weekly	Monthly	Other
			50 51 52	53 54 55	56 57	58 59	60 61	62 63	64 65	66

8. <u>Trend Data on Functions</u> (if available)

Item No.	Function	Number of Transactions per Year
		1949 50

APPENDIX 5A

ANALYSIS OF FUNCTIONS, FILING SECTION,
CATALOG MAINTENANCE, AND CATALOG PUBLICATION DIVISION
(Simplified Diagram)

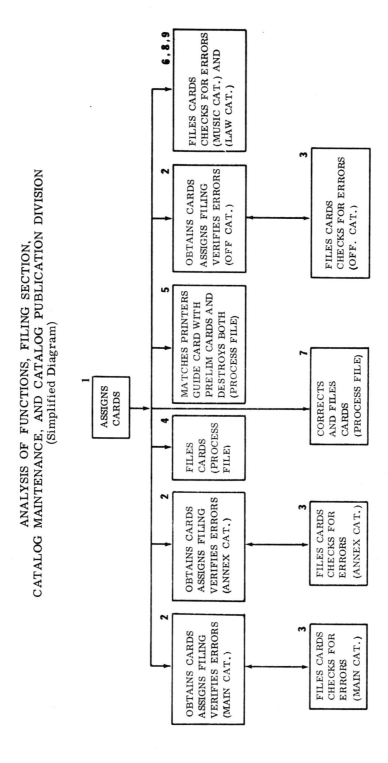

ANALYSIS OF FUNCTIONS

(Appendix 5A)

Catalog Maintenance and
Catalog Publication Division

Filing Section
Organizational Unit

1. Data Concerning Functions (No. transactions per year)

Item No.	Function	No. Pers. Perf. Funct.#	Title and Av. GS Level	Capacity per Person	Input(s) Type	Load (items/yr)	Funct. Trans. items/yr	Output(s) Type	Load (items/yr)
1	Assigns cards (this basically involves only logging no. of cards received. Section head spends most of his time on administrative duties)	.1	Filing Section Head-GS-10	22980 k	All cards	2298 k	2298k	All Cards	2298 k
2	Distributes cards to filers (this takes little time- most of supervisor time spent in verifying errors, training etc.)	.15 (.05 per person)	Main Catalog Annex Catalog and Official Catalog Supervisors GS-7		Main Cat. Cards Annex Cat. Cards Official Cat. Cards Process File Cards	595 k 544 k 735 k 424 k 2,298 k	595 k 544 k 735 k 424 k 2,298	Same	595 k 544 k 735 k 424 k 2,298 k
3	Files cards (in the 3 main catalogs)	6 (Main) 4.5 (Annex) 7 (Official)	Filers GS-6 (Trainee-GS-5)	About 53-54 per hour. slightly faster in Official since no rods in trays (Standards are 75-85 per hour)	Main Cat. Cards Annex Cat. Cards Official Cat. Cards				570 k 506 k 696 k
4	Files cards in Process Info. File	2	Filers GS-6	About 120 per hour	Prelim cards and Order cards	425 k	425 k		425 k

#Equivalent full time persons.

(Appendix 5A)

ANALYSIS OF FUNCTIONS (Cont.)

Catalog Maintenance and
Catalog Publication Division

Filing Section
Organizational Unit

1. Data Concerning Functions (No. transactions per year)

Item No.	Function	No. Pers. Perf. Funct.#	Title and Av. GS Level	Capacity per Person	Input(s) Type	Input(s) Load (items/yr)	Funct. Trans. items/yr	Output(s) Type	Output(s) Load (items/yr)
5	Matches new printed cards with Prelim Card in Process File and destroys	.4 (rough estimate)	PIF Investigator GS-7	125 per hour (rough estimate)	this procedure has just been started and is done on an available time basis. Probably will have to remove a slightly smaller number than total cards printed	about 100 k			
6	Files cards in Music Files (also has total responsibility for these catalogs)	1	Music Catalog Filer GS-7	48 per hour (this figure includes correction routines etc.)	Music Cards	86 k	86 k	Music Cards	86 k
7	Corrects and cancels preliminary cards	.3	PIF Investigator	24 per hour	Prelim Cards	13 k	13 k	Prelim Cards	13 k
8	Files cards in Law catalogs (total responsibility for these catalogs)	1.5	Law Catalog Filer-GS-7 (one GS-6 detailed half time)	17 per hour (this figure includes correction routines etc.)	All Cards	61 k	45 k	All Cards	45 k
9	Files in other special catalogs	.5 (rough estimate)	Filer GS-6 (detailed)	About 53 per hour (rough estimate)	Cards	47 k	47 k		47 k

#Equivalent full time persons.

Continued on following page

ANALYSIS OF FUNCTIONS (Cont.)

(Appendix 5A)

Catalog Maintenance and
Catalog Publication Division

Filing Section
Organizational Unit

2. Size of Arrearage

Size of Arrearage (specify units (e.g. uncataloged monographs))

Item No.	Function	Arrearage Prior to 1949	50	51	52	53	54	55	56	57	58	59	60	61	62	63	64	65	66
3	Files in Main Catalog							1 k	16 k	30 k		17 k	71 k	52 k	17 k	12 k	24 k	36 k	61 k
3	Files in Annex Cat.							121 k*	29 k*	29 k*		20 k*	44 k*	52 k*	21 k*	14 k*	23 k*	36 k*	74 k*
3	Files in Official Cat.							7 k	15 k	27 k		26 k	50 k	72 k	29 k	10 k	27 k	42 k	81 k
6	Files in Music (and Law beg. 1965)							4 k	1 k	1 k		1 k	2 k	1 k			1 k	7 k	
4	Files in PIF																	3 k	20 k**
	Total		10 k	130 k	38 k	105 k	107 k	134 k	61 k	88 k	71 k	64 k	167 k	177 k	68 k	36 k	75 k	122 k	216 k

* Does not include 1939-47 arrearage of 324,000
** Rough estimate

3. Effect of Title II on Function (List other significant programs if applicable)

Nine additional filers and 1 assistant section head requested for fiscal 1968

ANALYSIS OF FUNCTIONS *(Cont.)*

Catalog Maintenance and
Catalog Publication Division

Filing Section
Organizational Unit

(Appendix 5A)

4. Function - File Relationships

Item No.	Function	File Used	Est File Use per Transaction — No. Accesses	Est File Use per Transaction — Av. No. records access

(self survey - to be planned)

5. Trend Data on Functions (if available)

Item No.	Function	1949	50	51	52	53	54	55	56	57	58	59	60	61	62	63	64	65	66
3	Files - Main Catalog		347 k	343 k	337 k	346 k	372 k	376 k	375 k	374 k	403 k	399 k	329 k	383 k	408 k	417 k	440 k	487 k	570 k
3	Files - Annex Catalog		381 k	253 k	360 k	298 k	288 k	304 k	446 k	352 k	368 k	354 k	322 k	319 k	352 k	379 k	399 k	442 k	506 k
4	Files - Process Info. File		258 k	242 k	254 k	225 k	223 k	221 k	211 k	203 k	198 k	200 k	177 k	181 k	187 k	182 k	269 k	361 k	426 k
3	Files - Official		407 k	372 k	415 k	423 k	426 k	454 k	463 k	456 k	509 k	480 k	467 k	463 k	497 k	529 k	532 k	605 k	696 k
6	Files - Music		133 k	71 k	82 k	112 k	94 k	100 k	89 k	82 k	61 k	70 k	75 k	74 k	63 k	85 k	68 k	92 k	86 k
8	Files - Law																34* k	37 k	
	Files - Other												29 k	45 k	49 k	26 k	26 k	25 k	
	Total		1526 k	1281 k	1449 k	1404 k	1402 k	1455 k	1585 k	1467 k	1538 k	1503 k	1371 k	1464 k	1556 k	1618 k	1768 k*	2049 k	2198

* Filing Section took over filing in Law Library Catalog in November 1963

Continued on following page

(Appendix 5A)

ANALYSIS OF FUNCTIONS (Cont.)

Catalog Maintenance and Catalog Publication Division

Filing Section
Organizational Unit

	1949	50	51	52	53	54	55	56	57	58	59	60	61	62	63	64	65	66
6. Section Growth Information																		
a. No. people (by GS rating)																		
GS-10																		1
GS-7																		9
GS-6																		15
GS-5																		8
Total																		33
b. Space (square ft)																		
c. Facilities - dollars (other than office)																		
d. Activity Statistics																		

7. Critical skills needed   Posting asks for 2 years of college and 2 foreign languages; probably they sometimes take people with fewer languages or less education.

APPENDIX 6

HIGHER-LEVEL FLOW CHART
(A Portion of the Flow Chart for the Recording Section,
Serial Record Division)

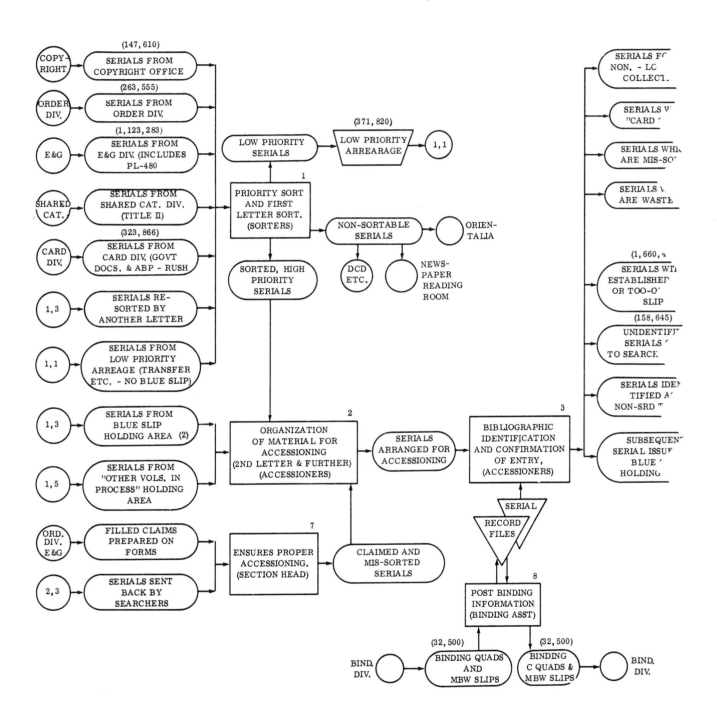

APPENDIX 7

DATA ELEMENTS

INFORMATION CATEGORIES (BIBLIOGRAPHIC ONLY)

ITEM NO.	INDICATOR	NAME
1	*	Main entry
2	*	Title statement
3	*	Place of publication
4	*	Publisher
5	*	Edition statement
6	*	Publication date
7	*	Series information
8		Author statement
9	*	Notes concerning bibliographical information
10	*	Number of pages or volumes
11	*	Dashed-on entries
12	*	Transliteration of title
13	*	Conventional title
14	*	Frequency of publication
15		Serial issue identifiers
16	*	LC call number
17	*	Tracings, subject
18	*	Tracings, cross-reference
19	*	Tracings, series
20	*	Tracings, nonsubject
21	*	Holdings
22	*	Illustration statement
23		Form of material designator
24		Date of beginning issue
25		LC card number
26		Cataloging treatment
27		Vernacular information
28		Price of item
29		Retention/acquisition decision
30		Language
31		Size of item
32		Outside library symbol and other identifier
33		Activity/inactivity indicator
34	*	Copy or set statement
35		Date of ending issue
36		Copyright status
37		Bibliographic annotation
38		LC ownership indicator
39		Bibliography number or other identification
40		Disposition of material not kept for LC
41		PL 480 number
42		Physical condition
43		Revised/edited indicator
44	*	Dewey decimal number
45		Page numbers of article in bibliographic citation
46		"In" analytic statement
47		NUC card number

* Indicates data can exist in raw or standardized form.

(Appendix 7)
INFORMATION CATEGORIES (NONBIBLIOGRAPHIC ONLY)

ITEM NO.	NAME	+	M	X
1	Special procedural instructions & control information handling; does not include control		M	
2	Date of transaction		M	
3	Priority treatment instructions		M	
4	Status indicator		M	
5	Source of information		M	
6	Addressor		M	
7	Custodial assignment, unbound	+		
8	Number of items needed		M	
9	Custodial assignment, bound	+		
10	Acquisition source, external			X
11	LC staff I.D. indicator		M	
12	Searched items relationship to system	+		
13	Period covered by serial issue	+		
14	Addressee		M	
15	Acquisition source, internal			X
16	Number of items received		M	
17	Price, estimated of item			X
18	Location in LC	+		
19	Biographical or background information			X
20	Routing information, internal		M	
21	Reason for action		M	
22	Record withdrawn notice	+		
23	Acquisition type indicator			X
24	Indication of gap in holdings			X
25	Cross reference between files		M	
26	Exchange indicator			X
27	First issue of serial received in LC			X
28	Date subscription ends			X
29	Date subscription begins			X
30	Identification control number		M	
31	Due date		M	
32	Title page and index information concerning			X
33	Claims outstanding indicator			X
34	Spine title			X
35	Subappropriation			X
36	Appropriation			X
37	Estimated U.S. dollars			X
38	LC classification number			X
39	Suballotment			X
40	LC card series			X
41	Data error indicator		M	
42	Allotment			X
43	Costs			X
44	Binding block & item number			X
45	Series/subseries indicator			X
46	Replacement orders outstanding indicator			X
47	Year of last receipt of discard item			X
48	Alphabetics & character set			X
49	Date of book catalog containing entry			X
50	Actual price			X
51	Subscriber identifier			X
52	Next available control number			X
53	No. of physical vols. bound			X
54	Outside library cataloging source			X
55	Amount to liquidate			X
56	Binding type			X
57	Color			X
58	Catalog identifier			X
59	Special characteristics of item			X
	TOTALS	6	16	37

+ - Widely used like most items on bibliographic list
M - In general, the category has a different definition when used in different divisions
X - Seldom used in more than a few divisions or types of activity. (e.g., cataloging)

APPENDIX 8

PORTION OF A DATA ELEMENT MATRIX

Legend:

\# - WIDELY USED LIKE MOST ITEMS ON BIBLIOGRAPHIC LIST (TABLE C-III)

M - IN GENERAL, THE CATEGORY HAS A DIFFERENT DEFINITION WHEN USED IN DIFFERENT DIVISIONS

X - SELDOM USED IN MORE THAN A FEW DIVISIONS OR TYPES OF ACTIVITY (EG, CATALOGING)

Data elements:

1 SPEC PROC INSTS & CONTR INFO
2 DATE OF TRANSACTION
3 PRIORITY TREATMENT INSTRUCTIONS
4 STATUS INDICATOR
5 SOURCE OF INFORMATION
6 ADDRESSOR
7 CUSTODIAL ASSIGNMENT-UNBOUND
8 NUMBER OF ITEMS NEEDED
9 CUSTODIAL ASSIGNMENT-BOUND
10 ACQUISITION SOURCE-EXTERNAL
11 LC STAFF ID INDICATOR
12 SEARCHED ITEMS RELATIONSHIP TO SYSTEM
13 PERIOD COVERED BY SERIAL ISSUE
14 ADDRESSEE
15 ACQUISITION SOURCE-INTERNAL
16 NUMBER OF ITEMS RECEIVED
17 PRICE-ESTIMATED OF ITEM

Task list:

OD-1-1	SCREEN REQUESTS
-2	DISTRIBUTE REQUESTS FOR MONOGRAPHS & SERIALS
-3	SEARCH SERIALS & MONOGRAPHS (REG BL ORD, TITLE II)
-4	GENERATE ORDER CONTROL DATA (PURCH REQ)
-5	PREPARE BIBLIOFAX ORDER FORMS
-6	PREPARE VARIOUS ORDER FORMS, HUMP CARDS, ETC
-7	REVIEW OF ORDERS
OD-2-8	APPROVAL OF SELECTIONS
9	FILE MAINTENANCE
OD-3-10	REVIEW DATA PROCESSING OFFICE LISTINGS
-11	ORIGINATE CANCELLATION NOTICE FORMS (CONTINUATIONS)
-12	MAILING OPERATIONS
OD-4-13	INVOICE CONTROL
-2	BATCH INV (MONOS) W/(PREQ, BL ORDS & TITLE II PR CARDS)
-3	BIBLIOGRAPHIC VERIFICATION (MONOGRAPHS)
-4	INVOICE EXAMINING (MONOGRAPHS)
-5	CLEAR PURCHASE REQUESTS (SERIALS)
-6	BEGIN INVOICE CLEARING & REVIEW (SERIALS)
OD-5-7	SERIAL CLAIMING & FOLLOW-UP
-8	INVOICE EXAMINING (SERIALS)
-9	CERTIFY INVOICE (MONOGRAPHS & SERIALS)
-10	COMPLETE INVOICE CLEARING; REVIEW DP OFFICE VOUCH LIST
-11	FILE MAINT & CLEARING (MONOGRAPHS & SERIALS)
-12	MAILING OPERATION
-13	REC REQ FOR MATL EVAL; PERFORM EVAL; PREP RESP
E&G-1-1	RECEIVE LC REQUESTS FOR E&G PROCUREMENT
-2	RECEIVE & DISTRIBUTE REQUESTS & OFFERS FOR E&G MATL
-3	BIBLIOGRAPHIC SEARCH
-4	OPERATIONAL SEARCH
-5	REQUEST LC DESIRED ITEMS UNDER TERMS OF AGREEMENTS
-6	PREPARE FORM CORRES IN REPLY TO REQUESTS, QUERIES, ETC
E&G-2-7	PREP OF NEGOTIATION CORR FOR E&G AGREEMENT
-8	PART IN PREP REVIEW & APPR OF REQ & NEG CORRES
E&G-3-9	ESTABLISH OR UPDATE E&G RECORDS
-10	PREPARE MATL & TRANSM CORR FOR FORW TO EX & POT PARTS
-11	FORWARD OUTGOING MATERIAL
-12	SELECT DUPS & TRANSF MATL & SET ASIDE FOR EXAM
-13	EXAMINE DUPLICATE MATL FOR POSS USE IN EXCHANGE
-14	MONITOR STATUS OF REQ & SEARCH FILES FOR OVERDUE REQ
-15	PURGE OUTSTANDING REQUESTS
-16	RE-REQUEST FROM SAME SOURCE; CONS PURCH; ABAND ATT
E&G-4-17	RECEIVE, SORT & DISTRIBUTE INC NON-PURCH, NON-GIFT MATL
-18	OPEN PACKAGES & ACKNOWLEDGE RECEIPT IF NECESSARY

Division headings (right margin):

Order Prep Rec & Clear'g — ORDER

Exchange & Gift S — EXCHA

Automated Serials Systems in Perspective

Bruce W. Stewart

Data Processing Supervisor
Texas Agricultural and Mechanical
University Library

The concept of applying data processing techniques to serials began to attract attention as early as 1949 when punched-card records were used in serials acquisition at the University of Texas Library. Since that time, punched-card equipment and computers have been applied in increasingly sophisticated ways in an effort to improve performance in processing serials.

While a great deal of work has been done in this area, the total number of existing computer-based serials systems is still very small compared to the total number of libraries. Most of the early pioneering systems are still operating, and a few have already been reconverted to make use of more modern computer hardware. There is a growing pool of common experience with operation of serials computer operations. Serials automation is still in its infancy, however, and no existing system operates to the complete satisfaction of its designers. "I would have done it differently if I knew then what I know now" is almost a basic axiom of systems analysts.

It should be noted that in every case of an operational system in a library, four basic developmental parameters are always found to be present. These parameters are:

1. Access to computer or data processing equipment
2. Availability of funds
3. Availability of technical knowledge
4. Interest and awareness on the part of both library and computer people.

It is beyond the scope of this paper to expand these points, which are reasonably self-explanatory; it is sufficient to emphasize that the lack of even one of these basic parameters will normally result in a severely constrained operation and possible complete discontinuance.

HISTORICAL CONTEXT

Computerized serial systems have developed side by side with advances in computer technology. Historically, data processing techniques were developed to accommodate what was considered a basic machine limitation. This limitation was the necessity for conserving internal storage processing time whenever possible. This concept dates from the early years of small computer and unit record equipment systems, when the relatively slow internal operating speeds and slow access to mass storage dictated heavy coding and extreme abbreviation in any application involving extensive computer processing. The resulting systems were oriented to accommodate the machines involved and not the people who must ultimately handle and analyze the information produced. Much of the criticism leveled at the pioneering systems was, in fact, leveled at extremely abbreviated titles, severely coded or truncated data, and other concessions to accepted data processing techniques.

The development and current sophistication of computer hardware now allows design of data processing systems which are concerned almost solely with the needs of the library staff and the patrons who will use the system. It is therefore the performance of the automated serials system as a whole, and not the efficiency of internal machine processing, which must be viewed as the paramount criterion.

The development of computer-based serials systems has also been influenced by the needs of particular types of libraries. Examples of computer techniques applied to serials in public libraries are almost nonexistent, probably due largely to the severe lack of the required developmental parameters.

Special libraries with their highly restricted clientele, often governed by needs set down by some parent organization, have historically been among the first to adopt computer systems for journal control. They have placed particular emphasis on current-receipt notification services for their specialized group of users. The small size of the serials collection in a special library seems to be a factor which has contributed to the relatively large number of successful operating systems. Early industrial applications of computers provided special librarians with readily available technical help as well as with hardware to do the job. A climate in which experimentation was commonplace and in which expenditures for research were a regular part of the budget also contributed.

In research and academic libraries, progress in applying computers to serials control has been much slower. The growing problems faced in daily routine operation of manual systems, however, have convinced many librarians that the flexibility of computer processing offers the only hope for real solutions. Beginning in 1960, several individual academic and research libraries which found themselves in a favorable environment began developmental work in this area. It is on these efforts that most existing systems are modeled.

Currently operating computerized serials systems may be characterized as one of three types:

1. Listing systems
2. Control systems
3. Combination systems.

The large majority of the operating systems are listing or report-generating systems. This is not to imply that they are simple systems. This implies, rather, that the primary processing involved is manipulation of stored data to produce various listings or reports. These listings are used by the library staff and by the library patrons. In a typical listing system, the sole or primary output intended is a title list, union list, or shelf list. One of these listings compiled by the computer may of course be used by the technical services staff to make administrative decisions which control the serials operation.

It is useful at this point to make a clear distinction between mechanization and automation. Mechanization is the process of replacing one or more individuals with a machine procedure that does the job essentially the same way. Automation, however, may be characterized as developing completely new solutions to the tasks, utilizing the speed and power of computers in the most efficient manner. While the library community is obviously in a less than embryonic state in development of truly automated systems, serial *control* systems, as opposed to listing operations, are a step closer to true automation.

The third type, the combination system, results from the fact that it is always possible to produce any desired listings as by-products of a control system. All operational control systems embody pure listing and report programs as a subset.

It is interesting to observe that many systems initially proposed as control systems became operational as pure listing systems. The sophistication of programming and complexity of operation of a control type system requires a commitment in programming effort, cost, and computer capability which far exceeds the pure listing system.

OPERATING PARAMETERS

In any discussion of computer applications in the serials area, some common operating parameters are apparent. This paper will discuss four of these: (1) Filing Method, (2) Timing Cycles, (3) Operating Philosophy, and (4) Coding Requirements. These particular parameters are significant because of the basic design considerations they introduce. Most computerized serials systems embody distinctly unique features, influenced by these parameters.

Filing Method

The problem of instructing a computer system so that it will automatically maintain a filing sequence which is in accordance with American Library Association filing rules has been almost insurmountable. The complexity of the programming necessary to achieve even a semblance of correct filing order has ruled out most efforts in the past which involved small, limited-capacity computer systems.

The method which has evolved achieves proper filing order "outside the machine" by manual assignment of a numeric sequencing number for each entry. Interfiling of new entries is achieved by leaving some arbitrary interval between each initially assigned number. One advantage of this method is that the sequencing number is available as the necessary, unique identifying factor required for computer processing.

One encouraging recent development is the advent of fairly sophisticated programming efforts involving large computers. These efforts are meeting with surprising success in developing computer filing systems which require only slight compromises in accepted filing rules. Future development of these efforts holds great promise.

Timing Cycles

A cycle is the time period from one computer processing run to the next. Computerized serials systems universally operate in cycles, for several reasons. Libraries ordinarily have access to a computer facility, usually through their host organizations, for only limited periods of time. Various inputs for computer processing normally must be held and batched until a regular run. Computer technology has not, until very recently, been able to provide remote-access capability to users on any feasible basis. This necessity for "batching" input for cyclic operation has long been a major constraint in the design of computer systems. The advent of feasible remote access on a real-time basis probably holds the most promise for future design improvements.

The operating cycle adopted by most existing systems is a monthly updating and reporting cycle, with alternate daily and weekly runs. The number of regular and special runs is usually a factor of policy decision, economic considerations, and the amount of computer time available for library processing.

Operating Philosophy

Computerized serials systems operate on the "exception principle." This is an operating procedure under which the computer handles routine tasks as much as possible, and only exceptions to this normal routine operation require attention or decision by staff personnel. This operating principle is basic to any data processing system and is the major method of increasing efficiency of operations in a computer environment.

This concept is implemented to a greater or lesser degree in all existing systems. Problems arise, however, because of the many variables and the lack of consistency inherent in any serials operation; it is almost impossible to plan in advance for all possible variations, because of the large numbers of serials. This problem is very critical in a computer system where consistency and uniformity become most important.

Coding Requirements

The severity of coding of information for a computerized serials system is a major factor affecting both design and operation. Existing systems range from the severe coding and truncated titles of the early pioneering systems to the entry of full bibliographic information in completely retrievable form.

The necessity of answering internal storage and processing time is not now as critical as it was with early small computer systems. The efficiency of handling abbreviated information within the computer must be weighted against the clerical effort required to code and decode information as it is used in day-to-day operations. Experience with existing systems indicates this is not a trivial amount of effort.

It is encouraging to note that current systems under development tend to incorporate features which alleviate the problems involved in coding effort. The tremendous speed and power of new computers foster design of systems which are divided into two subsystems: a clerical system and a computer system. Input of information and data-handling procedures are designed to accommodate staff personnel, and only very limited familiarity with the computer system is required on their part. The computer program then assumes the task of coding information in a form most convenient for internal processing.

FUNCTIONAL ASPECTS

In discussing computerized serials systems, it is helpful to consider several basic aspects on a functional level. Segmenting the discussion into these neat little packages must be done with some caution, however, because any such division may be very inappropriate for the technology of the future. Every existing automated serials system may be regarded as encompassing one or more of the following aspects:

1. Listing
2. Receiving
3. Claiming
4. Binding
5. Holdings and Lacks
6. Subscription Renewal and Budgeting
7. Operating Statistics.

The type of operating system is determined by the degree to which it provides automatic control of these various functions. Only a very few of the more sophisticated computer-based serials systems will be found to incorporate more than one half of these basic functions. By far the most common situation existing is the use of a computer in one or two areas, with the remaining aspects handled entirely by traditional manual methods.

This paper will not detail the computer procedures necessary for each individual operation; it will discuss instead operating considerations from a librarian's point of view, noting any significant variations from the method presented.

It should not be surprising to note that most existing computer systems evidence a remarkable similarity in those aspects which are handled by the computer. There is, however, a wide diversity of philosophies, methods, and techniques associated with the actual computer techniques developed. Discussion of detailed variations of these computer programs is beyond the scope of this paper.

Listing

The most basic aspect of a computerized serials operation is the production of various kinds of lists and reports. This is by far the most common application in the serials area, and experience has proven it the most successful. A multitude of systems, which have the sole purpose of producing and maintaining various lists and reports, exists. As mentioned earlier, the ability to produce these same lists as byproducts of more sophisticated control systems has more than once become the sole justification for keeping an otherwise unsatisfactory system active.

Once a data base is available in machine-readable form an infinite number of lists and reports can be produced. The speed with which the computer can easily manipulate the stored data provides a flexibility not possible in any manual system.

The most common types of lists and reports being regularly produced are intended for use by library patrons. The pressing need to maintain accurate, up-to-date public service files for serials information can be readily met by computer-produced title lists, location indexes, union holding lists, and catalogs. In addition, numerous working files for clerical and administrative use are readily available. As the data base is expanded by including other aspects as part of the computer system, the possibilities for meaningful control and for statistical reporting become even more numerous.

The library operating procedure involved in this activity is the clerical preparation of additions and changes for input to the computer to maintain the data base. The complexity of this clerical operation is determined by the complexity of coding and by the length of the processing cycle adopted. The computer programs used in merely updating and maintaining this data base, however, are usually as complex as for any other part of a complete central system.

Receiving

The operating procedure most widely used in existing computer-based serials systems revolves around what has become known as the "arrival card." One card is produced by the computer, at the beginning of each cycle, for each physical item expected during the cycle. Prepunched into each card is the necessary title identification and the identification (volume, number, and date) for the item expected. Information printed on the arrival card for use by clerical personnel includes this data, plus any other information required to check in and distribute the item.

Arrival cards are maintained in two separate files: cards for expected arrivals and cards for received arrivals. Clerical procedure involves matching cards to serial issues and marking issues for distribution, as well as transferring the arrival cards to the "received" file. These received cards are then returned as input to the computer processing run for the next cycle.

Several significant variations of this basic method exist which are used to handle irregular arrivals and other unexpected items. All receipts may be considered as regular or irregular arrivals. A regular subscription is by definition any predictable pattern of publication. All other irregular serials with completely unpredictable frequency are handled as exceptions to the basic system. The tremendous variation and lack of consistency in numbering schemes and publishing intervals present major problems, which are not completely resolved by any existing system. Variations to meet these problems are all basically attempts to let the event of arrival initiate the updating procedure, which can be accomplished in several ways. A dummy arrival card may be produced and interfiled permanently for each known irregular publication, or a listing of irregulars may be placed with the expected arrival file. Eventual receipt of an irregular item then requires that an update card be manually produced. While several other slight variations are used, no really satisfactory solution exists which has been proven by operation.

Experience with existing systems has also proven that no time savings can be expected with an arrival card check-in system. The significant feature is that the data involved is being handled and captured in machine-readable form. The real efficiency of operating a computer system accrues from the ability to do all succeeding file maintenance operations automatically. These advantages will exist even when a large percentage of receipts cannot be checked in automatically and must be handled manually as snags. But the eventual efficiencies may or may not then offset the additional clerical effort required.

The receiving aspect is the key to the successful operation of a complete control system. The experience of both proven and unsuccessful operating systems indicates that the size of the percentage of snags is of critical importance.

Claiming

The operating procedure most commonly used revolves around the "unreceived" arrival cards remaining in the "expected" arrivals file at the end of each cycle. The decision to claim missing material, however, is usually based on the judgment of an experienced staff member. "Claimed" cards are then marked and returned to the expected arrivals file. The computer system, when instructed that a claim is pending, can produce a form claim notice with address, ready for mailing. The form notice may be either on postcard stock or a letter for use in a window envelope.

A significant variation on this basic system involves automatic preparation of claim notices. This is accomplished by a variety of methods. The expected date of arrival of the next issue can be the triggering date for a claim slip. An elapsed period of more than a set number of days after expected receipt can be established as the point of automatic production.

Experience with existing systems, however, indicates that the variation in receipt of even known, predictable titles can result in excessive claiming notices. No existing system incorporates a completely automatic claiming procedure which has been proven by operation.

Binding

The operating procedure most commonly used revolves around a computer-produced file of cards or list which constitutes a "tickler" file for the bindery clerk. The clerk will receive one tickler notice at the beginning of each cycle for each title ready to be bound during the cycle. The binding candidates are then manually processed. If visual inspection indicates missing issues or insufficient bulk for binding, the tickler is refiled until the missing material is received, or until the next binding card for the title is produced.

A computer-controlled system such as the one just described has several significant advantages. The operation of such a system, however, requires that holdings information be recorded and updated by the computer system. Significant variations exist which will accommodate the need to maintain bindery records separate from holdings information. A binding information slip may be produced, for example, which gives full binding instructions to the binder. Information would include color, binding title, style, and any other data which had been previously entered into computer storage. The production of this slip can then be assigned to a given month so that the binding load is staggered evenly over a 12-month period. The backlog of slips in the file also gives an accurate estimate of unbound material in the collection.

Holdings and Lacks

Existing systems which incorporate the holdings and lacks maintain and update both bound and unbound holdings automatically. When the receipt of an individual item is recorded, the unbound holdings record is updated. The holdings then remain in the record as unbound until receipt of an update indicates that a particular volume has been bound. The computer system then deletes the entries for the unbound volume and substitutes an entry for the bound volume. This data base of retrospective holdings is then used to produce holdings records for public service use and shelf lists or other holdings statements for use as serials working files.

Two significant variations exist in the manner in which holdings are recorded in the computer. One widely accepted method provides that the holding statement be carried in condensed form in computer storage. This method is convenient to handle, and requirements for data storage are considerably reduced.

The other method also being used provides that holdings information indicate physical bound volumes only. Condensed holdings statements are then compiled by the computer for public service lists. This method has the advantage of an item-by-item entry which is available for inventory control or other analysis concerning physical volumes held.

Certain listing systems also incorporate a static statement of holdings which must be maintained and updated manually. Experience with existing systems has shown that where the complexity and sophistication required to maintain an automatic holdings record is not justifiable, a static statement of holdings is often acceptable.

Subscription Renewal and Budgeting

The operating procedure most commonly used is computer production of cards or lists as ticklers to initiate subscription renewal. The actual subscription renewal may either be printed by computer or be processed manually, depending on the complexity of the system. Initial acquisition and cataloging is normally handled by other operating units in the library. In addition to subscription and vendor information, financial information is stored in the computer. When a subscription renewal is processed, the ordering and payment part of the record is updated by manually produced input to the computer.

The significant feature of this system is that this data base is then available to programs which analyze serials expenditures and provide budgets and budget forecasting. In this area, as in the area of operating statistics, the flexibility of the computer provides a real advantage over any manual method of operation. This aspect of the serials operation is one that is often implemented in the type of combination system which does not otherwise incorporate complete control. Experience has shown that a high degree of computer control can be expected in this area. Proven applications of a similar nature have long been in existence in business and accounting systems.

Operating Statistics

Normal operating statistics desired for administration and control of the serials operation are readily available in a computer-based system. Nearly any analysis or report can be produced, provided the information base is part of the machine-readable data base. No other system can surpass the computer's ability to compile statistics.

The variation in kinds of reports produced is endless and is normally limited only by the ingenuity of the computer programmer and by the wishes of the library administration. All existing computer-based systems make use of a machine-readable data base for the production of statistics. The experience in many instances, in fact, indicates that the only problem is to resist the impulse to produce needless volumes of useless statistics.

SUMMARY

The premise of this paper is that computerized serials systems have started to proliferate and that it is desirable to recognize functional aspects of these systems to avoid overgeneralization. It is important to understand the operation of these various aspects in order to make critical comparisons between specific systems. This paper suggests that any specific computer-based serials system can be segmented for study into the seven fundamental aspects discussed above. No belief is held that these aspects are the only pertinent ones, or even the best that could be defined. A strong recommendation is made, however, that evaluation of any system will be most meaningful when the system is analyzed under coverage of one or more of the above aspects of operation.

DISCUSSION

FRED BELLAMY, University of California, Santa Barbara: Like most of the rest of us, I have been impressed with the possibility of cooperative ventures, and a few months ago, we decided to prepare a serials title list. It had nine data elements in it. A similar list had been prepared at the San Diego campus and a data base containing all of their titles was there. Experience at our Davis campus indicated that we could expect to find a rather large percentage of matches. So we called the San Diego campus and they sent us ten boxes of cards (20,000 cards), and we began comparing their cards against our files. We found about 70 percent of the titles matched. Then we gave our keypunch girls the San Diego cards and a bunch of blank cards and had them punch the additional information into the San Diego cards, and a full set of data into the blank cards for those titles which did not match.

We thought this was really a wonderful idea. Then about halfway through the project, I asked myself if this was really an effective way of doing the job. So we did a time study and it turned out that it took just as much time to punch the full blank card as it did to take the San Diego card, handle it, and run it through the machine to get to the point where we added the rest of our data elements. So in this one case, after the fact, and through an actual time study, we discovered that using available data was not time saving. This may not be a typical example, but I offer it for your consideration.

MR. STEWART: Let me comment on that. I think part of that might have been the situation. There may have been so little information that was of use to you that it may not have been of benefit. In our own case, we picked up a tape of something like 30,000 entries in what my serials librarian considered to be very acceptable form, and went through and picked information off by its identifying number. The amount of effort that would have been required to punch the bibliographic history, compared to the amount it took to write a computer program and keypunch several thousand 6-digit numbers, to go through and match and pull it off—why, there's no comparison. I think it depends on what you are trying to do.

MR. BELLAMY: Let me offer a counter comment, then. Of the nine data elements, only one was common and that was the full title. The other elements were peculiar to our local operation. The call number was peculiar, the location, holdings, certainly. All of these things were peculiar.

MR. STEWART: For just the title itself, would it have been cheaper to rekey the entire title or to pull it off the San Diego files?

MR. BELLAMY: I can't say. The operators had to

pass the card through the machine, you know, and that means duplicating the first portion of the card. I think the answer would be yes, though. Now, I'd like to hear your comments on on-line serials systems; what do you think the future holds for on-line operation of serials control?

MR. STEWART: I think the only significant difference that an on-line system is going to make is in the check-in operation, because the listing operations and the analysis and production of reports really don't require an on-line situation. You don't have to have in real time the notification that a subscription renewal is due. You can get along with this once a day or once a week or even once a month.

The one place where an on-line capability will make a real difference is in the check-in operation. Having a clerk sit down and type in on a keyboard the information about an issue which has been received, and then having the computer tell her whether it checks in or whether it doesn't, or whether it checks in and there is an issue missing there, is the same sort of situation as recording it on a Kardex card. It's not an attempt to predict anything at all, and the real complexity in programming a computer system to predict is in writing the programs that handle the prediction for 10,000 unique titles. The number of variations in the numberings, in the types of receipt, and so forth, defeats any attempt to write a really successful prediction program.

EUGENE JACKSON, IBM: I would like to add some numbers in so that we have an idea of the quantity of institutions involved here. In this connection, there was a survey of the extent of library automation, done by the Special Libraries Association and the ALA Library Technology Project. The results of this are summarized in an article in *Special Libraries* for May-June, and it shows that the serials control function, which Mr. Stewart has covered this morning, is the most popular mechanization function at this time. It is followed immediately by circulation control, which is the subject of the next discussion this morning. Out of 1130 institutions that were reported either as being users of automation at this time or planners of such automation, there were 209 that are actual users of serials control systems. This includes all varieties, from unit cards on up. There are 242 planners, making a total of 451, which is 40 percent of the 1130 institutions.

MR. STEWART: Out of the 14 references I included in this paper, I think only one or two are control systems; by that I mean they include automatic check-in and completely update the records from there on. Three or four of those 14 were purely listing systems based on unit record systems or computer systems. The rest were all combination systems that were listing systems with some degree of control over ordering or binding or something like that. When I say there is very little work being done in the completely automatic control system, I mean in perhaps two out of all the libraries in the country.

In reference to the survey Mr. Jackson mentioned, there is, if you look at the figures, a great deal of work being done in special libraries which concerns the application of computers to journal control. There is also very little that's being done in public libraries, and I think that the development of systems is obviously influenced by the type of library. A special library has a highly restricted clientele; it has particular emphasis, for instance, on current receipt notification and on SDI [Selective Dissemination of Information] and current awareness, the type of things that it is not possible to emphasize in a large university library. It looks to me as though the small size of the serials collection in a special library is one factor which contributes to a successful operating system; it's easier to program a system that will handle 1000 or 2000 journals or 500 or 100 than it is to program the one that will handle 15,000 or 20,000. As I have said, early industrial applications of computers have also provided special librarians with the ready availability of technical help and hardware to do the job, and a climate in which experimentation is accepted and in which appropriations for research are an accepted part of the budget. The development in academic libraries has been much slower.

Automated Circulation Systems

C. D. Gull

Professor, Graduate Library School
University of Indiana

This report identifies three basic functions and four kinds of basic data for circulation systems. It discusses computers and peripheral equipment, and describes eight major operations of circulation work and four operational records which ought to be consultable. Statistics and automated design objectives are identified as essential but greatly neglected by librarians.

Major improvements feasible with a computer are:

1. Routing of periodical issues to individuals (principally in special libraries)
2. Introduction of strict fines accounting
3. Collection from users of information on effective use of, and need for, library materials
4. Provision for the growth of library collections by feedback from effective use and need records
5. Introduction of rational, data-based management to replace intuitive management.

Circulation systems which use unit record (punched-card) equipment and which do not use electronic digital computers are excluded from this presentation.

The prospect for automated or computerized circulation systems has never been better than it is at this moment, and over the next few years, the prospect can be expected to improve materially as new equipment with greater capabilities becomes available at costs which are reasonable for libraries to bear. Any consideration of the prospect for computerized circulation systems, however, needs to be founded upon a clear understanding of circulation systems as they exist at the present time and upon an exploration of what an ideal circulation system may be able to provide within a reasonable number of years in the future. None of the principal accounts of circulation work provides the type of organized understanding of circulation work which is essential for computerizing a system. Consequently, the first eight sections of this presentation are intended to offer, very briefly, that type of understanding. It is important to note that no single library is engaged in all the activities

described in these sections, nor are all automated circulation systems together performing these activities.

BASIC FUNCTIONS

The basic functions of a library circulation system are:

1. To record and control the use of all kinds of library materials
2. To guide the continuing provision of library materials or the continuing growth of the collection
3. To guide the continuing growth and improvement of library services.

From the point of view of reader service, the second and third functions are the most important. While their importance has been recognized for many years by librarians, it has been impossible with the techniques at our disposal in the past to collect, process, and transfer circulation department experience to the other departments of the library so as to guide the way in which the collection is built and operated to improve services to users. Automated circulation systems show a tendency to emphasize the service aspects without reducing circulation controls.

BASIC DATA

Four kinds of basic data are required in a library circulation system. They are derived from:

1. The materials used by any kind of user in a library. This class of data is generated from the familiar activity of loaning books, periodical issues, films, pamphlets, etc., from libraries. There is very little distinction among various types of libraries about the treatment of materials, although some special libraries have the additional problems of controlling security-classified materials and of

routing periodical issues to members of the organization which they serve.

2. The time span for the use of the material, whether used in or out of the library. The common basic data are date of loan, date due, and date of return.
3. The borrowers or the users of the library, who generate information by their actions and by their own characteristics.
4. The borrowers' requests for unavailable items. These requests can be for materials unavailable because of current use within the library, loan outside the library, or absence from the library system altogether.

SERVICE LOCATIONS

The physical location of service points affects the generation and the collection of the basic data for circulation work. The service points can be as few as one in a library or there can be multiple service points, as in public libraries with service points in the main library, branches, bookmobiles, stations, etc. While this aspect of circulation work is sometimes considered by type of library, the categorization by type of library is less important here than distinguishing a single service point from multiple service points. If one service point is feasible, economies in personnel and equipment and improved control of materials can be realized.

COMPUTERS AND PERIPHERAL EQUIPMENT

The computers and peripheral equipment available to the library have a significant effect on the circulation system. Mechanical, manual, and photographic systems are the most common at the present time. The most recent comprehensive work, the *Study of Circulation Control Systems* prepared by George Fry and Associates, Inc., (Chicago: American Library Assn.—Library Technology Project, 1961) lists 27 such systems. It gives exhaustive information about the times required to perform the various operations, summaries of costs and recommendations, and, finally, a table which librarians can fill out in selecting one system. It does not, however, include computerized circulation systems.

Electronic digital computers are increasingly employed for circulation control. They require manual assistance and, in many instances, specialized peripheral equipment. Computers are used in all the systems considered in this presentation.

The extensive report on "The Use of Data Processing Equipment by Libraries and Information Centers" by Creative Research Services for the American Library Association and Special Library Association (1966) shows that there are some 80 libraries employing computers for circulation control and about 40 libraries using computers for classified

document loan control, which is a form of circulation work. The survey report also shows that 27 models of small computers are in use from eight manufacturers, 17 models of medium-sized computers from seven manufacturers, and 20 models of large computers from six manufacturers; in all, a total of 64 different models of computers from 10 different manufacturers. My survey of the literature shows only 14 computer models from three manufacturers; 12 models of International Business Machines computers, the GE 225 computer from General Electric Company and the UNIVAC 1107 computer from the Sperry Rand Corporation (see Tables I and II).

The literature survey shows the following peripheral equipment in use: six examples of the IBM 357 Data Collection System; one example of the IBM Administrative Terminal System; one using Dura Mach 10 paper-tape typewriter; one Friden Model 30 Collectadata; one Book-a-Matic system; one example of the Addressograph-Multigraph Data Recorder (the common gas station credit card imprinter) used with the Addressograph 9500 Optical Code Reader (to read the bar codes on credit cards). One library is using IBM 1305 Disc Storage, and two are using IBM 1311 Disc Storage Drive for random access to circulation information. To these, the CRS survey adds Data-Phones, Teletype, and Telex, but no remote consoles are listed for on-line, random-access computer systems. The diversity of computers and peripheral equipment suggests that there is no uniformity in the use of computers for circulation control.

THE MAJOR OPERATIONS OF CIRCULATION WORK

There are eight major operations performed in circulation work:

Provision of Information Service to Borrowers

The primary operation of a circulation system is provision of information service to borrowers. Borrowers want to know where an item is, whether an item is on loan, when it can be expected to be available, and, in some libraries, who is the borrower. Borrowers should be privileged to receive such information, but, unfortunately, this is one of the operations most neglected in many circulation systems. The Fry report notes that there have been no adverse effects stemming from the policy in some libraries of not offering any information about the location of books out of the library on loan. In the future, this conclusion ought to warn of a deplorable situation in a library, and the introduction of computers ought to be the principal means of improving performance in this area. That the Fry report can suggest there have been no adverse effects means to me that the users of libraries have resigned themselves to accept that some kinds of libraries do not offer this

TABLE I

LIBRARIES AND COMPUTERS - 1966

Function	In Use	On Order
Circulation Control	80	90
Classified Documentation Loan Control	40	20
Total	120	110

kind of service, and, consequently, the users do not complain about its absence. If the major objective of a library is to provide service, then it follows that information on the location of materials should be made available. Computers offer the opportunity to overcome this major deficiency which exists in most libraries today.

The library which accepts the responsibility of providing information service to borrowers ought to be prepared to act on the borrowers' responses to the information given out. These actions include acceptance of reserve requests for any library material unavailable for various reasons, recall of items from loan after accepting reserve requests, and acceptance of recommendations for materials which are absent for any reason. Libraries which have circulation systems using book cards and the IBM 357 Data Collection System or the IBM 026 Printing Card Punch are accepting reserve requests. The recall records usually go into the computer daily, and the recall of the items from the borrowers is accomplished by computer-printed notices. There is no indication in the literature, however, that computerized circulation systems now provide a point at which borrowers can recommend that materials be added to the library system. Perhaps the existing systems are not sufficiently integrated with the recommending and acquisitions procedures, or perhaps the libraries accept recommendations at other locations in the building, but certainly a computerized circulation system offers a good service point for the acceptance of recommendations.

Control of Borrowers or Users

The second major operation in a circulation system is the control of borrower or users, commonly called the registration of borrowers. This operation is neglected in many libraries now. Although the Fry report suggests that many libraries operate successfully without a registration list of borrowers, such a list is extremely useful and can be obtained at a minimum cost with computers. It would be relatively simple to maintain several files such as a numerical registration file, an alphabetical registration file, and an alphabetical list of delinquent borrowers.

When a computer is available, it will be desirable to obtain more information about borrowers when they register for library use. The early work of Margery C. Quigley at the Montclair Public Library, in New Jersey, during World War II, with the aid of IBM punched cards, is a pioneering example of this application (see Bibliography, No.261). Information such as age, sex, schooling, personal interests, language capabilities, community activities, etc., can be asked of the borrower and recorded for future processing and study. The potentiality of studying thoroughly the needs of borrowers through the production of correlated statistics is very significant. The distribution of statistics of borrowers' age, sex, education, location, language facilities, interests, community activities, in relationship to the materials borrowed, satisfaction in use, time of loans, etc., will afford library administrators opportunities to study their users in depth as never before.

Although the registration of borrowers is neglected in many libraries now, the introduction of computers is bringing about several innovations in borrower registration. In one system, a punched-card registration file is created and maintained for manual consultation, and lists are printed from these cards by the computer for use in other locations. Information on borrowers can also be gathered as the transactions are performed, and the computer is then used to identify borrowers' names and to sort them into alphabetic or borrower number order and to print lists at regular intervals; this method does not require borrowers to register before borrowing.

In systems using plastic, embossed borrowers' cards, the borrowers' cards and lists are frequently supplied by other parts of the organization which the library serves. Since these cards are only partly compatible with computer operations and since they are retained by the borrowers, in most cases, library files are sometimes created by imprinting the borrowers' information onto IBM cards which are subsequently punched and used to prepare borrowers' lists by computer. Some libraries are also making their borrowers' lists available for borrowers to consult, in both alphabetic and identification number orders.

Control of Materials

The third major operation is the control of materials, including some suboperations called loan

TABLE II

COMPUTER MODELS AND MANUFACTURERS BOOKS AND CLASSIFIED DOCUMENTS

Computers	Models	Mfrs.
Small	27	8
Medium	17	7
Large	20	6
Total CRS Survey	64	10
Total Literature Survey	14	3

transactions. The control of materials can be broken down further into charging materials, discharging borrowed materials, calculating fines, renewing loans, and identifying service points at which loans take place.

The charging of materials for use within the library or outside of the library is a process which requires the collection of information about the item loaned, about the borrower, and about the date of the loan and the specified date of return. For this process, the majority of libraries are using IBM punched cards as book cards and adding the borrowers' identification, service location, and time data. For most of the libraries, the charging process produces transaction cards bearing complete information for input to computers. If transaction cards are not made, the book cards are used as computer input. Two principal methods are used to record the loan transactions. One method combines a data-collector device and a cable-connected key punch. The other employs a manually operated key punch, but no data-collector device.

The first method uses the IBM 357 Data Collection System, which is probably the most widely used equipment to record the data about book, borrower, location, and date. In use, the borrower's plastic, punched, embossed card (often with a color photograph of the borrower) is inserted into one slot and the book card into another slot. The transaction card is produced on a cable-connected IBM 026 Printing Card Punch, either at the charging station or at a remote location. Duplicate book or transaction cards can be produced during the charging operation if desired for use as date due cards, an extra file, etc. The literature shows only that the IBM 357 Data Collection System is used by Washington University (see Bibliography, No.241), Florida Atlantic (see Bibliography, No.117), Oakland (see Bibliography, No.226, 228), Southern Illinois (see Bibliography, No.248, 251), Windsor, and Lehigh universities (see Bibliography, No.233), although over 50 libraries were known to be using the 357 in 1966. The systems using book cards and the 357 Data Collection System report that about four to six charges can be made per minute, which is a real improvement over the methods which were replaced.

Michigan State University (see Bibliography, No. 237) uses the Friden Collectadata System 3001 or 3002 Transmitter, with punched book and borrower cards. The intention is to convert to an embossed and punched borrower's badge.

The second method to record book, borrower, location, and date together uses the book card and a manually operated 026 Printing Card Punch, requiring the charging assistant to be a typist. The book card and keypunch method is used by Sandia Corporation, Argonne National Laboratory, IBM's Watson Research Center (see Bibliography, No.243), Redstone Scientific Information Center, and Arizona State (see Bibliography, No.242), and Rice universities (see

Bibliography, No.240, 268, 272). Transaction cards and duplicates can be produced with this method.

The School of Medicine of Washington University (see Bibliography, No.252, 266) and the Upstate Medical Center of the State University of New York in Syracuse (see Bibliography, No.239) use embossed book cards and embossed borrowers' plastic identification cards. The embossed information is recorded on a blank IBM book card, which is keypunched later as computer input. If there is a voided transaction card in the book remaining from a previous transaction, it is clipped to the blank imprinted card and used as the machine-readable source of book identification. Gaylord and Addressograph data recorders are used, respectively. With a Gaylord recorder, the borrower's number must be keypunched. With the Addressograph imprinter, the borrower's number is read optically later from the familiar bar code used on gasoline credit cards.

Two libraries charge out materials without using book or borrower cards. The NASA [National Aeronautics and Space Administration] Manned Spacecraft Center in Houston (see Bibliography, No.231) charges materials by writing into a daily logbook. The date is keypunched every morning for computer input. This charging method is acknowledged to be the major source of errors in their system. Columbia University is creating its charges by using the Dura Mach 10 paper-tape typewriter. These methods require no machine-readable book or borrowers' cards, although these cards could be produced as computer output if desired.

In considering the use of book cards, libraries have had to choose whether to prepare book cards for the entire collection or for a fraction of the collection before installing the computerized system. This problem was highlighted by the experience of Southern Illinois University (see Bibliography, No.248, 251) which required 1800 man-hours of student help to code worksheets for optical scanning and conversion of the data to magnetic-tape records by Science Research Associates in Chicago. The tape records were then converted into punched book cards at the University. This work was done for approximately 600,000 volumes.

In contrast, Lehigh University (see Bibliography, No.233) prepared book cards for only 40,000 of 450,000 volumes in advance. Arizona State (see Bibliography, No.242) prepared the book cards as required for loan or as books were cataloged or reclassified and found that 80 percent of the books presented for use after the first year had book cards already in them. The circulation analysis by Trueswell (see Bibliography, No.269) confirms that it is easier to prepare only a percentage of book cards in advance or as needed than to prepare all the book cards before a system is put into operation.

It is conceivable and very probable that the materials for loan can be provided at some time with machine-readable records. These records may be the call numbers on the spine, the front, or the back of the volumes, prepared in such a fashion that passing them under a reading head or passing a reading head over them will secure the record of the individual item without using a book card.

The discharging of borrowed materials adds further to the information collected at the time of charging or loaning an item. The additional information is the date returned and the cancellation of any record which shows that an item is still due to be returned. Some libraries check files for reserve or overdue status also. After discharge, the book can be returned to its original shelf location or loaned to another individual at once.

The libraries which use a 357 Data Collection System generally discharge a book by feeding the book card and a 357 discharge or return badge into the 357 terminal. The discharge transaction card is produced on a nearby or remote 026 Printing Card Punch to be sent later to the computing center, and the book card is returned to the pocket of the book. Some libraries produce extra copies of the book card at the time of discharge by keeping the punch at the circulation desk.

If the library maintains a reserve file or checks on overdues, it is necessary to check a computer print-out or a card file before a book can be supplied with its book card and made available for circulation or shelving. Some libraries maintain a discharge file by preparing a discharge card either at the time of charging or subsequently by computer. The use of a discharge file takes care of the problem of checking files for reserves and overdues.

A very interesting addition to the data on the discharge cards is found in the Watson Center Library of IBM (see Bibliography, No.243) where the computer-produced discharge cards show the number of times each item has circulated. The computer advances this record by one each time the discharge card is prepared. When the discharge card is placed in the book, it therefore shows the latest record of how many times the item has circulated. This information is also kept in tape storage for statistical uses. This capability will facilitate the weeding of the shelves by inspection or, if the librarians prefer, weeding the shelves by asking the computer to print out from complete tape storage the list of items which have circulated below a minimum number of times for a certain span of years after publication.

In systems which use embossed plastic cards, the charge card is pulled from the files, marked void, and placed in the book pocket to be used as the punched-card source of information for the next circulation. The disadvantage of this method is that the date of return is lost from the circulation figures kept on magnetic tapes.

The NASA Manned Spacecraft Center in Houston (see Bibliography, No.231) uses a manual discharge technique, entering the discharge in a logbook by hand, using the accession number. Later an artificial return date is added, which will make statistics on length of the use of items invalid.

Columbia University plans to discharge by keyboarding the data on the Dura Mach 10 paper-tape typewriter. This circulation method will reqire two keyboard efforts for every loan, and it will not build up a supply of machine-readable book cards in commonly circulating volumes.

One of the simpler uses of the computer will be to allow the peripheral charging and discharging equipment to add the date and loan station to each transaction. This kind of information could be controlled from the central computer so that the machinery is updated each day to accomplish this type of recording.

Since some materials are always retained longer than the specified loan period, the necessity arises to calculate fines for keeping that material too long. The records of this calculation and of the collection of the fines can be added to the charge-discharge record. Apparently, special libraries with automated circulation systems do not levy fines for overdue materials. Fines are levied in college and university libraries, where the computer is frequently used to calculate the amount of fines, to prepare lists of borrowers who owe money, and to prepare and send notices to the treasurer's or bursar's office for collection of the fines at a central point.

Many libraries permit the renewal of a loan. Whenever a loan is extended in any manner, the record of the extension of the loan should contain renewal status, date of renewal, and date due, so that a new date is available for calculation of the possible overdue status when the item is eventually returned. Libraries using book cards and data-collection devices appear to require a book to be returned to renew a loan. Renewals are accomplished in the same manner as the original charges, with additional information entered into the record to show the renewal status, the date of the renewal transaction, and the date due.

Since special libraries have very liberal loan periods and do not collect fines, they show a tendency to employ automatic renewal techniques, using the computer to make the renewals effective. At Sandia, for example, four automatic renewal notices are sent to a borrower; if the item is not returned after the fourth notice, the fifth notice goes to the department manager with a request that he take administrative action to have the item returned. The Redstone Scientific Information Center allows the borrower to renew after one year's use by signing and returning a punched-card renewal notice which contains the book card information in it.

As a part of the loan transaction, it is desirable not only to add the date on which the transaction takes place but also the identification of the service point at which the loan takes place. Sandia and the Argonne National Laboratory, however, are the only libraries which report that they record more than one service point. Information about the loan of materials by service points is generally unavailable in anything more than simple totals of items borrowed for time periods. With computers available, it will be possible to correlate the service points data with other information, such as materials and borrowers, or effective use information about the materials, or use within or without the buildings.

Control of Records

More commonly called file maintenance or updating by computer people, the control of records is the fourth major operation in circulation work. It includes the interfiling of newly charged records, the removing of charges for returned materials, and the changing of the records for items on which the loan has been extended or changed in any way. File maintenance is accomplished daily at the computing center in most computerized circulation systems, although Picatinny Arsenal reports that it is done every two days[1] and the NASA Manned Spacecraft Center (see Bibliography, No.231), Argonne National Laboratory, Watson Library of IBM (see Bibliography, No.243), and Redstone Scientific Information Center report file maintenance on a weekly schedule. In a computerized circulation system, file maintenance simply disappears from the circulation department work areas and is done at the computer.

Control of the Time of Loans

The control of the time of loans, the procedures required to accomplish the return of overdue items, constitutes the fifth group of operations for circulation work. Computers offer the opportunity to obtain a great deal of information about the time span for use of materials. Most systems provide very little information about this aspect, however, and, consequently, the loan periods are still established by intuition and experience. With computer-prepared information, they can be established by reference to the actual needs and practice of borrowers.

In libraries which use charging systems for the use of materials within the library, it will be possible to determine the elapsed time of such loans with the aid of a recording time clock as part of the peripheral equipment. Although this information is largely unknown at the present time in most libraries, Michigan State (see Bibliography, No.237) and Oakland universities (see Bibliography, No.226, 228) are collecting time data in hundredths of hours with their 357 Data Collection Systems.

Computers can be especially effective in accomplishing the return of overdue items. They can search the records for the overdue items, categorize them in various ways for statistical purposes, pre-

pare the overdue notices for mailing or other types of delivery, and prepare overdue lists arranged by materials, by dates, and by borrowers.

The loan periods which determine when overdues occur, range in the systems reported in the literature from one to two weeks, as the shortest interval, to ten years (at the Argonne National Laboratory, where items are overdue after ten years only because one punched-card column was allocated for the year date). The various frequencies of making searches for overdues by the computer are reported as once or twice a week, fortnightly, "two weeks from Friday," monthly, six months, one year, and ten years. At Lehigh (see Bibliography, No.233), an overdue is detected the day before the item is due back at the library, but the overdue notice is not sent immediately. Many of the items are not considered overdue in special libraries until someone requests them.

Very little information has been reported on the categorization of overdues by various classes. The most common one is to list borrowers alphabetically by name or numerically by identification number and to show the items overdue, how long they have been overdue, and the amount of fine. Evidently not much statistical analysis has been attempted on overdues.

Most of the libraries having computerized circulation systems prepare overdue notices with the aid of the computer. These are printed out on the printer and mailed to the delinquent borrowers. A variety of overdue notice forms is used. One of the interesting forms, used at Lehigh, is the UARCO Data Mailer form. A deleaver and burster machine was purchased to separate the UARCO carbon-paper sets and carbon paper before distribution.

Several libraries prepare overdue lists for the head librarian or the head of the circulation department. Among these libraries are the NASA Manned Spacecraft Center (see Bibliography, No.231), the Widener Library at Harvard (see Bibliography, No. 253), Florida Atlantic (see Bibliography, No.117), Rice (see Bibliography, No.240, 268, 272), and Columbia universities, Argonne National Laboratory, Watson Library of IBM (see Bibliography, No.243), and the Redstone Scientific Information Center.

Fines Accounting

Fines accounting, or the control of fine receipts, is the sixth operation in circulation work. The following steps are desirable here: From the records of the loan transactions, calculate the fines receivable and total these in the necessary categories; calculate the fines actually received by corresponding categories and totals; reconcile these accounts by loan stations, by totals over regular periods of time. Remote consoles can be used when overdue books are returned, to direct the computer to calculate the fines on the book and to check the delinquent filing record to see if the borrower owes additional money.

Reconciliation of the fines accounts will then in-

---

[1] I. Haznedari and H. Voos, "Automated Circulation at a Government R&D Installation," *Special Libraries*, 55:77-81 (Feb. 1964).

dicate what the library should have received from fines; compare this amount with what the library actually received for certain periods from the various stations and by totals for the system. The present procedures for the control of fine receipts in most libraries leave an extraordinary loophole. Since the information on fines receivable compared to fines received is not available and since many libraries have no effective method for recording the fines taken in, there are unusual opportunities for petty pilfering of the fine drawer. As in many other instances of petty pilfering, the total amounts can be large enough to constitute criminal acts. I well remember a public library in which something over 10 percent of the budget, or over $100,000 a year, came from the income from fines. The introduction of fines accounting by computer alone might pay for the cost of operating a computerized circulation system in a large public library because of increased fine receipts. There is no indication in the written accounts, however, that any library is yet undertaking to reconcile fines receivable with fines actually received over regular periods of time. Computers are used to calculate and print fines notices but not to reconcile accounts. Oakland University (see Bibliography, No.226, 228) reports one interesting variation. It uses a "Discharge Fine Paid" trigger card in its discharge process so that the computer receives positive directions that no fine is due on that overdue item.

Gathering of Effective Use Records

The seventh major operation in circulation work is gathering of effective use records. Practically no information, however, is now collected in circulation systems from borrowers about their effective use of library materials. A major consideration in the gathering of effective use records is whether the system and the equipment permit the borrowers to participate, thus presumably reducing the load on the staff, or whether the staff is the only group which can gather the records. The introduction of records of effective use will require the participation of borrowers.

Regular Routing of Periodical Issues

An important operation in some special libraries, and the eighth major operation to be considered, is the regular routing of periodical issues to individuals served by the library. This service requires the creation of a routing list, attachment of the routing slips to the individual issues of a periodical, and a record system which monitors the progress—sometimes slow—of the issues as they proceed through the organization until their eventual return to the library's custody. The procedures should include a periodic review by each reader of his own list of periodical titles and should permit him to direct changes in his list at any time by recommending the deletion, continuation, or addition of individual titles.

Although there is no report of computerized routing of serial issues in the literature, I am privileged to report on the procedures followed at the Scientific Library of Eli Lilly and Company, Indianapolis. Approximately 100 journals are routed there to more than 600 persons, using an IBM System/360 Model 30 computer. The tape and card records are also used to maintain master subscription control lists and vendor renewal lists. Over 300 changes are required a month. Routing slips are printed on 7 inch by 7 inch paper by computer in six copies for use when issues are checked in. Annual review notices are prepared in two copies, one for each recipient and one for the library.

OPERATIONAL RECORDS

There are four major types of operational records which ought to be available from a circulation system. First of all, loan records should be available by date. The date used may be the date of the loans, or the date when the materials are due. The loan records can be separated into those which are not due and those which are overdue. All of these records by date can be maintained in a subarrangement according to the subject classification or other useful characteristic of the material. There are no reports in the literature, however, of loan records being available by date on computerized circulation systems. This capability may not be implemented until on-line random-access computer systems are used by libraries.

Second, loan records should also be available by the characteristics of the items loaned. A common arrangement is by classification number, another common arrangement is by author, and sometimes the arrangement is by accession number or by form of the material. The most useful subarrangement for records of multiple copies is probably according to date due. There is an evident tendency towards the preparation of daily circulation loan records arranged by these characteristics. These records are usually placed where the borrowers can consult them. In many instances, the borrower's identification number is shown for each loan recorded on the list. If lists are provided weekly or fortnightly rather than daily, there is a tendency to use the IBM punch-card files as a manual loan record between the printings of the computerized list. Some lists are broken up into sections; e.g., long-term and short-term loans; books on loan, lost books, books recalled, and books returned; documents, pamphlets, journals, and books, in separate listings. Rice University provides a list of closed reserves in three parts—by course number, by author, and by title—for students to consult.

Third, records on borrowers should also be

available to administrators and to individual borrowers. In the sense that the borrowers' names are related to the individual items borrowed, this type of record is most frequently absent in libraries. In some special libraries and libraries dealing with security classified items, however, the borrower's record, showing all loans outstanding to each individual, is absolutely essential. The most common frequency for providing borrowers lists in computerized circulation systems appears to be daily, although some libraries have weekly and fortnightly lists. Lehigh (see Bibliography, No.233) finds that the borrowers list is only needed at the ends of the semesters. Some libraries break up these lists and send portions to individual borrowers. These lists are particularly useful in checking out employees or students who sever their relationships with the library and must clear their accounts before final departure. Lists can be arranged either alphabetically by borrowers' surnames or numerically by employee numbers; in the later case, alphabetic arrangement is usually provided also for administrative use.

The record of reserve items which individuals have requested upon return or of requests for unavailable items is the fourth major operational record which should be available. This record can be ordered by author, by subject classification, or by the name of the requester. The Watson Library of IBM (see Bibliography, No.243) has a weekly list of reserved loan requests arranged alphabetically by author for the use of the librarian; this was the only example of a printed list found in the literature.

CORRELATED USE RECORDS
OR STATISTICS

Correlated use records, or statistics, are provided by combining the basic data secured during all the circulation operations with service points data and with operational data. The statistical processing of these data can provide five major kinds of correlated use records which ought to be available from the circulation system.

First, there should be a record, based on the amount of time that the items have been used, showing whether the materials have been used in the library or outside the library. The subarrangements under the time periods can be made according to the types of subject material, the characteristics of the borrowers, the service locations, and the records of the effectiveness of use.

A few examples of statistics on time for use of materials were found in the literature. Oakland University (see Bibliography, No.226, 228) and Michigan State University (see Bibliography, No.237) both analyzed the use of materials every hour of every day. Oakland University discovered four major use peaks each day and learned that certain days of the week the library was more heavily used than on other days.

The findings enabled them to improve their personnel scheduling. Michigan State cumulated the time and use records for a full term. The School of Medicine of Washington University (see Bibliography, No.252, 266) analyzed its figures for materials both loaned and returned during one month, but since by their system the used IBM book cards are returned to the books after their return, cumulative statistics on usage are not obtainable.

Trueswell (see Bibliography, No.257) has suggested that the data on the amount of time the items are used and frequency of use can be used to guide the weeding of collections, to determine multiple copy needs, and to rearrange stacks for more efficient service from the collections.

Overdues are a special category of time records. Adequate overdue statistics can be used to establish a rational loan period, thus minimizing the number of overdues occurring in the system.

Second, statistics on materials which have been loaned are extremely important in guiding the future provision of library materials for users of the library. This aspect of library service is rarely attempted in any library except one which at least uses a punched-card installation as its minimum equipment. With a computer, the materials can be categorized easily by subject classes, by language, by date of publication, by the kinds of borrowers, by service location, by time, and by effective use.

Arizona State University (see Bibliography, No. 242) reported that the study of the statistics of its active subject areas was of material assistance for its acquisitions planning. Oakland University (see Bibliography, No.226, 228) has obtained experimental statistics, arranging the record of use by Library of Congress classification against the number of charges and by the various curricula against the number of charges. Lehigh University (see Bibliography, No. 233) obtains daily statistics on charges by Dewey classification and totals by type of loan the number of missing books, reserves, and items sent out for binding and mending. These statistics are provided in cumulative monthly and yearly totals also.

Third, information should also be collected about borrowers in order to indicate their characteristics in the use of the library. This information can be broken down by the characteristics of borrowers and subordered by subject classes, time of borrowing, service location, and effective use.

Picatinny Arsenal obtains monthly statistics about user organizations. Lehigh University obtains daily statistics by type of borrower, with cumulative monthly and yearly figures. Oakland University has obtained experimental figures on use by classes of use compared to grade-point average and by grade-point average compared to use. They suggest that the statistics ought to be provided to identify nonborrowers and to show borrower records by groups, such as commuters, dormitory students, students by courses, part-time students, and faculty members.

Fourth, records should be maintained according to the locations from which service was rendered to show the comparative use and effectiveness of each service location. Again, the subarrangements can be by class of material, class of borrower, time of use, and effective character of use. At the Redstone Scientific Information Center, for example, they can ask for a list of all patrons with over fifty loans. The conclusion might be that such patrons are hoarding the items, but there is also the possibility that such a list might reveal where branches ought to be established. This need could be determined by plotting the locations of heavy borrowers on a map of the George C. Marshall Space Flight Center (see Bibliography, No.231).

The effective use of library materials, the fifth item on which statistics should be collected, is something about which professional librarians know almost nothing. Materials are borrowed within the library or taken home, but librarians have only the remotest idea what happens to these materials in the hands of the users. The only way to gather this information is to collect it from the users as suggested earlier. The collection of this information requires borrower participation and some kind of a record for the borrower or a staff member to fill out. The types of information requested could be obtained from the following questions, for example:

1. Did you read all of this book?
2. Did you read portions of this book?
3. Did you enjoy this book as a literary production?
4. Did you find the information you wanted in this book? (Answer by percentages.)
5. Did you take some action after reading this item, e.g., visit a city, national park, restaurant, museum, etc., buy a product, or change your personal or business activities?
6. Did other persons in your family, or friends, visitors, etc., make additional use of this book during the loan period?

Although no information on this category was found in the literature on computerized circulation systems, Project MARC (for Machine-Readable Cataloging) at the Library of Congress holds significant promise for effective use studies, because the circulation data can be compared with collected data about the bibliographical elements of catalog cards, all of which are tagged for computer processing in Project MARC. For example, users' profiles can be derived by matching circulation data with certain bibliographical elements, and the profiles can be used to provide selective notice of new material at regular intervals to individual users.

MINIMUM OBJECTIVES IN DESIGNING A CIRCULATION SYSTEM

The minimum objectives of a circulation system need to be carefully considered and carefully specified before a computerized circulation system is finally designed. There are a number of minimum objectives, which can be described as follows:

1. The convenience of the users and of the library staff is paramount in the adoption of the system. In designing the system, every effort should be made to assure convenience.
2. The operational records should be accessible at all times in an easy manner. Accessibility can be defined in physical terms as well as in terms of time. It is physical accessibility which argues for the use of computers in circulation work. Computers offer the only possibility of physical accessibility and a short response time to reach the operational records in the four basic orders of date due, type of material, name of borrower, and reserve items or requests for unavailable items.
3. The record should be complete and accurate.
4. The system adopted should be economical in relation to the total library budget.

The absence of information on designing automated circulation systems in the current literature suggests that this important area is largely ignored and misunderstood by librarians. The best information on design is in the reports from Johns Hopkins, Lehigh, and Rice universities. The information available about libraries planning to introduce automated circulation systems is somewhat more extensive, but it is primarily found in memoranda which are not generally available. The great lack of information in the literature about plans for automating circulation work emphasizes the value of the survey report prepared by Creative Research Services for ALA and SLA in 1966, and shows that only LC, ALA, and SLA possess the basic information, in the returned questionnaires. My literature survey provided some information about the plans of *ten* libraries, but the CRS report shows that 428 libraries are planning for automation for circulation control and that 244 have authorized automation studies underway for circulation control. Similarly, for classified document loan control, some 80 libraries have plans, and some 50 have an authorized study underway. For both uses, existing orders for computers exceed orders for punched card equipment about two to one, 90 for circulation control and 20 for classified document control.

Information on the cost of computerized information systems, expressed either in dollars or in time, is uncommon. The NASA Manned Spacecraft Center (see Bibliography, No.231) notes that its manual key-punching method with computer control costs 6 cents per transaction based on 6000 transactions per month. The Picatinny Arsenal noted that its early figures showed that the circulation methods saved two minutes per transaction over the manual method. Washington University (see Bibliography, No.241) showed an estimate of $500 to $1000 a month saved over its manual Gaylord charging system. Southern Illinois University (see Bibliography, No.248, 251), which

TABLE III

AUTOMATION IN USE AND PLANNED FOR CIRCULATION WORK IN LIBRARIES
(Source: Creative Research Services, 1966, Pages 9, 11, 39, 41, 43, 45, 50, 51)

LIBRARIES	SYSTEMS IN USE—1966[1]			SYSTEMS PLANNED			AUTHOR-IZED AUTO-MATION STUDY UNDER-WAY	WHEN PLANNED TO IMPLEMENT AUTHORIZED STUDY				
	Total EAM ADP[2]	EAM	ADP	Total EAM ADP	EAM on Order	ADP on Order		Next Year	1-2 Years	2-5 Years	Other Period	Don't Know
CIRCULATION CONTROL												
Col. & Univ.	62/79	37/47	25/32	206	29	50	113	20	36	30	3	24
Industrial	63/69	27/34	36/35	73	5	11	42	13	17	7	0	5
Public	28/33	20/22	8/11	65	11	17	43	11	10	14	0	8
Govt.	15/16	8/9	7/7	47	4	9	29	6	12	4	1	6
Other	10/12	8/8	2/4	35	4	2	16	3	3	6	1	3
Total	179/209	100/120	79/89	428	53	90	244	53	79	61	5	46
CLASSIFIED DOCUMENT CONTROL												
Col. & Univ.	6/8	2/4	4/4	17	2	4	10	2	2	2	2	2
Industrial	40/42	14/21	26/21	33	3	9	20	8	8	2	0	2
Public	0/0	0/0	0/0	0	0	0	0	0	0	0	0	0
Govt.	8/12	4/7	4/5	21	1	5	13	7	2	1	0	3
Other	14/15	5/7	9/8	8	0	0	4	1	1	0	0	2
Total	68/77	25/39	43/38	79/87	6	18/20	47/52	18	14	6	2	12

[1]The internally inconsistent figures for Systems in Use 1966 come from p.9 and 11 for lower (right-hand) figure and from p.25 and 26 for upper figure.

[2]Since most computer (ADP) systems use punched-card equipment (EAM) to some extent, these totals may be much too large. As a worst possible example, 89 ADP plus 120 EAM for circulation control may represent only 120 libraries (not 209) of which 89 use ADP and EAM and 31 use EAM alone. The data were gathered in questions 8 and 9 but not presented in this manner in the report.

previously used McBee Keysort edge-notched cards and borrowers' cards, was able to reassign to other tasks 12 full-time persons working on returns and two full-time persons working on overdues, after their IBM 357-1401 system was installed. The best reports have been provided by Rice University (see Bibliography, No.240, 268, 272), which gives its conversion costs, and by Lehigh University (see Bibliography, No.233), which offers conversion and operating costs.

Most of the statistical correlations useful for management which have been found in the literature have been discussed above, but Rice University registered an interesting experience which relates to design objectives. Mr. Ruecking was predicting a 9 percent increase in circulation for the forthcoming year, based on previous statistics. With the introduction of the IBM 357 Data Collection System, the increase proved to be 33 percent in the first year. It remains to be seen whether this increase will continue or is a jump to a new plateau of library use; it is possible that there is a parallel here between circulation in a library and traffic flow on a highway, which increases noticeably whenever a highway is improved.

The CRS report also shows that 57 percent of the libraries with authorized studies underway plan to implement their studies in two years or less (see Table III).

MAJOR IMPROVEMENTS FEASIBLE WITH COMPUTERS

In summary, there are four major improvements which are becoming feasible with the introduction of computers into circulation work. First, the requirement of routing periodical issues to individuals served by the library of an organization can be accomplished much more expeditiously with the aid of a computer than with any other method we know. It is a relatively easy matter for a computer to correlate the title of a periodical, its issue number, and its copy number, with the names, addresses, telephone numbers, and administrative units of the several individuals to which the periodical title should be routed regularly upon the receipt of new issues. It is also relatively easy for the computer to change this routing list whenever the individuals wish or whenever they change employment. The computer can also maintain a record of where an individual issue of a periodical is to be found during its routing period. If such a reporting system is needed, machine-readable punched cards can be returned by each person on the routing list when he finishes an issue. The computer can also check on the eventual return of all issues and report about those which have not yet been returned to the library.

These capabilities mean that many special libraries have an opportunity to maintain the required control of security matter and periodicals in a convenient manner never available to them before. Some special libraries with access to computers are already taking advantage of the computer in this way.

Fines accounting represents the second major improvement feasible with the computer. Now that the computer makes it possible to calculate the amount of fines to be collected and to compare this figure with the actual amount of money received by each collecting station, there is the opportunity to introduce fines accounting that will satisfy the fiscal authorities of the library or of the jurisdiction to which the library belongs. The introduction of adequate fines accounting may in certain situations virtually pay for the introduction of the computer to the circulation system if there has been any appreciable pilfering of the fine receipts. I anticipate that the fiscal authorities will strongly urge, if they do not insist, that computers be employed for this purpose once they become aware that strict control can be obtained over fine income. The only rational reason for no controls over fine income at the present time is that it is virtually impossible to accomplish such control with manual methods.

The collection of effective use and need records is the third, and important, improvement made feasible by the introduction of the computer into circulation work. In the past, librarians have acquired their collections by intuition and by calling upon years of experience in dealing with the needs of the users of their libraries. Their success in using this method is obvious. The failures of this method are concealed, however, because people give up asking for

things which they recognize from past experience they cannot obtain. I suggest that there are large and significant latent needs for information among our population. After the users of libraries become aware that the expressions of their needs and the expressions of their satisfaction with the materials which they have used in libraries are being recorded, analyzed, and used to guide the growth of library collections, they will start to ask for the kinds of information which they need but which they could not get before.

Fourth, by employing the principle of feedback from the operational records and by using the effective use and need records obtained from the borrowers, the librarian will be in a position to guide the future growth of the library by responding to actual needs rather than to estimated needs. The growth of a collection based on actual needs ought to be somewhat different from that based on estimated needs. I am not suggesting that estimated needs should be neglected; experience and intuition should be followed very much as in the past, but the collection should also grow as a direct response to what people have said about materials and about their needs.

PROSPECTS FOR COMPUTERIZED CIRCULATION SYSTEMS

The prospects for computerized circulation systems are therefore very good indeed in the next five to ten years. The introduction of computers into circulation systems will mean a growing trend toward rational management to replace intuition in management. We can expect that the costs will be reasonable in relation to the rest of the library budget and in relation to the requirements of the users. We can confidently predict that there will be materially improved library service for all users. We will be able to offer to governing bodies and fiscal authorities, in many cases for the first time in history, adequate justification for a library's financial needs. For these reasons, I conclude that computerized circulation systems are already a demonstrated necessity for many library systems.

Trends Affecting Library Automation

Charles P. Bourne

Director, Advanced Information Systems Division
Programming Services, Inc.

The terms "library automation" and "library mechanization" as used in this paper refer to the use of new technology in the libraries, including copying machines and communications equipment as well as data processing equipment. This new technology is an area of increasing interest in the library field, as evidenced by such factors as the volume of published literature on this topic, the number of positive returns submitted to the American Library Association-Library Technology Program Automation Survey, the establishment of the new ALA Information Science and Automation Division, and, of course, by the attendance at this ALA Preconference Institute on Library Automation.

Much of the early work in library mechanization placed great emphasis on computer file searching, but this is only one area of interest today, and usually a topic of only minor interest to most libraries. There is currently more emphasis and interest on the mechanization of libraries' technical processing activities.

SIGNIFICANT RECENT EVENTS AND TRENDS

Federal Involvement

One significant trend recently has been the increasing federal involvement in information-handling activities. This includes the federal involvement in such things as the direct publication or indirect support of primary and secondary journals, support of translation services, support of new library construction, granting of book purchase funds, sponsorship of library research and development projects, sponsorship of library school fellowships, implementation of centralized and regional information and data centers, and establishment of a National Commission on Libraries. This federal involvement is likely to grow during the next few years.

Machine-Language Records

There has been an increase in the distribution of catalog and index records in machine-language form (e.g., computer magnetic tapes) from a central service organization. The following list provides some examples of organizations that are planning, developing, or operating such distribution systems:

Library of Congress—Project MARC catalog records
Chemical Abstracts Service—*Chemical Titles* tapes
National Library of Medicine—MEDLARS tapes
Defense Documentation Center–TAB tapes (planned)
National Aeronautics and Space Administration—STAR tapes
Institute for Scientific Information—*Science Citation Index* tapes
Biological Abstracts—(in planning)
American Society for Metals—ASM *Metals Review* tapes
Abel—catalog record paper tapes
Stacey's—catalog record tapes

This type of activity will undoubtedly grow rapidly during the next few years.

Increased Microform Use

There has been an increase in the publication and use of microform for library material and in the emergence of several relatively low-cost ($100) viewers. The main types of microform use to date, with examples, have been the following:

Federal dissemination of report material—DDC [Defense Documentation Center], OTS [Office of Technical Services] Clearinghouse, NASA report distribution
Commercial publication—microform book and periodical publication (e.g., by University Microfilms, 3M, Microcard Corporation); manufacturer catalog files (e.g., subscription services to several million pages of catalog material provided by Information Retrieval, Inc., Information Handling Services, Thomas Register)
In-house reference—document collections (e.g., Patent Office conversion of 3 million patents); parts listings (e.g., Eastern Airlines' 4 million pages of

maintenance manuals and parts catalogs on film); business records (e.g., retail customer files); library catalogs (e.g., at Lockheed, Redstone Arsenal)

In two library applications, microfilm editions or equivalents of the entire card catalog file are distributed on a periodic basis to a number of branch libraries. In several of the commercial catalog publications, the publishers talk in terms of processing 36 million feet of 16-millimeter film and 1-1/2 million microfiche a year. This is an activity that is expected to grow during the next few years, particularly with respect to commercial publication.

Manufacturer Mergers with Information Services

There has also been an increased involvement by equipment manufacturers in the publication and distribution of information. Examples of such joint merger activities during the last several years are: Xerox Corporation with University Microfilms, Basic Systems, American Educational Publications, and Professional Library Service; International Business Machines with Science Research Associates; National Cash Register with Microcard Corporation; Radio Corporation of America with Random House; Raytheon with D. C. Heath; Litton Industries with American Book Company; Bell and Howell with Charles E. Merrill Books, Inc., and Microphoto; 3M Company with the International Microfilm Press; and International Telephone and Telegraph with Howard Sams.

Library Recognition of Need for Special Staff

An increasing number of libraries have recognized the need to establish on their staff a member who has the specific responsibility of investigating the possibility of technology utilization in that library. A typical job title is Associate Director for Systems Research. Libraries have been finding that in many cases the success of the library-mechanization activity depends in large part upon having some key individual—one spark plug—to initiate and guide the library in this work. This person could be a programmer, librarian, or administrator; he could appear in any of these roles. Many libraries are also finding that proximity to a computer center or data processing staff is not enough to ensure success to the library's mechanization activity.

EXPANSION AND CONTINUATION OF EARLIER WORK

Most of the recent library-mechanization work has been simply a continuation and follow-up, by increased numbers of people, in the mechanization of library technical processes (e.g., circulation control, acquisitions, cataloging, serials records). This literature is covered by the ADI [American Documentation Institute] *Annual Review of Information Science and Technology, Documentation Abstracts,* and the bibliographies of Neeland and McCune.[1]

Most of the work to date has been for the development of fragmented subsystems (e.g., Library A has a circulation control system, Library B has a serials records system). There are few examples of what might be called a completely mechanized library, or total system, where all of the functions are handled by one master system in an integrated manner.

An increasing number of organizations are converting catalog records to machine-language versions by a number of ways (e.g., key punch, paper tape, online terminals, optical character readers), with key punch and paper tape the predominant methods. Work is under way by the United States of America Standards Institute Z-39 committee to develop the basis for a standardization of machine-language bibliographic format.[2] The Library of Congress MARC [Machine-Readable Cataloging] tape format is also gaining widespread acceptance as a de facto standard format and method of representation for communication of catalog records between libraries.[3]

There has been an increase in the number and activity of Selective Dissemination of Information (SDI) systems. In addition to an estimated twenty to forty in-house systems, there are now several more generally available services planned or in operation (e.g., American Society for Metals, Institute for Scientific Information, Chemical Abstracts Service, Share Research). There is also an increase in the number of instances in which an organization has used a computer to prepare reference tools for manual use. Examples are KWIC [Key-Word-in-Context] indexes, book form catalogs, and indexes to journals.

NEW WORK

There has been some work on the further development and utilization of new techniques and systems. Some of the main examples are:

1. On-line file search from remote terminals (e.g., the NASA Recon system developed by Bunker-Ramo, the NASA file search system developed by Lockheed, the BOLD [Bibliographic On-Line Display] system

[1] Frances Neeland, *A Bibliography on Information Science and Technology for 1966,* Pt. II (Santa Monica, Calif.: System Development Corp., 1967); Louis C. McCune and Stephen R. Salmon, "Bibliography of Library Automation," *ALA Bulletin,* 61:674-94 (June 1967).

[2] Ann T. Curran and Henriette D. Avram, *The Identification of Data Elements in Bibliographic Records:* Final report of the special project on data elements for the subcommittee on machine input records (SC-2) of the sectional committee on library work and documentation (Z-39) of the U.S.A. Standards Institute (n.p.: 1967).

[3] *Project MARC—An experiment in Automating Library of Congress Catalog Data* (Washington, D.C.: Library of Congress, 1967).

developed by System Development Corporation, the Datrix system demonstrated by Xerox, the TIP [Technical Information Project] file developed at Massachusetts Institute of Technology)

2. Utilization of time-shared computer time for processing work from remote terminals (e.g., input for catalog conversion at the Santa Clara Public Library and the State University of New York, input processing at Syntex and IBM-Los Gatos, patron identification and circulation control at Redstone Arsenal)

3. Increasing numbers of cooperative technical processing services planned or in operation that will use data processing techniques to improve their operating efficiency

4. Expansion of services by book dealers to provide machine-language catalog records as an extension of the cards-with-book programs (e.g., Abel paper-tape plan, Stacey's magnetic-tape plan).

IDEAS STILL ON THE SHELF

A number of technical approaches have been shown to be helpful for libraries, but they have not gone into extensive use primarily because of their unfavorable economics. Examples of these approaches are facsimile transmission of interlibrary loan or other requested material; large, mechanized microform storage and retrieval systems; large associative memories; and machine translation. These approaches will have to be reviewed again as the technology and cost picture improves.

Aside from the economic question, there are still some areas where the libraries have not fully taken advantage of the computer capability that is available to them. For example, it is possible to do the following tasks now, and with benefit to the libraries, but they have generally not been done to date:

1. Use of urban-planning information files, census data, and other sources of regional resource information, in order to determine more closely the characteristics and requirements of library-user populations in a given geographic area

2. Use of circulation data to record the history of use of each item in the collection, in order to obtain better information for the planning of acquisition and book-retirement programs

3. Use of catalog data to provide special types of listings for special administrative purposes (e.g., lists in order by date of publication, to identify and locate "rare" books in the total collection; lists in order by height of book in order to simplify reshelving by book height).

SUMMARY

One final word of encouragement: do not wait for developments that are reported to be just around the corner or in the development laboratories; you may be better off using the tools and resources that are presently known and available. And a word of warning: no library mechanization project will proceed smoothly and easily; you can expect trials and tribulations, sweat and tears.

DISCUSSION

JOHN KOUNTZ, Orange County Library System: I want to thank Mr. Bourne for bringing the operations research gaming or modeling aspect into the discussion. I would like to draw attention to an article in the May *ALA Bulletin* which may be a first move in this direction in gaming with populations for the establishment of new libraries for a system.

MR. BOURNE: I would like to see machines used more to aid in the regular management reporting of the library operations: the actual physical inventory of the collections, perhaps even the per unit production rates of individual staff members in some of the processing areas.

Question: We've heard quite a bit in the last couple of days about digital computer technology; I wonder whether you have thought at all about high-density television techniques and what their role might be.

MR. BOURNE: If you are thinking of it just as a mechanism for storage, I would say it's only one of many different mechanisms that you could use. Regardless of the mechanism, the large, mechanized storage and retrieval systems have all been fairly expensive and very difficult for people to justify. I don't think high-density TV recording would be much different from that, if used as a large, mechanized image storage and retrieval system.

Response: I am thinking of a system in which the basic medium is a film clip or microfiche of some kind and in which the dissemination function is primarily performed by a high-resolution TV.

MR. BOURNE: This again runs into the problem that it may be very simple to reproduce and distribute multiple copies in this form, but now you require the user to have another special viewing mechanism. You face a situation in which the individual user now has to have a TV playback unit, or he has got to have a microfiche viewer and perhaps other microform viewers.

Question: I was at an IFIPS [International Federation of Information Processing Societies] Conference in Rome last week, and one member of my panel was seriously proposing a very high-resolution TV network, coupled with a centralized film store.

MR. BOURNE: A lot of problems have been concerned with a resolution of the image that you could store with the band width and the coding pattern that's used for most of the TV images. It would be difficult, I think, for a lot of library material with small footnotes and graphics to be adequately represented by a video file or a video representation.

Question: There seems to be a growing number of users, especially in industry, who are interested in the maintenance of small files. Traditionally, industry is tied to scientific computation machinery and hardware of large volume, and it seems to be a hard selling job for people to convince management that a small machine is possibly just as applicable to the maintenance of small files as a large data processing system.

I wondered if you had any feeling about this matter, or if you saw any growing effort on the part of hardware and software producers either to make this plainer or to suppress this type of solution.

MR. BOURNE: There have been very few instances in which a library by itself had sufficient work that it could justify having its own machine, so in almost all applications either the library found the application after they had the machine in the company, in which case they designed their implementation around the machine that was available, or the library had the application in mind before the company got the machine, in which case they could hopefully make their point of view known to the computer-selection committee within the company so that at least their kinds of requirements could be taken into account when the company was acquiring a machine.

The trend today is toward machines that have a composite capability for handling both scientific and textual types of material equally well, so that it's not necessarily as much of a drawback as it was in the past, when there were purely scientific machines and purely business-type machines. Similarly, the trend has been for much more machine for the dollar, so that for the same amount of money today, you can get a pretty comprehensive and powerful machine.

Question: It seems that smaller libraries, public libraries or academic libraries, that have been forced to look at the larger machines simply because they happen to be there, as they are in industry, might have an out in that they can now begin to deal with service companies on such an arrangement as "bought" time, real-time, or time-shared operation.

MR. BOURNE: If we remember that every library has the option of going to service bureaus and shopping around to find out which machine configuration or which service bureau can do its processing at the least total cost, a particular library needn't be limited to any particular machine.

MARY ELLEN JACOB, Sandia Corporation, Livermore: When you start talking about computers, one of the things that we have found in our system to be of prime importance is sorting of records. We store the

data on the machine, but we do more manipulating of it than we do anything else. We happen to have a dictionary catalog, and maintaining it involves a great deal of sorting. The more data we put into the file, the longer our sorts become; so in considering the smaller machines, you've got to be extremely careful about how much data is going to be involved, how much you have to manipulate it and to sort it.

CARL SPAULDING, Council on Library Resources: Recently we've seen some fairly severe cold water dashed on the matter of machine translation, particularly as concerned with whether or not it was economical and done quickly enough in terms of the editing that had to follow in order to make it really useful.

Another area that a very great deal of money has been put into is information retrieval involving a really large file and no especially good way of knowing in advance what kind of detail will be requested from it. Are you optimistic or pessimistic about the probability that we will get a good percentage return in this application in a reasonable length of time?

MR. BOURNE: First, machine translation. I imagine you are referring to the ALPAC [National Research Council, Automatic Language Processing Advisory Committee] reports on the evaluation of machine translation, which I think were done in the context of a specific, operating machine-translation system. I think the report described the fact that the products of the machine-translation system required very extensive editing, so that almost as much time was spent post-editing as had been on the original translation. I would be pessimistic about having in production machine-translation systems for five years or so. There just have been too many problems in the production of a large corpus of material. I wouldn't expect machine translation to be working economically and with a response time that was competitive with manual translations for at least another five years.

On the problem of trying to do a file search on a data base when you're not sure how you are going to query it later, one approach is simply to make a full text search of the system. This has been the approach suggested and used in a couple of instances. The IBM labs in New York are doing full text searching on the abstracts of technical journal articles, for example, as well as on titles.

Another approach would be to try at least to characterize the kinds of elements of data that are included in the file record, and then to use a formatted file structure in which everything is recorded to start with in some tag form so that you've at least got the capability for searching it later, once you decide how to do it.

JOHN HARRISON, Klein Science Library, Yale: You mentioned a few of the SDI services, I believe, *Chem Abstracts* and the one located in Philadelphia, *Science Citation Index.* Have you found any university-based SDI systems that seem successful, or would you suppose there would be a trend in this direction within some of the larger universities?

MR. BOURNE: Traditionally, industrial organizations seem to have provided more information services for the professional staff than academic organizations have, so a lot of custom-tailored services are provided that you'd never find in an academic library. SDI systems traditionally have been implemented in industrial-type environments. There haven't been any that I know of in an academic organization, although I understand university people are trying to run SDI experiments on the MARC tapes. I don't see any reason why they wouldn't work in a university environment.

DON BLACK: Wayne State University has a rather extensive SDI system both within the university and to people without.

MR. GULL: One of our graduate students in the Graduate Library School is preparing his PhD thesis on an SDI experiment. He has the profiles of 40 faculty members. Nearly 300 responded to his original question, and he was embarrassed to have to turn most of them down. He is searching on subject headings and classification numbers from Project MARC. This thesis is one instance of a limited application.

MR. HARRISON: All of this leads into the question of whether we shouldn't think about expanding MARC data with more extensive subject coverage. I realize that this is a big dose for the Library of Congress, but I think it's an area in which we are going to be doing more work in the universities. Do you have any idea right now that they will expand the MARC data to include deeper subject work? We have, I believe, the figure of something like 1.4 subject headings per monograph title, and in science library work I find this insufficient. The MARC data is continuing this trend, and I don't think we have a reason to continue this trend any more, because we're not turning out cards. We are thinking about a data base that we can access at a later time to do a retrieval job, a literature search job.

MR. SALMON: This seems to me almost totally unrelated to the question of automation or information retrieval. It's the problem of subject cataloging, which we have trouble doing on a current basis anyway. If you are going to increase the work load there, it's a problem of staffing subject analysts.

MR. ANGELL: I do not believe that the concept of depth indexing has been stated. The 1.4 average subject headings on LC cards, which is the average for those that get subject headings at all, does not, in my opinion, give an accurate idea of the number of access points that the subject heading system provides.

Depth indexing could be defined in various ways. Indexing to the chapter level, which has been men-

tioned, is a possibility, but I have in my own mind a serious question whether we want in a large collection an entry for every chapter on banking in every book on economics. For the kind of work that conventional subject headings are trying to do and the kind of service that a large monographic collection is trying to provide, I don't think that depth indexing has been defined. I would be delighted to return to Washington with a good definition of it.

MR. HARRISON: Obviously, for monographic work, subject cataloging in broad headings is sufficient, but we've got another world here, that of what somebody called vertical files or report literature. The people in the business want to be able to control this.

MR. SALMON: My point was not that this shouldn't be done, but that our problem is not an automated one or a mechanical one. It is a problem of finding the staff and the money to do the indexing. Except to the extent that automatic indexing can do this for us—and that's been only to a very limited degree—we have to do this analysis manually, and we have to have people to do it. This is, to me, the problem; the mechanical one comes later.

MR. HARRISON: I've got some figures on this problem because we are trying to get the money. We figured that for LC classifications Q, R, S, and T—around 370 titles —it would probably cost about $26,000 a year to do deep indexing or match type headings for this monographic material. Compared to a book budget of $70,000, this seems to be getting a little out of proportion. That's why I was hoping it could be done nationally.

MR. SALMON: We could use 60 catalogers at the moment just for what we are already trying to do. If you've got more than that, we can talk about doing more work.

MISS JACOB: We happen to have an SDI system, and we have in our system both books and reports. We are just in the process of starting to put in periodical literature. We use maybe the same thing LC does— 1.4, maybe 2 to 3 subject headings on an average per book, certainly not more than that. As far as the SDI system is concerned, this coverage has proved adequate, and one of the reasons for it is the fact that we use both a subject indexing aspect and also key words from the title. In the case of symposia or materials of this type which become more complex and more difficult to handle, we are able to put the titles of the papers in, which gives us certainly a much wider breadth of coverage than we could have otherwise.

Our main trouble with indexing is more with reports; the thing is that reports are more specific in their very nature. Therefore, the amount of indexing that has to be done for them is not in the same category as that for a book . What I am trying to say is that, as far as our book collection is concerned, we have found little or no trouble with the headings that LC uses or with the few additional ones we may have had to assign.

Bibliography

Bibliography
of Library Automation

by *Lois C. McCune and Stephen R. Salmon*

The items listed in this bibliography have been selected primarily for their potential value to the librarian beginning an investigation of the field of library automation. For this reason, only material pertaining to the automation or mechanization of traditional library functions is cited (material on information retrieval, mechanized indexing, selective dissemination of information), and such related, but peripheral, topics as computer printing, photocomposition, and facsimile transmission have been omitted. Emphasis has also been placed primarily on recent writings; most of the literature appearing before the early 1960's is now of historical interest only and hence is not included.

To facilitate use, citations have been arranged by subject and, within subject areas, in reverse chronological order. Starred items are for first reading.

General and miscellaneous

1967

1. BRYAN, HARRISON. American automation in action. Library journal, v. 92, Jan. 15, 1967: 189–196.
2. COX, N. S. M., J. D. DEWS, *and* J. L. DOLBY. The computer and the library; the role of the computer in the organization and handling ,of information in libraries. Hamden, Conn., Archon Books, 1967. 95 p.
3. SEMINAR ON AUTOMATION IN BRITISH COLUMBIA UNIVERSITY LIBRARIES. *3d, Vancouver, 1966.* Report. Vancouver [University of British Columbia] 1967, 8 p.

1966

4. BLACK, DONALD V., *and* EARL A. FARLEY. Library automation. *In* Annual review of information science and technology.

v. 1, 1966. Edited by Carlos A. Cuadra. New York, Interscience: Wiley. p. 273–303.
5. BURKE, FRANK G. Automated techniques in the Manuscript Division. *In* U.S. *Library of Congress.* Information bulletin, v. 25, July 14, 1966: 389–390.
6. CLAPP, VERNER W. Closing the circuit: automation and data processing for libraries. Library journal, v. 91, Mar. 1966: 1165–1171.
7. COBLANS, HERBERT. Use of mechanized methods in documentation work. London, Aslib, 1966. 89 p.
8. GREINER, WILLIAM E. Data processing equipment and the library. *In* Clinic on Library Applications of Data Processing, *University of Illinois, 3d, 1965.* Proceedings. Edited by Francis B. Jenkins. Champaign, Ill., Distributed by the Illini Union Bookstore [1966] p. 175–192.
9. GULL, C. DAKE. The present state of library automation; a study in reluctant leadership. *In* Clinic on Library Applications of Data Processing, *University of Illinois, 3d, 1965.* Proceedings. Edited by Francis B. Jenkins. Champaign, Ill., Distributed by the Illini Union Bookstore [1966] p. 1–14.
10. KRAFT, DONALD H. The influence and impact of mechanization on libraries and society today and tomorrow. *In* Texas Conference on Library Mechanization,

Reprinted from the ALA Bulletin, June 1967

1st, Austin, 1966. Proceedings. Edited by John B. Corbin. Austin, Texas Library & Historical Commission, 1966. (Texas. State Library [Austin] Monograph no. 6) p. 31–36. Available on loan from LOCATE, Library of Congress, Washington, D.C. 20540.

11. Los Angeles County Public Library to study computerized techniques. Library journal, v. 91, Aug. 1966: 3673.

12. MEISE, NORMAN R. Conceptual design of an automated national library system. [Hartford] 1966. 246 p. Thesis (MA)—Rensselaer Polytechnic Institute, Hartford Graduate Center. Available on interlibrary loan from United Aircraft Corporate Systems Center, Farmington, Conn.

13. ORMSBY, JEANNE. Cuyahoga automates! Ohio Library Association. Bulletin, v. 36, Jan. 1966: 19–21.

14. OVERHAGE, CARL F. J. Plans for project Intrex. Science, v. 152, May 20, 1966: 1032–1037.

15. PAPAZIAN, PIERRE. The old order and the new breed; or, Will automation spoil Mel Dewey? ALA bulletin, v. 60, June 1966: 644–646.

16. Recent developments in automation at British Columbia University Libraries; University of British Columbia, University of Victoria, Simon Frazer University. No. 1 + Vancouver, B.C., Nov. 1966 + irregular.

17. STUART-STUBBS, BASIL. Conference on Computers in Canadian Libraries, Université Laval, Québec, March 21–22, 1966. A report prepared for the Canadian Association of College and University Libraries. [Vancouver] University of British Columbia Library, 1966. 13 p.

18. VICKERY, B. C. The future of libraries. The Library Association record, v. 68, July 1966: 252–260.

19. WELSH, WILLIAM J. Compatibility of systems. *In* Harvey, John, *ed.* Data processing in public and university libraries. Washington, Spartan Books, 1966. (Drexel Information Science series, v. 3) p. 79–93.

20. WHITE, HERBERT S. To the barricades! The computers are coming! Special libraries, v. 57, Nov. 1966: 631–635.

1965

21. BENKIN, JAMES. Automated procedures at Purdue University Library: accounting procedures. *In* Meeting on Automation in the Library—When, Where, and How, *Purdue University, 1964.* Papers. Edited by Theodora Andrews. Lafayette, Ind., Purdue University, 1965. p. 36–38.

22. DUNKIN, PAUL S. 1964: peek into paradise. Library resources & technical services, v. 9, spring 1965: 143–148.

23. FELTER, JACQUELINE W. From tedium to apathy. *In* Medical Library Association. Bulletin, v. 53, July 1965: 451–453.

24. GULL, C. DAKE. Attitudes and hopes where automation is concerned. *In* Meeting on Automation in the Library—When, Where, and How, *Purdue University, 1964.* Papers. Edited by Theodora Andrews. Lafayette, Ind., Purdue University, 1965. p. 53–64.

25. GULL, C. DAKE. The hardware of data processing. Library resources & technical services, v. 9, winter 1965: 6–18.

*26. HAMMER, DONALD P. Automated operations in a university library; a summary. College & research libraries, v. 26, Jan. 1965: 19–29, 44.

27. HAYES, ROBERT M. Implications for librarianship of computer technology. *In* Clinic on Library Applications of Data Processing, *University of Illinois, 2d, 1964.* Proceedings. Edited by Herbert Goldhor. Champaign, Ill., Distributed by the Illini Union Bookstore [1965] p. 1–6.

28. HOWE, MARY T. Mechanization in the Decatur Public Library. *In* IBM Library Mechanization Symposium, *Endicott, N.Y., 1964.* [Proceedings. White Plains, N.Y., International Business Machines Corp., 1965] p. 1–13.

29. JAHODA, GERALD, *and* FERROL ANN ACCOLA. Library records prepared with the aid of data processing equipment. College & research libraries, v. 26, Mar. 1965: 129–137.

30. KRAFT, DONALD H. Basic computer information for librarians. *In* Meeting on Automation in the Library—When, Where, and How, *Purdue University, 1964.* Papers. Edited by Theodora Andrews. Lafayette, Ind., Purdue University, 1965. p. 3–22.

31. LAZORICK, GERALD J., *and* HUGH C. ATKINSON. Gift and exchange department automation study. Buffalo, State University of New York at Buffalo, 1965. 2 p. + illus.

Bibliography . . .

32. LICKLIDER, J. C. R. Libraries of the future. Cambridge, Mass., M.I.T. Press, 1965. 219 p.

*33. PARKER, RALPH H. The machine and the librarian. Library resources & technical services, v. 9, winter 1965: 100–103.

34. PFLUG, GÜNTHER. Problems of electronic data processing in libraries. Libri, v. 15, 1965: 35–49.

35. PLANNING CONFERENCE ON INFORMATION TRANSFER EXPERIMFNTS, *Woods Hole, Mass., 1965.* Intrex; report of a Planning Conference on Information Transfer Experiments, Sept. 3, 1965. Edited by Carl F. J. Overhage and R. Joyce Harmon. Cambridge, Mass., M.I.T. Press, 1965. 276 p.

36. WEISS, RUDI. The state of automation? A survey of machinery used in technical services departments in New York State libraries. Library resources & technical services, v. 9, summer 1965: 289–302.

37. WERTZ, JOHN A. Possible applications of data processing equipment in libraries. *In* Clinic on Library Applications of Data Processing, *University of Illinois, 2d, 1964.* Proceedings. Edited by Herbert Goldhor. Champaign, Ill., Distributed by the Illini Union Bookstore [1965] p. 112–117.

1964

38. ADKINSON, BURTON W. Trends in library applications of data processing. *In* Clinic on Library Applications of Data Processing, *University of Illinois, 1st, 1963.* Proceedings. Edited by Herbert Goldhor. Champaign, Ill., Distributed by the Illini Union Bookstore [1964] p. 1–8.

39. BOLT, BERANEK, *and* NEWMAN, INC. Toward the library of the 21st century; a report on progress made in a program of research sponsored by the Council on Library Resources. Cambridge, Mass., 1964. 41 p.

40. BRODMAN, ESTELLE, *and* CHESTER R. GOUGH. Computers in medical and university libraries; a review of the situation in the U.S. in 1964. St. Louis, Washington University School of Medicine [1964] 14 p.

41. CLAPP, VERNER W. Mechanization and automation in American libraries. Libri, v. 14, 1964: 369–375.

*42. CLAPP, VERNER W. The future of the re-search library. Urbana, University of Illinois Press, 1964. 114 p.

43. Conference on Libraries and Automation, *Airlie Foundation, 1963.* Libraries and automation: proceedings. Edited by Barbara Evans Markuson. Washington, Library of Congress, 1964. 268 p. Available from Government Printing Office, Washington, D.C., 20401. $2.75.

44. CULBERTSON, DON S. New library science: a man-machine partnership. PNLA quarterly, v. 29, Oct. 1964: 25–31.

45. GORCHELS, CLARENCE. Of new libraries and futuristic libraries. College & research libraries, v. 4, 1964: 267–268, 284.

46. GRIFFIN, HILLIS L. Estimating data processing costs in libraries. College & research libraries, v. 25, Sept. 1964: 400–403.

47. HEILIGER, EDWARD M. Florida Atlantic University; new libraries on new campuses. College & research libraries, v. 25, May 1964: 181–185.

48. HEILIGER, EDWARD M. Staffing a computer based library. Library journal, v. 89, July 1964: 2738–2739.

49. JACOBS, JAMES W. Present and future applications of data processing equipment for school libraries [Montgomery County, Md.]. *In* Clinic on Library Applications of Data Processing, *University of Illinois, 1st, 1963.* Proceedings. Edited by Herbert Goldhor. Champaign, Ill., Distributed by the Illini Union Bookstore [1964] p. 37–42.

50. MELIN, JOHN S. Libraries and data processing: where do we stand? Urbana, University of Illinois, Graduate School of Library Science, 1964. 44 p. Occasional paper no. 72.

51. MORSE, PHILIP M. The prospect for mechanization. College & research libraries, v. 25, Mar. 1964: 115–119.

*52. PARKER, RALPH H. What every librarian should know about automation. Wilson library bulletin, v. 38, May 1964: 752–754.

53. SCHULTZ, CLAIRE K. Automation of reference work. Library trends, v. 12, Jan. 1964: 413–424.

*54. STEIN, THEODORE. Automation & library systems. Library journal, v. 89, July 1964: 2723–2734.

1963

55. AMERICAN LIBRARY ASSOCIATION. The library and information networks of the future. Prepared for U.S. Air Force Sys-

tems Command, Rome Air Development Center. Chicago, 1963. 43 p. AD-401 347.

56. DUBESTER, HENRY J. The librarian and the machine. *In* Institute on Information Storage and Retrieval, *1st, University of Minnesota, 1962.* Information retrieval today. Minneapolis, 1966. p. 167–176.

57. GOLDHOR, HERBERT. New technology; promise and reality. The library quarterly, v. 33, Jan. 1963: 102–114.

58. TAMS, MADGE P. Libraries and computers, the state of the art. Southeastern librarian, v. 13, winter 1963: 229–234.

1962

59. GRIFFIN, MARJORIE. The library of tomorrow. Library journal, v. 87, Apr. 15, 1962: 1555–1557.

60. HAYES, ROBERT M. The meaning of automation to the library profession. PNLA quarterly, v. 27, Oct. 1962: 7–16.

61. KEMENY, JOHN G. A library for 2000 A.D. *In* Greenberger, Martin, *ed.* Management and the computer of the future. [Cambridge, Mass.] Published jointly by M.I.T. Press and Wiley, New York, 1962. p. 134–178.

62. KRAFT, DONALD H. Data processing equipment for library use in clerical tasks and dissemination of information. Illinois libraries, v. 44, Nov. 1962: 587–592.

63. SCHULTHEISS, LOUIS A. Automation of library operations. *In* Computer Applications Symposium, *Chicago.* Computer applications; proceedings. 1961. Edited by Robert S. Hollitch and Benjamin Mittman. New York, Macmillan [1962] p. 35–44.

64. SCHULTHEISS, LOUIS A., DON S. CULBERTSON, *and* EDWARD M. HEILIGER. Advanced data processing in the university library. New York, Scarecrow Press, 1962. 388 p.

65. SWANSON, DON R. Library goals and the role of automation. Special libraries, v. 53, Oct. 1962: 466–471.

Before 1962

66. ASHLEY, EDWIN M. Clerical automation. Library journal, v. 82, July 1, 1957: 1725–1729.

67. BERRY, MADELINE M. Applications of punched cards to library routines. *In* Casey, Robert S., *and others, ed.* Punched cards: their applications to science and industry. 2d. ed., New York, Reinhold Publishing, 1959. p. 279–302.

68. CLAPP, VERNER W. The computer in the

library. *In* Computer Applications Symposium, *Chicago.* Computer applications; proceedings. 1960. Edited by Benjamin Mittman and Andrew Ungar. New York, Macmillan [1961] p. 35–45.

69. MAXFIELD, DAVID K. Library punched card procedures; past experience and future possibilities. Library journal, v. 71, June 15, 1946: 902–905, 911.

70. PARKER, RALPH H. Library applications of punched cards; a description of mechanical systems. Chicago, American Library Association, 1952. 80 p.

71. SHAW, RALPH R. Management, machines, and the bibliographic problems of the twentieth century. *In* Shera, Jesse H., *and* Margaret E. Egan, *eds.* Bibliographic organization. Chicago, University of Chicago, 1951. p. 200–225. '

72. WAGMAN, FREDERICK H. Libraries in the age of automation. Texas library journal, v. 35, June 1959: 42–55.

General (Library of Congress)

For additional citations about Library of Congress projects see *CATALOGING* (Library of Congress).

1966

*73. MARKUSON, BARBARA EVANS. A system development study for the Library of Congress automation program. The library quarterly, v. 36, July 1966: 197–273.

1965

74. MARKUSON, BARBARA EVANS. The United States Library of Congress automation survey. Unesco bulletin for libraries, v. 19, Jan.-Feb. 1965: 24–34.

75. SNYDER, SAMUEL S. Automation at LC: philosophy, plans, progress. Library journal, v. 90, Nov. 1, 1965: 4709–4714.

1964

76. HAYES, ROBERT M. Automation and the Library of Congress: three views; information scientist. The library quarterly, v. 34, July 1964: 229–232.

77. KING, GILBERT W. Automation and the Library of Congress: three views; chairman of survey team. The library quarterly, v. 34, July 1964: 234–239.

78. PARKER, RALPH H. Automation and the Library of Congress: three views; university librarian. The library quarterly, v. 34, July 1964: 232–234.

79. VOIGT, MELVIN J. LC and automation.

Library journal, v. 89, Mar. 1964. 1022–1025.

80. WALSH, JOHN. Library of Congress: automation urged for bibliographic control but not prescribed as a panacea. Science, v. 143, Jan.–Mar. 1964: 452–455.

1963

*81. KING, GILBERT W., *and others*. Automation and the Library of Congress. Washington, Library of Congress, 1963. 88 p. Available from Government Printing Office, Washington, D.C., 20401. $2.

Acquisitions

1967

82. AHN, HERBERT K. Computer-assisted library mechanization (CALM); acquisition (ACQ); CALMACQ Project notebook. Irvine, University of California, 1967.

83. ALANEN, SALLY, DAVID E. SPARKS, *and* FREDERICK G. KILGOUR. A computer-monitored library technical processing system. *In* American Documentation Institute. Proceedings of the annual meeting. v. 3; 1966. [Woodland Hills, Calif.] Adrianne Press [1966] p. 419–426.

1966

84. BRODMAN, ESTELLE, *and* GERALDINE S. CO-HEN. Communications to the editor; changes in acquisitions-cataloging methods at Washington University School of Medicine Library. *In* Medical Library Association. Bulletin, v. 54, July 1966: 259–260.

85. CORBIN, JOHN BOYD. The acquisitions programs of the centralized processing center of the Texas State Library. *In* Texas Conference on Library Mechanization, *1st, Austin, 1966*. Proceedings. Edited by John B. Corbin. Austin, Texas Library & Historical Commission, 1966. (Texas. State Library [Austin] Monograph no. 6) p. 36–46. Available on loan from LOCATE, Library of Congress, Washington, D.C. 20540.

86. GEDDES, ANDREW. Data processing in a cooperative system—opportunities for service [Nassau Library System]. *In* Harvey, John, *ed.* Data processing in public and university libraries. Washington, Spartan Books, 1966. (Drexel Information Science series, v. 3) p. 25–35.

87. HOLZBAUR, FREDERIC W., *and* EUGENE H.

FARRIS. Library information processing using an on-line, real-time computer system. Poughkeepsie, N.Y., International Business Machines Corp., 1966. 47 p. TR 00.1548.

*88. KOZLOW, ROBERT D. Report on a library project conducted on the Chicago campus of the University of Illinois. [Washington, National Science Foundation] 1966. 1 v. (various paging). NSF grants 77 and 302.

89. LINE, MAURICE B. Automation of acquisition records and routine in the university library, Newcastle upon Tyne. *In* Program; news of computers in British university libraries, no. 2, June 1966. 4 p.

90. RIFT, LEO R. Automation of library acquisitions procedures at Bowling Green State University. Bowling Green, Ohio, 1966. 3 p. + illus.

91. RIFT, LEO R. Automation of standing order acquisitions procedures at Bowling Green State University. Bowling Green, Ohio, 1966. 5 p. + illus.

92. RIFT, LEO R. Automation of subscriptions and periodicals records of Bowling Green State University. Bowling Green, Ohio, 1966. 6 p. + illus.

93. RIFT, LEO R. Use of the IBM 1050 system for library acquisition procedures at Bowling Green State University. Bowling Green, Ohio, 1966. 2 p. + illus.

1965

*94. COX, CARL R. Mechanized acquisitions procedures at the University of Maryland. College & research libraries, v. 26, May 1965: 232–236.

95. FERRIS, H. DONALD. Automated procedures at Purdue University Library: order department. *In* Meeting on Automation in the Library—When, Where, and How, *Purdue University, 1964*. Papers. Edited by Theodora Andrews. Lafayette, Ind., Purdue University, 1965. p. 39–42.

*96. MINDER, THOMAS L. Automation—the acquisitions program at the Pennsylvania State University Library. *In* IBM Library Mechanization Symposium, *Endicott, N.Y., 1964*. [Proceedings. White Plains, N.Y., International Business Machines Corp., 1965] p. 145–156.

97. MINDER, THOMAS L., *and* GERALD J. LAZOR-ICK. Automation of the Penn State University acquisitions department. (Reprinted from Automation and scientific communication. ADI proceedings, 1963)

In IBM Library Mechanization Symposium. *Endicott, N.Y., 1964.* [Proceedings. White Plains, N.Y., International Business Machines Corp., 1965] p. 157–163.

98. MOORE, EVELYN A., ESTELLE BRODMAN, *and* GERALDINE S. COHEN. Mechanization of library procedures in the medium-sized medical library: III. acquisitions and cataloging. *In* Medical Library Association. Bulletin, v. 53, July 1965: 305–328.

99. SCHULTHEISS, LOUIS A. Data processing aids in acquisitions work. Library resources & technical services, v. 9, winter 1965: 66–68.

Before 1965

100. BAATZ, WILMER H., *and* EUGENE H. MAURER. Machines at work [Milwaukee Public Library]. Library journal, v. 78, Aug. 1953: 1277–1281.

101. BROWN, GEORGE B. Use of punched cards in acquisitions work. College & research libraries, v. 10, July 1949: 219–220.

102. BUTCHER, S. J. Acquisition of books [Hampstead Public Libraries]. The Library Association record, v. 54, Aug. 1952: 259–262.

103. CULBERTSON, DON S. The costs of data processing in university libraries; in book acquisition and cataloging. College & research libraries, v. 24, Nov. 1963: 487–489.

104. JUHLIN, ALTON P. The use of IBM equipment in order procedures at Southern Illinois University Library. Illinois libraries, v. 44, Nov. 1962: 598–602.

105. KELLER, ALTON H. Book records on punched cards [Library of Congress]. Library journal, v. 71, Dec. 1946: 1785–1786.

106. MOFFITT, ALEXANDER. Punched card records in serial acquisitions. College & research libraries, v. 7, Jan. 1946: 10–13.

107. PARKER, RALPH H. Automatic records system at the University of Missouri Library. College & research libraries, v. 23, May 1962: 231–232, 264–265.

108. PARKER, RALPH H. Development of automatic systems at the University of Missouri Library. *In* Clinic on Library Applications of Data Processing, *University of Illinois, 1st, 1963.* Proceedings. Edited by Herbert Goldhor. Champaign, Ill., Distributed by the Illini Union Bookstore [1964] p. 43–54.

*109. RANDALL, G. E., *and* ROGER P. BRISTOL. PIL (Processing Information List) ; or,

A computer-controlled processing record. Special libraries, v. 55, Feb. 1964: 82–86.

Cataloging

1967

110. BREGZIS, RITVARS. The bibliographic information network: some suggestions for a different view of the library catalogue. *In* Brasenose Conference on the Automation of Libraries, *Oxford, Eng., 1966.* Proceedings of the Anglo-American Conference on the Mechanization of Library Services. Edited by John Harrison and Peter Laslett. [London and Chicago] Mansell, 1967. p. 128–142.

111. PALMER, FOSTER M. Conversion of existing records in large libraries with special reference to the Widener Library Shelflist. *In* Brasenose Conference on the Automation of Libraries, *Oxford, Eng., 1966.* Proceedings of the Anglo-American Conference on the Mechanization of Library Services. Edited by John Harrison and Peter Laslett. [London and Chicago] Mansell, 1967. p. 57–76.

112. WEISS, IRWIN J., *and* EMILIE V. WIGGINS. Computer-aided centralized cataloging at the National Library of Medicine. Library resources & technical services, v. 11, winter 1967: 83–96.

113. WELLS, A. J. The British National Bibliography. *In* Brasenose Conference on the Automation of Libraries, *Oxford, Eng., 1966.* Proceedings of the Anglo-American Conference on the Mechanization of Library Services. Edited by John Harrison and Peter Laslett. [London and Chicago] Mansell, 1967. p. 24–29.

1966

114. BRODMAN, ESTELLE, *and* GERALDINE S. COHEN. Communications to the editor; changes in acquisitions-cataloging methods at Washington University School of Medicine Library. *In* Medical Library Association. Bulletin, v. 54, July 1966: 259–260.

115. CURLEY, WALTER W. The data processing program in operation at the Suffolk Cooperative Library System, Patchogue, N.Y. *In* Clinic on Library Applications of Data Processing, *University of Illinois, 3d, 1965.* Proceedings. Edited by Francis B. Jenkins. Champaign, Ill., Distributed by the Illini Union Bookstore [1966] p. 15–42.

116. DODENDORF, MARY SEELY. 870 Document Writing System of International Business Machine Corporation in the Library Section, Los Angeles City Schools. *In* Clinic on Applications of Data Processing, *University of Illinois, 3d, 1965.* Proceedings. Edited by Francis B. Jenkins. Champaign, Ill., Distributed by the Illini Union Bookstore [1966] p. 43–64.

117. HEILIGER, EDWARD M. Florida Atlantic University Library. *In* Clinic on Library Applications of Data Processing, *University of Illinois, 3d, 1965.* Proceedings. Edited by Francis B. Jenkins. Champaign, Ill., Distributed by the Illini Union Bookstore [1966] p. 92–111.

118. HOLZBAUR, FREDERICK W., *and* EUGENE H. FARRIS. Library information processing using an on-line, real-time computer system. Poughkeepsie, N.Y., International Business Machines Corp., 1966. 47 p. TR 00.1548.

119. KILGOUR, FREDERICK G. Library catalogue production on small computers. American documentation, v. 17, July 1966: 124–131.

120. LAZORICK, GERALD J. Proposal for conversion of shelf list bibliographic information to machine readable form and production of book indexes to shelf list. In collaboration with Hugh Atkinson and John Herling. Buffalo, State University of New York at Buffalo, University Libraries, 1966. 13 p.

121. NELSON ASSOCIATES, INC. The feasibility of further centralizing the technical processing operations of the public libraries of New York City; a survey conducted for the Brooklyn Public Library, The New York Public Library, and the Queens Borough Public Library. In collaboration with The Theodore Stein Co., New York, 1966. 45 p. + appendices.

122. NEW YORK PUBLIC LIBRARY, *Reference Dept.* Catalog study report. No. 1 + New York, Mar. 9, 1966 + irregular. Latest received in LC no. 15 dated August 1966, prepared by The Theodore Stein Co.

123. RICHMOND, PHYLLIS A. Note on updating and searching computerized catalogs. Library resources & technical services, v. 10, spring 1966: 155–160.

1965

*124. BURNS, LORIN R. The use of IBM unit record equipment in the Lake County Public Library. *In* IBM Library Mechanization Symposium, *Endicott, N.Y., 1964.* [Proceedings. White Plains, N.Y., International Business Machines Corp., 1965] p. 15–36.

*125. DeGENNARO, RICHARD. A computer produced shelf list. College & research libraries, v. 26, July 1965: 311–315, 353.

126. DIVETT, ROBERT T. Mechanization in a new medical school library: I. acquisitions and cataloging. *In* Medical Library Association. Bulletin, v. 53, Jan. 1965: 15–25.

127. INTERNATIONAL BUSINESS MACHINES CORPORATION. *Federal Systems Division.* Report of a pilot project for converting the pre-1952 National Union Catalog to a machine readable record. A study sponsored by the Council on Library Resources, Inc. Rockville, Md., 1965. 52 p. + appendices.

128. JOHNS HOPKINS UNIVERSITY. Progress report on an operation research and systems engineering study of a university library. Baltimore, Milton S. Eisenhower Library, Johns Hopkins University, 1965. 110 p. PB-168 187. NSF grant GN-31.

*129. KILGOUR, FREDERICK G. Development of computerization of catalogs in medical and scientific libraries. *In* Clinic on Library Applications of Data Processing, *University of Illinois, 2d, 1964.* Proceedings. Edited by Herbert Goldhor. Champaign, Ill., Distributed by the Illini Union Bookstore [1965] p. 25–35.

130. KILGOUR, FREDERICK G. Mechanization of cataloging procedures. *In* Medical Library Association. Bulletin, v. 53, Apr. 1965: 152–162.

131. MOORE, EVELYN A., ESTELLE BRODMAN, *and* GERALDINE S. COHEN. Mechanization of library procedures in the medium-sized medical library: III. acquisitions and cataloging. *In* Medical Library Association. Bulletin, v. 53, July 1965: 305–328.

132. PERREAULT, JEAN M. On bibliography and automation; or, How to reinvent the catalog. Libri, v. 15, 1965: 287–339.

1964

133. BUCKLAND, LAWRENCE F. Problems confronting machine processing of shared catalog data. *In* Association of Research Libraries. Minutes of the sixty-fourth meeting, June 27, 1964. p. 13–24.

134. HIGHUM, CLAYTON D. Cataloging for document retrieval at Florida Atlantic University. College & research libraries, v. 25, May 1964: 197–199.

135. KRAFT, DONALD H. Library automation with data processing equipment. Chicago, Ill., International Business Machines Corp., 1964. 19 p.

*136. SIMONTON, WESLEY C. The computerized catalog: possible, feasible, desirable? Library resources & technical services, v. 8, fall 1964: 399–407.

137. SWANSON, DON R. Dialogues with a catalog. The library quarterly, v. 34, Jan. 1964: 113–125.

Before 1964

138. CULBERTSON, DON S. The costs of data processing in university libraries: in book acquisition and cataloging. College & research libraries, v. 24, Nov. 1963: 487–489.

139. DURKIN, ROBERT E., *and* HERBERT S. WHITE. Simultaneous preparation of library catalogs for manual and machine applications. Special libraries, v. 52, May-June 1961: 231–237.

140. GULL, C. DAKE. How will electronic information systems affect cataloging rules? Library resources & technical services, v. 5, spring 1961: 135–139.

141. INTERNATIONAL BUSINESS MACHINES CORPORATION. Library processing for the Albuquerque Public School System. White Plains, N.Y., International Business Machines Corp. [1962?] 9 p. Brochure K20-0048-0.

142. LIPETZ, BEN-AMI. Labor costs, conversion costs and compatibility in document control systems. American documentation, v. 14, Apr., 1963: 117–122.

143. SPARKS, DAVID E. A machine interpretable format for library cataloging. Unpublished paper, 1962. 18 p. + illus. Available on loan from author, Science and Technology Division, Library of Congress.

Cataloging (automatic typewriters)

1966

144. LANE, DAVID O. Automatic catalog card production [Boston University]. Library resources & technical services, v. 10, summer 1966: 383–386.

145. SALMON, STEPHEN R. Automation of library procedures at Washington University. Missouri Library Association. Quarterly, v. 27, Mar. 1966: 11–14.

1965

*146. JACKSON, WILLIS CARL, EUGENE PETRIWSKY, *and* JAMES G. STEPHENS. Catalog card production by Flexowriter: the University of Colorado system. The Colorado academic library, v. 2, fall 1965: 4–7.

1964

147. MOORE, MILTON. Flexowriter versus multilith: a time and cost study. California librarian, v. 25, Oct. 1964: 257–259.

*148. PARKER, RALPH H. Development of automatic systems at the University of Missouri Library. *In* Clinic on Library Applications of Data Processing, *University of Illinois, 1st, 1963.* Proceedings. Edited by Herbert Goldhor. Champaign, Ill., Distributed by the Illini Union Bookstore [1964] p. 43–54.

149. SIEVERS, PATRICIA T., *and* PAUL J. FASANA. Automated routines in technical services; research report. Bedford, Mass., U.S. Air Force Cambridge Research Laboratories, 1964. 16 p. AD 435 615.

150. WILSON, C. W. J. Use of the Friden Flexowriter in the library of the Atomic Energy Research Establishment, Harwell. Journal of documentation, v. 20, Mar. 1964: 16–24.

Before 1964

*151. FASANA, PAUL J. Automating cataloging functions in conventional libraries. Library resources & technical services, v. 7, fall 1963: 350–363.

152. FASANA, PAUL J. Automating cataloging functions in conventional libraries. a technical report. Lexington, Mass., Itek, 1963. AD 613 337.

153. ISOTTA, N. E. C. A suggested first step toward automation. Aslib proceedings, v. 14, Oct. 1962: 333–341.

154. JOHNSON, NOEL W. Automated catalog card reproduction [California State Library]. Library journal, v. 85, Feb. 15, 1960: 725–726.

155. LIPETZ, BEN-AMI, DAVID E. SPARKS, *and* PAUL J. FASANA. Techniques for machine-assisted cataloging of books. Prepared for U.S. Air Force Cambridge Research Laboratories. Lexington, Mass., Itek, 1962. 22 p. AD 636 977.

156. LUCKETT, GEORGE R. Partial library automation with the Flexowriter automatic writing machine. Library resources & technical services, v. 1, fall 1957: 207–210.

157. MOOERS, CALVIN N. The tape-typewriter plan. *In* Aslib proceedings, v. 12, Aug.

1960: 277–291.
158. WITTY, FRANCIS J. The Flexowriter and catalog card reproduction: perfect solution for short runs. D.C. libraries, v. 28, July 1957: 2–4.

Cataloging (book catalogs)
1967
*159. CARTWRIGHT, KELLEY L., *and* RALPH M. SHOFFNER. Catalogs in book form; a research study of their implications for the California State Library and the California Union Catalog, with a design for their implementation. [Berkeley, Calif.] Institute of Library Research, University of California, 1967. 69 p. + illus.

1966
160. BREGZIS, RITVARS. The ONULP bibliographic control system; an evaluation. *In* Clinic on Library Applications of Data Processing, *University of Illinois, 3d, 1965.* Proceedings. Edited by Francis B. Jenkins. Champaign, Ill., Distributed by the Illini Union Bookstore [1966] p. 112–140.
*161. HAYES, ROBERT M., RALPH M. SHOFFNER, *and* DAVID C. WEBER. The economics of book catalog production. Library resources & technical services, v. 10, winter 1966: 57–90.
162. HEALEY, JAMES S. An automated library in New England [New Bedford, Mass., Public Library]. Wilson library bulletin, v. 41, Dec. 1966: 411–413, 438.
163. KIEFFER, PAULA. The Baltimore County Public Library book catalog. Library resources & technical services, v. 10, spring 1966: 133–141.
164. McCASLIN, O. R. The book catalog program of the Austin Public Library: the programmer's viewpoint. *In* Texas Conference on Library Mechanization, *1st, Austin, 1966.* Proceedings. Edited by John B. Corbin. Austin, Texas Library & Historical Commission, 1966. (Texas. State Library [Austin] Monograph no. 6) p. 17–20. Available on loan from LOCATE, Library of Congress, Washington, D.C. 20540.
165. McCURDY, MAY LEA. The book catalog program of the Austin Public Library: the librarian's viewpoint. *In* Texas Conference on Library Mechanization, *1st, Austin, 1966.* Proceedings. Edited by John B. Corbin. Austin, Texas Library & Histori-

cal Commission, 1966. (Texas. State Library [Austin] Monograph no. 6) p. 13–16. Available on loan from LOCATE, Library of Congress, Washington, D.C. 20540.
166. MORELAND, GEORGE B. An unsophisticated approach to book catalog and circulation control. *In* Harvey, John, *ed.* Data processing in public and university libraries. Washington, Spartan Books, 1966 (Drexel Information Science series, v. 3) p. 53–63.
167. NELSON ASSOCIATES, INC. Centralized processing for the public libraries of New York State; a survey conducted for the New York State Library. In collaboration with The Theodore Stein Co., New York, 1966. 34 p. + appendices.
168. RIFT, LEO R. Production of the science library catalog at Bowling Green State University on the IBM 1050 unit record system. Bowling Green, Ohio, 1966. 4 p. + illus.
169. SANTA CLARA VALLEY LIBRARY SYSTEM. Implementation of BALANCE [Bay Area Libraries Associated Network for Cooperative Exchange] phase I and II, book catalog production. [Santa Clara, Calif.] 1966. 52 p.
170. STANFORD UNIVERSITY. Stanford Undergraduate Library book catalog: fact sheet. [Stanford, Calif.] 1966. 3 p. + illus.

1965
171. BREGZIS, RITVARS. The Ontario New Universities Library Project—an automated bibliographic data control system. College & research libraries, v. 26, Nov. 1965: 495–508.
172. BLACKBURN, ROBERT H. On producing catalogues in book form for five libraries at once [Ontario New Universities Library Project]. *In* Canadian Library Association. Library automation projects; a collection of papers by Canadian librarians. Ottawa, 1965. p. 20–22. Occasional paper no. 48.
173. HEILIGER, EDWARD M. Use of a computer at Florida Atlantic University Library for mechanized catalog production. *In* IBM Library Mechanization Symposium, *Endicott, N.Y., 1964.* [Proceedings. White Plains, N.Y., International Business Machines Corp., 1965] p. 165–186.
174. JOHNSON, RICHARD D. Book catalog for the Undergraduate Library. *In* Stanford University Libraries. Bulletin, v. 27, July 16, 1965: 87–88.

175. JONES, ROBERT C. A book catalog for libraries—prepared by camera and computer [The Junior College District of St. Louis]. Library resources & technical services, v. 9, spring 1965: 205–206.

176. MATTA, SEOUD MAKRAM. The card catalog in a large research library: present condition and future possibilities in the New York Public Library. [New York] 1965. 248 p. Thesis (D.L.S.)—Columbia University.

177. PERREAULT, JEAN M. Computerized cataloging: the computerized catalog at Florida Atlantic University. Library resources & technical services, v. 9, winter 1965: 20–34.

178. PIZER, IRWIN H. Book catalogs versus card catalogs. In Medical Library Association. Bulletin, v. 53, Apr. 1965: 225–238.

179. ROBINSON, CHARLES W. The book catalog: diving in [Baltimore County Public Library]. Wilson library bulletin, v. 40, Nov. 1965: 262–268.

180. VAVREK, BERNARD. The book catalog: one step backward. Wilson library bulletin, v. 40, Nov. 1965: 269–270.

181. WEINSTEIN, EDWARD A., and VIRGINIA GEORGE. Notes toward a code for computer-produced printed book catalogs. Library resources & technical services, v. 9, summer 1965: 319–323.

182. YALE UNIVERSITY. Administrative Data Systems. Library Projects Staff. The Kline [Science Library] book catalogues; a progress report. [New Haven, Conn.] 1965. 17 p.

1964

*183. BECKER, JOSEPH. Automatic preparation of book catalogs. ALA bulletin, v. 58, Sept. 1964: 714–718.

184. BROWN, MARGARET C. A book catalog at work [Free Library of Philadelphia]. Library resources & technical services, v. 8, fall 1964: 349–358.

185. CLINE, CATHERINE. Procedures for developing Timberland's book catalog. PNLA quarterly, v. 28, Jan. 1964: 128–132, 136.

186. GELLER, WILLIAM SPENCE. Duplicate catalogs in regional and public library systems [Los Angeles County Public Library system]. The library quarterly, v. 34, Jan. 1964: 57–67.

187. HAGLER, RONALD. The place of the book catalog in the university library. PNLA quarterly, v. 28, Jan. 1964: 125–127.

188. HAKE, SHIRLEY. Book catalogs in the public library system [King County, Wash.]. PNLA quarterly, v. 28, Jan. 1964: 132–133, 136.

189. HARRIS, IRA. Reader services aspects of book catalogs. Library resources & technical services, v. 8, fall 1964: 391–398.

190. HENDERSON, JOHN D. The book catalogs of the Los Angeles County Public Library. In Clinic on Library Applications of Data Processing, University of Illinois, 1st, 1963. Proceedings. Edited by Herbert Goldhor. Champaign, Ill., Distributed by the Illini Union Bookstore [1964] p. 18–32.

191. JOHNS, LOETA L. P[acific] N[orthwest] B[ook] C[atalog] past and future. PNLA quarterly, v. 28, Jan. 1964: 120–123.

192. JONES, BOB. The compact book catalog by photographic process [The Junior College District of St. Louis]. Library resources & technical services, v. 8, fall 1964: 366–369.

193. KENNEDY, JAMES H., and MERLE N. BOYLAN. IBM 1401 computer produced and maintained printed book catalogs at the Lawrence Radiation Laboratory. Livermore, University of California, Lawrence Radiation Laboratory, 1964. 25 p. UCRL-7555.

194. MACQUARRIE, CATHERINE. The metamorphosis of the book catalogs [Los Angeles County Public Library]. Library resources & technical services, v. 8, fall 1964: 370–378.

195. MORELAND, GEORGE B. Montgomery County book catalog. Library resources & technical services, v. 8, fall 1964: 379–389.

*196. PARKER, RALPH H. Book catalogs. Library resources & technical services, v. 8, fall 1964: 344–348.

197. PERREAULT, JEAN M. The computerized book catalog at Florida Atlantic University. College & research libraries, v. 25, May 1964: 185–197.

198. PIZER, IRWIN H. Another look at printed catalogs. Special libraries, v. 55, Feb. 1964: 119.

199. RICHMOND, PHYLLIS A. Book catalogs as supplements to card catalogs. Library resources & technical services, v. 8, fall 1964: 359–365.

200. WEINSTEIN, EDWARD A., and JOAN SPRY. Boeing SLIP: computer produced and maintained printed book catalogs. American documentation, v. 15, July 1964: 185–190.

1963

*201. KINGERY, ROBERT ERNEST, *and* MAURICE F. TAUBER, *eds.* Book catalogs. New York, Scarecrow Press, 1963. 330 p.

202. RICHMOND, PHYLLIS A. A short title catalog made with IBM tabulating equipment [University of Rochester]. Library resources & technical services, v. 7, winter 1963: 81–85.

203. VERTANES, CHARLES A. Automating the school library: an advance report. Wilson library bulletin, v. 37, June 1963: 864–867.

Before 1963

204. ALVORD, DOROTHY. King County Public Library does it with IBM. PNLA quarterly, v. 16, Apr. 1952: 123–131.

205. DEWEY, HARRY. Punched card catalogs—theory and technique. American documentation, v. 10, Jan. 1959: 36–40.

206. GRIFFIN, MARJORIE. Printed book catalogs. Special libraries, v. 51, Nov. 1960: 496–499.

207. HEWITSON, THEODORE. The book catalog of the Los Angeles County Public Library: its function and use. Library resources & technical services, v. 4, summer 1960: 228–232.

208. MacDONALD, RUTH M. Book catalogs and card catalogs. Library resources & technical services, v. 6, summer 1962: 217–222.

209. MacQUARRIE, CATHERINE. IBM book catalog [Los Angeles County Public Library]. Library journal, v. 82, Mar. 1, 1957: 630–634.

210. MacQUARRIE, CATHERINE, *and* BERYL L. MARTIN. Book catalog of the Los Angeles County Public Library: how it is being made. Library resources & technical services, v. 4, summer 1960: 208–227.

Cataloging (filing)

1966

211. HINES, THEODORE C., *and* JESSICA L. HARRIS. Computer filing of index, bibliographic, and catalog entries. Newark, N.J., Bro-Dart Foundation, 1966. 126 p.

212. NUGENT, WILLIAM R. The mechanization of the filing rules for the dictionary catalogs of the Library of Congress. A report prepared for the Council on Library Resources, Inc. Maynard, Mass., Inforonics, 1966. 32 p.

1965

213. PERREAULT, JEAN M. The computer and catalog filing rules. Library resources & technical services, v. 9, summer 1965: 325–331.

214. POPECKI, JOSEPH T. A filing system for the machine age. Library resources & technical services, v. 9, summer 1965: 333–337.

1962

215. CULBERTSON, DON S., *and others.* An investigation into the application of data processing to library filing rules. Chicago, University of Illinois, Chicago Undergraduate Division, 1962. 27 p. + appendices. PB 164 441

1961

216. GULL, C. DAKE. How will electronic information systems affect cataloging rules? Library resources & technical services, v. 5, spring 1961: 135–139.

Cataloging (Library of Congress)

1967

*217. AVRAM, HENRIETTE D., *and* BARBARA EVANS MARKUSON. Library automation and Project MARC: an experiment in the distribution of machine-readable cataloging data. *In* Brasenose Conference on the Automation of Libraries, *Oxford, Eng., 1966.* Proceedings of the Anglo-American Conference on the Mechanization of Library Services. Edited by John Harrison and Peter Laslett. [London and Chicago] Mansell, 1967. p. 97–127.

1966

218. AVRAM, HENRIETTE D. The philosophy behind the proposed format for a Library of Congress machine-readable record. *In* Institute on Information Storage and Retrieval, *2d, University of Minnesota, 1965.* Information retrieval with special reference to the biomedical sciences. Minneapolis, 1966. p. 155–174.

219. CONFERENCE ON MACHINE-READABLE CATALOG COPY, *3d, Library of Congress, 1966.* Proceedings (Discussion of the MARC Pilot Project). Washington, 1966. 30 p.

*220. SHUART, RODNEY A. Application of information processing techniques to library systems [MARC Pilot Project].

In American Institute of Aeronautics and Astronautics, Annual Meeting, *3d, Boston, 1966*. Paper, New York, 1966. AIAA Paper no. 66–832.

221. U.S. *Library of Congress. Information Systems Office*. A preliminary report on the MARC (MAchine Readable Catalog) Pilot Project. Washington, 1966. 101 p.

222. Washington State Library. MARC Project participation. Olympia, 1966. 18 p. + appendices. Available on interlibrary loan from author.

1965

223. BUCKLAND, LAWRENCE F. The recording of Library of Congress bibliographical data in machine form; a report prepared for the Council on Library Resources, Inc. Revised. Washington, Council on Library Resources, Inc., 1965. 54 p. A photocopy is available from the Photoduplication Service, Library of Congress, Washington, D.C. 20540. $8 postpaid.

224. CONFERENCE ON MACHINE-READABLE CATALOG COPY, *2d, Library of Congress, 1965*. Proceedings. Sponsored by Council on Library Resources, Inc., and Library of Congress. Washington, 1965. 35 p.

225. U.S. *Library of Congress. Information Systems Office*. Planning memorandum number 3. A proposed format for a standardized machine-readable catalog record. A preliminary draft prepared by Henriette D. Avram, Ruth S. Freitag, and Kay D. Guiles. Washington, 1965. 110 p.

Circulation

1967

226. CAMMACK, FLOYD, *and* DONALD MANN. Institutional implications of an automated circulation study [Oakland University]. College & research libraries, v. 28, Mar. 1967: 129–132.

1966

*227. STOCKTON, PATRICIA ANN. An IBM 357 circulation procedure. College & research libraries, v. 28, Jan. 1967: 35–40.

228. AULD, LAWRENCE. Automation report. Rochester, Mich., Kresge Library, Oakland University, 1966. 8 p. + appendices.

229. BASS, DAVID W. LAPL [Los Angeles Public Library] and the Data Service Bureau. Wilson library bulletin, v. 41, Dec. 1966: 405–408.

230. Binghamton (N.Y.) State College automates library circulation. Library jour-

nal, v. 91, June 15, 1966: 3134.

231. BRADLEY, ALBERT P. The NASA Manned Spacecraft Center Library—practical mechanization of library functions on a daily basis. Special libraries, v. 41, Dec. 1966: 692–697.

232. COX, JAMES R. Automation advances in the Research Library. UCLA librarian, v. 19, Mar. 1966: 22–24.

233. FLANNERY, ANNE, *and* JAMES D. MACK. Mechanized circulation system, Lehigh University Library. Bethlehem, Pa., Center for Information Sciences, Lehigh University, 1966. (Library systems analysis, report no. 4) 17 p. + appendices.

234. HEALEY, JAMES S. An automated library in New England [New Bedford, Mass., Public Library]. Wilson library bulletin, v. 41, Dec. 1966: 411–413, 438.

235. KIMBER, RICHARD T. Studies at the Queen's University of Belfast on real-time computer control of book circulation. Journal of documentation, v. 22, June 1966: 116–122.

236. LAZORICK, GERALD J. Proposal for a real-time circulation system. In collaboration with Hugh Atkinson and John Herling. Buffalo, State University of New York at Buffalo, University Libraries, 1966. 10 p.

237. MARTIN, FRANK, *and* JACK BANNING. Library circulation control at Michigan State University. East Lansing, Mich., 1966. 11 p.

238. PAYNE, LADYE MARGARETE, LOUISE SMALL, *and* ROBERT T. DIVETT. Mechanization in a new medical school library: II. serials and circulation. *In* Medical Library Association. Bulletin, v. 54, Oct. 1966: 337–350.

239. PIZER, IRWIN H. A mechanized circulation system. College & research libraries, v. 27, Jan. 1966: 5–12.

240. RUECKING, FREDERICK. The circulation system of the Fondren Library, Rice University. *In* Texas Conference on Library Mechanization, *1st, Austin, 1966*. Proceedings. Edited by John B. Corbin. Austin, Texas Library & Historical Commission, 1966. (Texas. State Library [Austin] Monograph no. 6) p. 21–30. Available on loan from LOCATE, Library of Congress, Washington, D.C. 20540.

241. SALMON, STEPHEN R. Automation of library procedures at Washington University. Missouri Library Association. Quarterly, v. 27, Mar. 1966: 11–14.

1965

242. Arizona State University. Computerized circulation summary. [Tempe, Ariz.] 1965. 3 p.

243. BECKER, JOSEPH. IBM circulation control. Drexel library quarterly, v. 1, Jan. 1965: 29–32.

244. CALIFORNIA, UNIVERSITY. *University at Los Angeles. Library Systems Staff.* Automated circulation control in the University Research Library at UCLA; a progress report. Los Angeles, 1965. 3 p. + illus.

245. CAMMACK, FLOYD M. Remote-control circulation [University of Hawaii]. College & research libraries, v. 26, May 1965: 213–218. See also Ralph R. Shaw's "Machine Application at the University of Hawaii" (entry 255).

*246. COX, CARL R. The mechanization of acquisition and circulation procedures at the University of Maryland Library. *In* IBM Library Mechanization Symposium, *Endicott, N.Y., 1964.* [Proceedings. White Plains, N.Y., International Business Machines Corp., 1965] p. 205–236.

*247. COX, JAMES R. Circulation control with IBM unit record equipment at UCLA. *In* IBM Library Mechanization Symposium, *Endicott, N.Y., 1964.* [Proceedings. White Plains, N.Y., International Business Machines Corp., 1965] p. 95–132.

*248. DE JARNETT, L. R. Library circulation control using IBM 357's at Southern Illinois University. *In* IBM Library Mechanization Symposium, *Endicott, N.Y., 1964.* [Proceedings. White Plains, N.Y., International Business Machines Corp., 1965] p. 77–94.

249. HARRIS, MICHAEL H. The 357 data collection system for circulation control. College & research libraries, v. 26, Mar. 1965: 119–120, 158.

*250. JOHNS HOPKINS UNIVERSITY. Progress report on an operations research and systems engineering study of a university library. Baltimore, Milton S. Eisenhower Library, Johns Hopkins University, 1965. 110 p. PB-168 187. NSF grant GN-31.

251. MCCOY, RALPH E. Computerized circulation work: a case study of the 357 data collection system [Southern Illinois University]. Library resources & technical services, v. 9, winter 1965: 59–65.

252. MOORE, EVELYN A., *and* ESTELLE BRODMAN. Communications to the editor; circulation system changes, serial record changes [at Washington University School of Medicine Library]. *In* Medical Library Association. Bulletin, v. 53, Jan. 1965: 99–101.

*253. PALMER, FOSTER M. Punch card circulation system for Widener Library—Harvard University. Cambridge, Mass., 1965. 39 p.

254. RIFT, LEO R. The IBM 357 charging system proposed for Bowling Green State University; to become operational early in 1967. Bowling Green, Ohio, 1965. 22 p. + illus.

255. SHAW, RALPH R. Machine application the University of Hawaii. College & search libraries, v. 26, Sept. 1965: 3(382, 398. See also Floyd M. Cammacᴋ ᴊ "Remote-control circulation" (entry 245).

256. SOUTER, THOMAS A. Automated procedures at Indiana University Library: circulation department. *In* Meeting on Automation in the Library—When, Where, and How, *Purdue University, 1964.* Papers. Edited by Theodora Andrews. Lafayette, Ind., Purdue University, 1965. p. 43–45.

257. TRUESWELL, RICHARD W. A quantitative measure of user circulation requirements and its possible effect on stack thinning and multiple copy determination. American documentation, v. 16, Jan. 1965: 20–25.

258. Use of data processing equipment in circulation control. *In* American Library Association, *Library Technology Project.* Library technology reports. Chicago, July 1965. 24 p.

259. YABROFF, ARTHUR. Circulation control at the Detroit Public Library. *In* IBM Library Mechanization Symposium, *Endicott, N.Y., 1964.* [Proceedings. White Plains, N.Y., International Business Machines Corp., 1965] p. 37–42.

1964

*260. BECKER, JOSEPH. Circulation and the computer. ALA bulletin, v. 58, Dec. 1964: 1007–1010.

261. BULL, MARGARET G. Statistics and the Montclair Public Library IBM circulation control system. *In* IBM Library Mechanization Symposium, *Endicott, N.Y., 1964.* [Proceedings. White Plains, N.Y., International Business Machines Corp., 1965] p. 61–76.

262. COX, JAMES R. IBM circulation control at the University of California Library at

Los Angeles; progress and change. Los Angeles, UCLA Library, 1964. 13 p.

263. KENNEDY, JAMES H. IBM 1401 computer produced and maintained library circulation records. Livermore, University of California, Lawrence Radiation Laboratory, 1964. UCRL-7555.

*264. KRAFT, DONALD H. IBM library circulation systems. Chicago, International Business Machines Corp., 1964. 15 p.

265. LEFFLER, WILLIAM L. A statistical method for circulation analysis. College & research libraries, v. 15, Nov. 1964: 488–490.

266. PIZER, IRWIN H., ISABELLE T. ANDERSON, and ESTELLE BRODMAN. Mechanization of library procedures in the medium-sized medical library: II. circulation records. In Medical Library Association. Bulletin, v. 52, Apr. 1964: 370–385.

267. ROY, ROBERT H. Utilization of computer techniques for circulation and inventory control in a university research library [Johns Hopkins University]. In Association of Research Libraries. Minutes of the sixty-third meeting. Jan. 26, 1964. p. 20–39.

*268. RUECKING, FREDERICK. Selecting a circulation-control system: a mathematical approach. College & research libraries, v. 25, Sept. 1964: 385–390.

*269. TRUESWELL, RICHARD W. Two characteristics of circulation and their effect on the implementation of mechanized circulation control systems. College & research libraries, v. 25, July 1964: 285–291.

270. WEYHRAUCH, ERNEST E. Automation in the reserved books room. Library journal, v. 89, June 1, 1964: 2294–2296.

1963

271. COX, JAMES R. The costs of data processing in university libraries: in circulation activities. College & research libraries, v. 24, Nov. 1963: 492–495.

272. RUECKING, FREDERICK. An automatic charging system for the Fondren Library; a recommendation for the 1964–65 budget year. [Houston, Rice University] 1963. 30 p. + appendices.

Before 1963

273. BIRNBAUM, HENRY. IBM circulation control at Brooklyn College Library; general information manual. White Plains, N.Y., International Business Machines

Corp., 1960. 32 p. Brochure E 20-0072.

274. HOWE, MARY T., and MARY K. WEIDNER. Data processing in the Decatur Public Library. Illinois libraries, v. 44, Nov. 1962: 593–597.

275. KLAUSNER, MARGARET. IBM circulation control [Stockton and San Joaquin County, Calif.]. Library journal, v. 77, Dec. 15, 1952: 2165–2166, 2168.

276. McCORD, JOHN G. W. A data processing system for circulation control at the Illinois State Library; a preliminary report. Illinois libraries, v. 44, Nov. 1962: 603–607.

277. PARKER, RALPH H. The punched card method in circulation work [University of Texas Library]. Library journal, v. 61, Dec. 1, 1936: 903–905.

278. PRATT, E. CARL. International Business Machines' use in circulation department, University of Florida Library. Library journal, v. 67, Apr. 1, 1942: 302–303.

279. QUIGLEY, MARGERY C. Library facts from International Business Machine cards. Library journal, v. 66, Dec. 1941: 1065–1067.

280. QUIGLEY, MARGERY C. Ten years of IBM. Library journal, v. 78, July 1952: 1152–1157.

Serials

1966

281. EYMAN, ELEANOR G., and others. Periodicals automation at Miami-Dade Junior College. Library resources and technical services, v. 10, summer 1966: 341–361.

282. CURRAN, ANN T. The mechanization of the serial records for the moving and merging of the Boston Medical and Harvard Medical serials. Library resources & technical services, v. 10, summer 1966: 362–372.

283. FELTER, JACQUELINE W. The union catalog of medical periodicals of New York. In Institute on Information Storage and Retrieval, 2d, University of Minnesota, 1965. Information retrieval with special reference to the biomedical sciences. Minneapolis, 1966. p. 117–131.

284. KOZLOW, ROBERT D. Report on a library project conducted on the Chicago campus of the University of Illinois. [Washington, National Science Foundation] 1966. 1 v. (various paging). NSF grants 77 and 302.

285. LAUCUS, CAROL A., and SUSAN RUSSELL.

Serials automation project at Baker Library; preliminary report. Boston, Harvard University, Graduate School of Business Administration, 1966. 47 p.

286. McGrath, William E., *and* Helen Kolbe. A simple, mechanized non-computerized system for serials control in small academic libraries: a primer. Library resources & technical services, v. 10, summer, 1966: 373–382.

287. Payne, Ladye Margarete, Louise Small, *and* Robert T. Divett. Mechanization in a new medical school library: II. serials and circulation. *In* Medical Library Association. Bulletin, v. 54, Oct. 1966: 337–350.

288. Rift, Leo R. Automation of subscriptions and periodicals records of Bowling Green State University. Bowling Green, Ohio, 1966. 6 p. + illus.

289. Rift, Leo R. Automation of standing order acquisitions procedures at Bowling Green State University. Bowling Green, Ohio, 1966. 5 p. + illus.

290. Stewart, Bruce Warren. The serials mechanization program of the Texas A & M University Library. *In* Texas Conference on Library Mechanization, *1st, Austin, 1966.* Proceedings. Edited by John B. Corbin. Austin, Texas Library & Historical Commission, 1966. (Texas. State Library [Austin] Monograph no. 6) p. 40–45. Available on loan from LOCATE, Library of Congress, Washington, D.C. 20540.

1965

291. Bishop, David, Arnold L. Milner, *and* Fred W. Roper. Publication patterns of scientific serials. American documentation, v. 16, Apr. 1965: 113–121.

292. Computer Usage Company, Inc. Serial library system [U.S. Army Biological Laboratory, Ft. Detrick, Md.]. Baltimore, Computer Usage, 1965. 61 p. AD 621 067.

293. Creager, William A., *and* David E. Sparks. A serials data program for science and technology. Final report to the National Science Foundation. Reading, Mass., Information Dynamics, 1965. 190 p. NSF-C-413.

*294. Culbertson, Don S. Computerized serial records. Library resources & technical services, v. 9, winter 1965: 53–58.

295. Felter, Jacqueline W., *and* Djoeng S. Tjoeng. A computer system for a union catalog: theme and variations. *In* Medical Library Association. Bulletin, v. 53, Apr. 1965: 163–177.

296. Hammer, Donald P. Automated procedures at Purdue University Library serials department, including binding. *In* Meeting on Automation in the Library— When, Where, and How, *Purdue University, 1964.* Papers. Edited by Theodora Andrews. Lafayette, Ind., Purdue University, 1965. p. 26–35.

297. Hammer, Donald P. Automated serials control in the Purdue University Libraries. *In* IBM Library Mechanization Symposium, *Endicott, N.Y., 1964.* [Proceedings. White Plains, N.Y., International Business Machines Corp., 1965] p. 133–144.

298. Hammer, Donald P. Reflections on the development of an automated serials system. Library resources & technical services, v. 9, spring 1965: 225–230.

299. Moore, Evelyn A., *and* Estelle Brodman. Communications to the editor; circulation system changes, serial record changes [at Washington University School of Medicine Library]. *In* Medical Library Association. Bulletin, v. 53, Jan. 1965: 99–101.

300. Schultheiss, Louis A. Two serial control card files developed at the University of Illinois, Chicago. Library resources & technical services, v. 9, summer 1965: 271–287.

*301. Stewart, Bruce Warren. A computerized serials record for the Texas A & M University Library. College Station, Tex., The Library, Texas A & M University, 1965. 123 p. Available from author.

302. Wilkinson, John P. A.A.U. [Association of Atlantic Universities] mechanized union list of serials. *In* APLA [Atlantic Provinces Library Association]. Bulletin, v. 29, May 1965: 54–59.

1964

*303. Becker, Joseph. Automating the serial record. ALA bulletin, v. 58, June 1964: 557–558.

304. California. University. *University at Los Angeles. Biomedical Library. Library System Planning Committee.* Biomedical library computer project for serials. [Los Angeles, University of California, 1964] 6 p.

*305. Ohio. State University, Columbus. *Libraries. Committee on Information Science. Subcommittee on Automated Serials Record.* Automated serials control project [report]. Columbus, Ohio, Feb. 1964. 13 p.

306. ROPER, FRED W. Preparation of records for the automated [serials] system at the Biomedical Library, University of California at Los Angeles. [Los Angeles, University of California, 1964] 6 p.

307. SRYGLEY, TED F. Serials record instructions for a computerized serial system [Florida Atlantic University]. Library resources & technical services, v. 8, summer 1964: 248–256.

*308. VDOVIN, GEORGE, and others. Serials computer project; final report. La Jolla, University of California, San Diego, 1964. 1 v. (various paging).

1963

309. PIZER, IRWIN H., DONALD R. FRANZ, and ESTELLE BRODMAN. Mechanization of library procedures in the medium-sized medical library: I. the serial record. In Medical Library Association. Bulletin, v. 51, July 1963: 313–338.

310. VDOVIN, GEORGE. The serials computer project, University of California Library, San Diego. In Institute on Information Storage and Retrieval, 1st, University of Minnesota, 1962. Information retrieval today. Minneapolis, 1966. p. 109–118.

311. VDOVIN, GEORGE, and others. Computer processing of serial records. Library resources & technical services, v. 7, winter 1963: 71–80.

312. VOIGT, MELVIN J. The costs of data processing in university libraries: in serials handling. College & research libraries, v. 24, Nov. 1963: 489–491.

Before 1963

313. ANTHONY, L. J., and J. E. HAILSTONE. Use of punched cards in preparation of lists of periodicals. Aslib proceedings, v. 12, Oct. 1960: 348–360.

314. CALIFORNIA. UNIVERSITY, San Diego. Report on serials computer project, University Library and UCSD Computer Center, 1961/62. La Jolla, Calif., 1962. 1 v. (various paging).

315. FETTERMAN, LOIS. Mechanization of magazine orders. In National Association of Secondary-School Principals. Bulletin, v. 43, Nov. 1959: 120–122.

316. McCANN, ANNE. Applications of machines to library techniques: periodicals. American documentation, v. 12, Oct. 1961: 260–265.

317. MOFFITT, ALEXANDER. Punched card records in serials acquisition. College & research libraries, v. 7, Jan. 1946: 10–13.

318. NICHOLSON, NATALIE, and WILLIAM THURSTON. Serials and journals in the MIT Libraries. American documentation, v. 9, Oct. 1958: 304–307.

319. YOUNG, H. H. Use of punched cards in the serials acquisitions department of the University of Texas. Special Libraries Association, Texas Chapter. Bulletin, v. 11, 1959: 1–3.

Systems analysis

1967

320. BOLLES, SHIRLEY W. The use of flow charts in the analysis of library operations. Special libraries, v. 58, Feb. 1967: 95–98.

321. COVILL, GEORGE W. Librarian + systems analyst = teamwork? Special libraries, v. 58, Feb. 1967: 99–101.

322. JACKSON, IVAN F. An approach to library automation problems. College & research libraries, v. 28, Mar. 1967: 133–137.

323. LAMKIN, BURTON E. Systems analysis in top management communication. Special libraries, v. 58, Feb. 1967: 90–94.

*324. MOORE, EDYTHE. Systems analysis: an overview. Special libraries, v. 58, Feb. 1967: 87–90.

1966

325. CHAPMAN, EDWARD A., and PAUL L. ST. PIERRE. Systems analysis and design as related to library operations. Troy, N.Y., Rensselaer Libraries, Rensselaer Polytechnic Institute, 1966. 78 p. A lecturer's manual and basis of a textbook sponsored by the Council on Library Resources to be published by John Wiley & Sons, late 1967.

326. HAMMER, DONALD P. Scheduling conversion. In Harvey, John, ed. Data processing in public and university libraries. Washington, Spartan Books, 1966. (Drexel Information Science series, v. 3) p. 103–123.

*327. HAYES, ROBERT M. Library systems analysis. In Harvey, John, ed. Data processing in public and university libraries. Washington, Spartan Books, 1966. (Drexel Information Science series, v. 3) p. 5–20.

328. KILGOUR, FREDERICK G. Basic systems assumptions of the Columbia-Harvard-Yale Medical Libraries computerization project. In Institute on Information Storage and Retrieval, 2d, University of Minnesota, 1965. Information retrieval with

special reference to the biomedical sciences. Minneapolis, 1966. p. 145–154.

329. LEIMKUHLER, FERDINAND F. System analysis in university libraries. College & research libraries, v. 27, Jan. 1966: 13–18.

330. MARKUSON, BARBARA EVANS. A system development study for the Library of Congress automation program. The library quarterly, v. 36, July 1966: 197–273.

1965

*331. BECKER, JOSEPH. System analysis—prelude to library data processing. ALA bulletin, v. 59, Apr. 1965: 293–296.

332. CORNELL UNIVERSITY. *Libraries.* System requirements. [Ithaca, N.Y.] 1965. 12 p.

333. FLOOD, MERRILL M. The systems approach to library planning. *In* Chicago. University. *Graduate Library School.* The intellectual foundations of library education; the twenty-ninth annual conference of the Graduate Library School, July 6–8, 1964. Edited by Don R. Swanson. Chicago, University of Chicago Press [1965] p. 38–50.

334. HAAS, WARREN J. Computer simulations at the Columbia University Libraries. *In* Clinic on Library Applications of Data Processing, *University of Illinois, 2d, 1964.* Proceedings. Edited by Herbert Goldhor. Champaign, Ill., Distributed by the Illini Union Bookstore [1965] p. 36–46.

335. HAYES, ROBERT M. The development of a methodology for system design and its role in library education. *In* Chicago. University. *Graduate Library School.* The intellectual foundations of library education; the twenty-ninth annual conference of the Graduate Library School, July 6–8, 1964. Edited by Don R. Swanson. Chicago, University of Chicago Press [1965] p. 51–63.

336. JOHNS HOPKINS UNIVERSITY. Program report on an operations research and systems engineering study of a university library. Baltimore, Milton S. Eisenhower Library, Johns Hopkins University, 1965. 110 p. PB-168 187. NSF grant GN-31.

337. LEIMKUHLER, FERDINAND F. Operations research in the Purdue Libraries. *In* Meeting on Automation in the Library—When, Where, and How, *Purdue University, 1964.* Papers. Edited by Theodora Andrews. Lafayette, Ind., Purdue University, 1965. p. 82–89.

338. SCHULTHEISS, LOUIS A. System analysis and planning. *In* Harvey, John, *ed.* Data processing in public and university libraries. Washington, Spartan Books, 1966. (Drexel Information Science series, v. 3) p. 92–102.

339. SPARKS, DAVID E., MARK M. CHODROW, *and* GAIL M. WALSH. A methodology for the analysis of information systems. Final report to National Science Foundation. Wakefield, Mass., Information Dynamics, 1965. 1 v. (various paging). Contract NSF-C-370.

340. SWENSON, SALLY. Flow chart of library searching techniques. Special libraries, v. 56, April 1965: 239–242.

341. TAYLOR, ROBERT S., *and* CAROLINE E. HIEBER. Manual for the analysis of library systems. Bethlehem, Pa., Center for Information Sciences, Lehigh University, 1965. (Library systems analysis, report no. 3) 44 p. + appendices.

1964

342. HAAS, WARREN J. A description of a project to study the research library as an economic system [Columbia University Libraries]. *In* Association of Research Libraries. Minutes of the sixty-third meeting, Jan. 26, 1964. p. 40–46.

343. MORELOCK, MOLETE, *and* FERDINAND F. LEIMKUHLER. Library operations research and systems engineering studies. College & research libraries, v. 25, Nov. 1964: 501–503.

344. MORSE, PHILIP M. Probabilistic models for library operations; with some comments on library automation. *In* Association of Research Libraries. Minutes of the sixty-third meeting, Jan. 26, 1964. p. 9–19.

Before 1964

345. BLACK, DONALD V. Library mechanization. Sci-tech news, v. 16, fall 1962: 115–117.

346. KILGOUR, FREDERICK G. Recorded use of books in the Yale Medical Library. American documentation, v. 12, Oct. 1961: 266–269.

347. SCHULTHEISS, LOUIS A., DON S. CULBERTSON, *and* EDWARD M. HEILIGER. Advanced data processing in the university library. New York, Scarecrow Press, 1962. 388 p.

348. SPRENKLE, PETER M., *and* FREDERICK G. KILGOUR. A quantitative study of characters on biomedical catalogue cards—a preliminary investigation. American documentation, v. 14, July 1963: 202–206.

Total systems

1967

*349. FUSSLER, HERMAN H. University of Chicago library automation program. *In* Association of Research Libraries. Minutes of the sixty-ninth meeting, Jan. 8, 1967.

350. FUSSLER, HERMAN H. University of Chicago library automation program. *In* Hamer, Elizabeth E. Report on the sixty-ninth meeting of the Association of Research Libraries. U.S. *Library of Congress.* Information bulletin, v. 26, Jan. 26, 1967: 72–73.

351. KILGOUR, FREDERICK G. Comprehensive modern library systems. *In* Brasenose Conference on the Automation of Libraries, *Oxford, Eng., 1966.* Proceedings of the Anglo-American Conference on the mechanization of library services. Edited by John Harrison and Peter Laslett. [London and Chicago] Mansell, 1967. p. 46–56.

352. PARKER, RALPH H. Library records in a total system. *In* Brasenose Conference on the Automation of libraries, *Oxford, Eng., 1966.* Proceedings of the Anglo-American Conference on the mechanization of library services. Edited by John Harrison and Peter Laslett. [London and Chicago] Mansell, 1967. p. 33–45.

1966

353. BAY AREA LIBRARY WORKING COMMITTEE. BALANCE [*Bay Area Libraries Associated Network for Cooperative Exchange*] a report on computerized procedures. [San Jose, Calif.] 1966. 78 p.

*354. GEDDES, ANDREW. Data Processing in a co-operative system—opportunities for service [Nassau Library System]. *In* Harvey, John, *ed.* Data processing in public and university libraries. Washington, Spartan Books, 1966. (Drexel Information Science services, v. 3) p. 25–35.

355. GORDON, GALVY E. Columbus conversion to data processing. Wilson library bulletin, v. 41, Dec. 1966: 414–417.

356. HAGE, ELIZABETH B. Computer potential in Maryland [Prince Georges County Memorial Library]. Wilson library bulletin, v. 41, Dec. 1966: 401–403.

*357. HOWE, MARY T. The establishment and growth of the data processing department in the Decatur Public Library. *In* Harvey, John, *ed.* Data Processing in public and university libraries. Washington, Spartan

Books, 1966. (Drexel Information Science series, v. 3) p. 37–52.

358. KRAFT, DONALD H. Total systems approach to library mechanization. *In* Texas Conference on Library Mechanization, *1st, Austin, 1966.* Proceedings. Edited by John B. Corbin. Austin, Texas Library & Historical Commission, 1966. (Texas. State Library [Austin] Monograph no. 6) p. 7–12. Available on loan from LOCATE, Library of Congress, Washington, D.C. 20540.

359. MEISE, NORMAN R. Conceptual design of an automated national library system. [Hartford] 1966. 246 p. Thesis (MA)—Rensselaer Polytechnic Institute, Hartford Graduate Center. Available on interlibrary loan from United Aircraft Corporate Systems Center, Farmington, Conn.

360. PARKER, RALPH H. Concept and scope of total systems in library records. *In* Harvey, John, *ed.* Data processing in public and university libraries. Washington, Spartan Books, 1966. (Drexel Information Science series, v. 3) p. 67–77.

361. PITTSBURGH. UNIVERSITY. Library automation plan; preliminary statement. [Pittsburgh] Nov. 1966. 5 p.

362. Québec (City) Université Laval. Bibliothèque. *Comité pour l'automatisation des services de la bibliotheque.* Rapport. Québec, Université Laval, 1966. 46 p.

*363. STEWART, BRUCE WARREN. Data processing in an academic library [Texas A & M University]. Wilson library bulletin, v. 41, Dec. 1966: 388–395.

*364. WEIDNER, MARY K. Decatur: pioneer in data processing. Wilson library bulletin, v. 41, Dec. 1966: 409–410, 438.

1965

365. BECKER, JOSEPH. Using computers in a new university library. ALA bulletin, v. 59, Oct. 1965: 823–826.

366. COMPUTER USAGE COMPANY. Specifications for an automated library system. Prepared for University of California at Santa Cruz. Palo Alto, Calif., 1965. 122 p.

367. CORBIN, JOHN BOYD. Automatic data processing in the Texas State Library. Texas library journal, v. 41, spring 1965: 12–14.

368. DILLON, HOWARD W. Program for the utilization of automatic data processing equipment. Columbus, Ohio State University, 1965. 7 p.

369. EDP Systems Development Services. Report of the survey of data processing feasibility for the Prince Georges County Memorial Library System. Hyattsville, Md., 1965. 48 p.

370. HAYES, ROBERT M. The concept of an online, total system. *In* American Library Association, *Library Technology Project*. Library technology reports. Chicago, May 1965. 13 p.

371. STONE, C. WALTER, *and others*. A library program for Columbia [Md.]. Pittsburgh, 1965. 54 p. CLR grant.

1964

372. BURNS, LORIN R. Automation in the public libraries of Lake County, Indiana. *In* Clinic on Library Applications of Data Processing, *University of Illinois, 1st, 1963.* ˙Proceedings. Edited by Herbert Goldhor. Champaign, Ill., Distributed by the Illini Union Bookstore [1964] p. 9–17.

373. MELIN, JOHN S. Libraries and data processing: where do we stand? Urbana, University of Illinois, Graduate School of Library Science, 1964. 44 p. Occasional paper no. 72.

374. OPTNER, STANFORD L., & ASSOCIATES. Report on an integrated data processing system for library technical services to the Public Library, City of Los Angeles. Los Angeles, 1964. 71 p.

Before 1964

375. CULBERTSON, DON S. Data processing for technical procedures at the University of Illinois Library. *In* Institute on Information Storage and Retrieval, *1st, University of Minnesota, 1962.* Information retrieval today. Minneapolis, 1966. p. 99–107.

376. HOWE, MARY T., *and* MARY K. WEIDNER. Mechanization in public libraries; data processing department in the Decatur Public Library. Unesco bulletin for libraries, v. 15, Nov. 1961: 317–321.

377. VERTANES, CHARLES A. Automating the school library; an advance report. Wilson library bulletin, v. 37, June 1963: 864–867.